# CONTESTED CIVIL SOCIETY IN MYANMAR

## Local Change and Global Recognition

Maaike Matelski

BRISTOL
UNIVERSITY
PRESS

First published in Great Britain in 2025 by

Bristol University Press
University of Bristol
1-9 Old Park Hill
Bristol
BS2 8BB
UK
t: +44 (0)117 374 6645
e: bup-info@bristol.ac.uk

Details of international sales and distribution partners are available at bristoluniversitypress.co.uk

© Bristol University Press 2025

British Library Cataloguing in Publication Data
A catalogue record for this book is available from the British Library

ISBN 978-1-5292-3054-3 hardcover
ISBN 978-1-5292-3652-1 paperback
ISBN 978-1-5292-3055-0 ePub
ISBN 978-1-5292-3056-7 ePdf

Cover design: Lyn Davies
Front cover image: Artwork by Dawei Lay

# Contents

List of Abbreviations and Acronyms                                          iv
Acknowledgements                                                            vii

Introduction: Contested Representation in Burma/Myanmar                       1

1    Conflict, Repression and Resistance from Colonialism to                 17
     Military Rule
2    Constructing Civil Society in Myanmar                                   31
3    Diversity and Fault Lines in Burmese Civil Society                      49
4    Room to Manoeuvre under Authoritarian Rule                             72
5    Transnational Advocacy Strategies and Pathways to Change                90
6    Competing Frames around the 2010 Elections                             103
7    Foreign Aid and the (De)politicization of Civil                        117
     Society Assistance
8    Interrupted Transition and Post-coup Resistance                        136

Conclusion                                                                  157

Notes                                                                       166
References                                                                  175
Index                                                                       199

# List of Abbreviations
# and Acronyms

| | |
|---|---|
| AAPP(B) | Assistance Association for Political Prisoners (Burma) |
| ABFSU | All Burma Federation of Student Unions |
| ABSDF | All Burma Students' Democratic Front |
| AFPFL | Anti-Fascist People's Freedom League |
| ALTSEAN | Alternative ASEAN Network (on Burma) |
| ASEAN | Association of Southeast Asian Nations |
| BBC | British Broadcasting Corporation |
| BCN | Burma Center Netherlands |
| BSPP | Burma Socialist Programme Party |
| BWU | Burmese Women's Union |
| CBI | Capacity Building Initiative |
| CBO | community-based organization |
| CDM | Civil Disobedience Movement |
| CPB | Communist Party of Burma |
| CRPH | Committee Representing Pyidaungsu Hluttaw |
| CSO | civil society organization |
| EAO | ethnic armed organization |
| EBO | Euro-Burma Office |
| EU | European Union |
| FBC | Free Burma Coalition |
| FTUB | Federation of Trade Unions of Burma |
| GCBA | General Council of Burmese Associations |
| GDP | gross domestic product |
| GONGO | government-organized non-governmental organization |
| HREIB | Human Rights Education Institute of Burma |
| ICC | International Criminal Court |
| ICG | International Crisis Group |
| ICJ | International Court of Justice |
| ICRC | International Committee of the Red Cross |
| IDP | internally displaced person |
| IIFFMM | Independent International Fact-Finding Mission on Myanmar |

| | |
|---|---|
| ILO | International Labour Organization |
| INGO | international non-governmental organization |
| KBC | Kachin Baptist Convention |
| KIA | Kachin Independence Army |
| KIO | Kachin Independence Organization |
| KNLA | Karen National Liberation Army |
| KNU | Karen National Union |
| LGBTIQ | Lesbian, Gay, Bisexual, Transgender, Intersex and Queer |
| MI(S) | Military Intelligence (Service) |
| MMCWA | Myanmar Maternal and Child Welfare Association |
| MP | Member of Parliament |
| MSF | Médecins Sans Frontières |
| MOU | Memorandum of Understanding |
| NCA | Nationwide Ceasefire Agreement |
| NCGUB | National Coalition Government of the Union of Burma |
| NDF | National Democratic Force |
| NGO | non-governmental organization |
| NLD | National League for Democracy |
| NUCC | National Unity Consultative Council |
| NUG | National Unity Government |
| NUP | National Unity Party |
| ODA | official development assistance |
| OIC | Organisation of Islamic Cooperation |
| PDF | People's Defence Force |
| R2P | Responsibility to Protect |
| RNDP | Rakhine Nationalities Development Party |
| SAC | State Administration Council |
| SLORC | State Law and Order Restoration Council |
| SNDP | Shan Nationalities Democratic Party |
| SPDC | State Peace and Development Council |
| TNI | Transnational Institute |
| UEC | Union Election Commission |
| UK | United Kingdom |
| UN | United Nations |
| UNDP | United Nations Development Programme |
| UNICEF | United Nations Children's Fund |
| US | United States |
| USAID | United States Agency for International Development |
| USDA | Union Solidarity and Development Association |
| USDP | Union Solidarity and Development Party |
| UWSA | United Wa State Army |

| | |
|---|---|
| WLB | Women's League of Burma |
| YMBA | Young Men's Buddhist Association |
| YMCA | Young Men's Christian Association |
| YWBA | Young Women's Buddhist Association |
| YWCA | Young Women's Christian Association |

# Acknowledgements

This book is dedicated to the people of Myanmar, and particularly the inspirational activists and civil society workers I was fortunate to meet during my research. It testifies to their courage, determination and strength, as well as their generosity even in times of extreme hardship. May your country see better days soon.

Special thanks to all the unnamed respondents in and from Myanmar who took time to talk to me in the course of this research. I am grateful for having met each of you and hope that you see your experiences reflected in this book. Thank you for your collaboration and sharing your insights.

I am fortunate to have a large support network inside and outside academia that provided feedback and distraction at appropriate times, so I will not attempt to name everyone here. A few persons deserve special mention, as this book would not have existed without them. Freek Colombijn supported my research at the Vrije Universiteit Amsterdam from the PhD application phase until the final version of this book. A big thank you to Freek, Oscar Salemink and Henk Schulte Nordholt for their supervision and all colleagues at the VU and elsewhere who proofread and provided peer support. Thanks also to the Anthropology Department and other institutes that helped to fund this research.

Rose Metro and an anonymous reviewer provided invaluable comments on the draft manuscript which helped to clarify my arguments. Aung Myo Hein, Myo Win, Seng Bu and Tun Lin Oo provided important feedback on the final chapter covering the post-coup period since 2021. Thank you to my various language instructors for teaching me about Burmese language and culture, and to the experts on Myanmar who took the time to provide guidance, especially in the early research phase. The growing Myanmar community in the Netherlands has been another source of inspiration and companionship, and I look forward to continue working with them.

Glen, my family and friends have been patient and supportive throughout the research and writing phases. Many thanks and love to you all.

Finally, I would like to thank Zoe Forbes, Stephen Wenham, Helen Nicholson and colleagues at Bristol University Press and Newgen Publishing for their professional support in the publishing process, and Dawei Lay for giving permission to use his beautiful artwork on the book cover.

Thank you, dank jullie wel, cezutinbadeh!

# Introduction: Contested Representation in Burma/Myanmar

Myanmar (also known as Burma; see the discussion of terminology later in the chapter) has endured prolonged periods of military rule and hosts some of the world's lengthiest internal conflicts. In the early 2010s, cautious hopes for democratic reform flared up on the local and international level, as the military initiated a top-down political transition process. These hopes were extinguished as the military continued to dominate the political landscape and terrorize the population, notably with its horrific violence against the Rohingya in 2017 and with a new military coup in 2021 and the subsequent violent repression of dissent. Throughout the long periods of military rule, the country has faced fierce contestation over political legitimacy and territorial control between the military and various armed and non-armed resistance groups. Burmese society, moreover, has historically been divided along the lines of ethnicity, class, age, gender, religion and rural or urban background. Diversity within the population gained political relevance when Burma was colonized by the British and during the subsequent independence struggle. Ethnic minorities, generally referred to in Myanmar as 'ethnic nationalities', make up over 30 per cent of the population and have borne the brunt of the military violence directed against populations in the border areas.[1] The nominally socialist military government which took power in 1962 was confronted with a large-scale popular uprising, resulting in a military reshuffle in 1988. This era of military change-over marked the rise of Aung San Suu Kyi as leader of the political opposition; her party won the elections of 1990 but was not allowed to take power. Meanwhile, armed ethnic resistance continued in the borderlands, while a Burman-dominated 'democracy movement' was established, partly from exile, in the 1990s.

In 2003, the military announced its 'Roadmap to Democracy', which resulted in a new constitution in 2008 and elections held in 2010. These developments intensified existing debates around the desired future of the country and how this should be achieved. By the time a quasi-civilian government under President Thein Sein took power in 2011, Myanmar's political transition had caught international attention. Aung San Suu Kyi's release from house arrest just days after the 2010 elections and her re-entrance into national politics in 2012 increased international interest during what some call Myanmar's 'honeymoon period'. A period of intense contestation followed, as Buddhist nationalism, communal conflict and renewed fighting in some of the ethnic states developed amid nominal progress towards democracy. This period of contestation was followed by five years of controversial rule by Aung San Suu Kyi and her party the National League for Democracy (NLD) from 2015 to 2020, during which military violence against the Rohingya and other minority groups intensified. The military's continued political influence culminated in another coup in response to the NLD's second victory in the 2020 elections, and a military junta called the State Administration Council (SAC) was created in February 2021. The years since this latest coup have seen an escalation of military violence against ethnic nationalities and political dissidents. As resistance and violence intensified in more regions than before, however, it also brought together previously dispersed opposition groups, cutting across some of the existing divisions within Myanmar's population.

This book focuses on the political transition period between 2010 and 2020 and analyses the factors that contributed to the various contestations before and during these political developments. While Myanmar's recent history is often told from the perspective of power holders – either the military or the main political opposition led by Aung San Suu Kyi, whose father headed the colonial independence movement – the focus here is on relatively young, educated, mostly urban citizens who sought to bring about social and political change by organizing under the banner of civil society. Within this framework, the book explores the dynamics surrounding the representation of Myanmar's diverse population, the various activities under authoritarian rule, and the influence of foreign actors. It explores the international optimism during Myanmar's early years of transition and the diverse responses to these sudden changes by civil society groups inside the country and in exile. While earlier Western involvement mostly took the shape of support for the democracy movement and limited levels of humanitarian assistance to ethnic nationalities in the border areas, the political transition period brought in a range of new external actors. Diplomats, donors and business actors entered in search of partnerships as the country opened up to outside influences. This provided local activists with new opportunities but also presented them with new challenges.

In this introduction, the framework and methodology of the research conducted for this study is introduced, as is the concept of civil society that serves as a lens throughout this book. Chapter 1 provides an overview of political developments that preceded the transition period of the early 2010s, centring on episodes of conflict, repression and resistance that characterize Myanmar's recent history. Chapter 2 discusses what constitutes civil society in Myanmar over time, and what activities these actors engaged in. The religious origins of most of the older non-state organizations and nationalistic forces are acknowledged, but the book focuses primarily on a growing number of progressive young actors driven by other motives and ideologies, some of whom have long remained outside public view. The chapter ends with the rise of Buddhist nationalism during the political transition period and the NLD's electoral victory in 2015. Chapter 3 describes the identities of various Burmese civil society actors along five broad fault lines, while Chapter 4 discusses how civil society actors engaged in various types of collective organization during the final stages of the pre-2010 military era and the early years of the political transition. This chapter counters depictions of civil society in authoritarian environments as mostly constrained by repressive structures. While the freedom to operate in the public sphere was severely restricted by the military government, some civil society actors managed to conduct politically sensitive work, either by disguising their activities or by turning to international platforms and soliciting the help of foreign supporters.

Chapter 5 describes what depictions of civil society gained international prominence, and what role civil society actors themselves played in influencing these depictions through their transnational advocacy strategies. Progressive sections of civil society interacted with a range of domestic and foreign actors, including relevant ministries and local authorities, fellow activists and donors, in order to achieve their goals for social and political change. However, the governmental and non-governmental actors they engaged with sometimes pulled them in opposite directions in terms of the preferred tactics and prioritization of issues and actions to achieve domestic change. This tension is exemplified by the campaigning around the 2010 elections, which forms the focus of Chapter 6. These were the most contentious elections to date and were preceded by a coordinated election boycott campaign of activists protesting the unfair playing field for the political opposition. While the elections of 2015 and 2020 were considered largely free and fair, the 2010 elections were heavily disputed both before and after they took place. Nevertheless, as Chapter 6 illustrates, they were the first opportunity in decades for people in Myanmar to openly discuss politics. Chapter 7 zooms in on the role of foreign supporters and discusses the influence of the largely Western donor support on civil society's room to manoeuvre before and during the transition. It provides examples of the way aid to Myanmar became politicized at various moments: first as a tool to sanction the military government, then as an attempt to bring about democratization from below, and next as a battleground over the rights of ethnic and religious minorities, particularly Rohingya and other Muslim populations.

The period between 2012 and 2017 saw not only political liberalization and increased civil liberties, but also hate speech emanating from Buddhist nationalists, communal violence in various parts of the country and the murder and expulsion of large groups of Rohingya as a result of military violence in Rakhine State. The subsequent lack of response from Aung San Suu Kyi and many prominent democracy activists sparked surprise and outrage among Western observers and the international human rights community. This book covers some of the internal dynamics that may help explain this increased discrepancy between local and international perspectives. The local responses to communal violence and hate speech cannot be understood without taking into account the legacy of decades of authoritarian rule, where the military dominated not only politics but also large sections of the media and the education system. Moreover, the military continuously portrayed itself as a guardian of Buddhist national identity and set various ethnic and religious groups against each other. The selective international attention on Myanmar, which focused on business opportunities on the one hand and human rights violations against the Rohingya on the other, further exacerbated the sense of victimhood among various sections of the Burmese population.

Lastly, Chapter 8 zooms in on civil society's responses to the military coup of 2021 and its subsequent search for inter-group solidarity and renewed international attention. After the coup a number of elected politicians and civil society representatives joined forces in the National Unity Government (NUG), a shadow body to the SAC. At the time of writing in 2022–23, the military and the NUG compete for local legitimacy and international recognition in platforms such as the UN and international courts, while developments in Afghanistan, Ukraine, Sudan and elsewhere have taken over global headlines. After months of peaceful protest and violent repression in 2021, some citizens turned to violent resistance by forming People's Defence Forces, many of which were trained by ethnic armed organizations (EAOs) in the border regions.[2] This led to new questions regarding representation and agenda setting on behalf of the Myanmar population, as well as debates over effective and acceptable forms of resistance. The Civil Disobedience Movement, in which striking public servants refuse to provide public services such as health care or education, also intensified pressure on various sides. Meanwhile, the nationwide anti-coup protests also had an emancipatory effect on various marginalized groups. Ethnic nationalities, women, youth and sexual minorities played a more prominent and visible role than before, and protesters showed increasing public support for the plight of the Rohingya and other minorities. While these events are ongoing, the book assesses their preliminary impact on the future of Myanmar as well as the continued role of various civil society actors.

## Researcher positionality

This book is based on PhD research conducted between 2009 and 2015, an important time of transition when Myanmar opened up to the outside world. Before starting my PhD in late 2009, I had worked as a volunteer for Burma Center Netherlands (BCN) and written a master's thesis on the debate around economic sanctions in response to human rights violations in Myanmar. Both these experiences pointed towards a gap in knowledge about inside perspectives as opposed to foreign perceptions. Up to the early 2000s, the country was regarded internationally as a pariah state with a largely repressed population under military rule. The results of the 1990 elections had been ignored, Aung San Suu Kyi remained under house arrest, and armed conflict in the ethnic regions continued. The number of political prisoners reached a peak after the so-called 'Saffron Revolution' in 2007, which occurred while I submitted my master's thesis. Throughout this period, foreign policy and development actors relied largely on the advocacy messages of democracy activists in exile. Few academics or policy makers conducted extensive research inside the country, and those who did were constrained in what they could share publicly, in order not to jeopardize the safety of their respondents or their own access to the country (Matelski, 2014). When I started my PhD, elections had just been announced for 2010. In the following years, I conducted fieldwork in central Myanmar, as well as with various Myanmar activists in the Thai border area. During this period, I witnessed the unfolding political transition and followed a number of respondents as they stepped up activities throughout the country. During the transition, many civil society actors sought and found new opportunities to contribute to social and political change. Various activists in exile, moreover, moved their organizations partly or completely back to Myanmar. My fieldwork ended just before the 2015 elections, in which Aung San Suu Kyi's NLD party gained its first country-wide victory since the unhonoured election results of 1990.[3]

By the time I defended my thesis in 2016, international optimism about Myanmar's political transition was at its height. In debates in academia, policy making and journalism in the Netherlands and elsewhere, I tried to refute suggestions that the transition had been completed, or that civil society should take on a less critical role towards the Myanmar government. I organized seminars and wrote op-eds highlighting the increasing hostility towards religious minorities and the continued side-lining of opponents to the military. These warnings were not based on particular insider information, as I only returned to the country for brief visits after 2015, while continuing to follow the situation through (social) media. Rather, my research experiences compelled me to join the more critical analysts and researchers on Myanmar who warned against international optimism regarding political developments, business opportunities and country-wide improvement of human rights, although not many had predicted the level of deterioration witnessed since (Cheesman, 2015; Callahan, 2018; Walton, 2018; Renshaw, 2019; Brooten et al, 2019; Campbell, 2023; Mon Mon Myat, 2023 and others).

This book describes the background as well as the development of selected civil society actors' identities, activities and perspectives throughout the political transition period. It does so through the eyes of an 'engaged observer', since I have long been involved in activism on Myanmar but have never lived in the country for a prolonged period and thus have not experienced the cycles of repression and resistance first-hand. As a White woman from Europe, moreover, with limited knowledge of Burmese language and no understanding of ethnic languages, I can only convey what my respondents were able and willing to share with me and add to this my personal analysis. It is important to acknowledge this position as an outsider, as there are many people in and from Myanmar who can share their inside perspectives on developments in the country yet often lack the international platform to do so. I fully support the increasing calls for Burma/Myanmar studies and policy discussions to become more inclusive of local voices (Chu May Paing and Than Toe Aung, 2021; Metro, 2023). Nevertheless, it is my hope that this personal account and analysis of an important period in Myanmar's political history contributes to a better understanding of the country's past, present and future and the situation of populations living under prolonged periods of conflict and repression in particular.

## Introducing the lens of civil society

This book discusses political developments in Myanmar through the lens of civil society. The contestations over the nature of civil society, and the question who is part of it, form an integral part of this discussion. Up to 2010, relatively little was known about varying views among Myanmar non-state actors. Donors and policy makers relied on messaging from the NLD as the main opposition party, and on the views of a number of prominent activists in exile. These categories were often conflated, for example through the National Coalition Government of the Union of Burma founded by a group of politicians elected in 1990 who had never been allowed to take office, many of whom had taken refuge outside the country. Discussions on ethnic affairs were usually held with leaders of EAOs, who constitute elite voices in their own environment. The research undertaken for this book explores the views of organized citizens in Myanmar who did not occupy such positions of political power, yet were particularly active within the socio-political sphere. After a concise discussion of the social scientific theory of civil society, the respondents for this study will be introduced. Chapters 2 and 3 will further unpack their various identities.

The concept of civil society originates largely in Western political thought, from Greek and Roman philosophers such as Plato, Aristotle and Cicero, to Enlightenment scholars such as Hegel and Ferguson (Cohen and Arato, 1994; Lewis, 2001). The positive connotations of civil society in the West, which strongly influenced the practice of foreign democracy promotion by the United States and other Western countries, emanates from Alexis de Tocqueville's work on 19th-century America, which explicitly identified an associational sphere independent from the state with the potential to contribute to democratization. Critical Marxist theorists, however, argue that such positive assessments ignore the importance of power inequalities within society and the potential for civil society to become complicit in repressive and exploitative practices (Howell and Pearce, 2002; Edwards, 2009). Antonio Gramsci in particular conceptualized civil society as a sphere of contestation between all forces in society, not just between citizens and the state, implying that the hegemony of a particular social group will also be reflected in civil society (Cohen and Arato, 1994; Glasius, 2012). Others similarly view civil society as a sphere that can be transformed through social movement struggles (Chandhoke, 2007) or suggest that attention should be paid to class struggles as well as foreign financial and ideological influences on local movements, such as the hegemonic role of US government agencies in the case of the Philippines (Hedman, 2006).

Contemporary civil society can be defined as 'citizens acting collectively in a public sphere' in order to achieve collective goals and is located between the private sphere and the realm of the state (Diamond, 1999: 221). Yet such definitions are inevitably partial and contested, and should be viewed in light of their particular cultural and geographic origins. Civil society theories gained empirical relevance when highly politicized movements brought about democratization processes in various Latin American and Eastern European countries in the 1970s and 1980s, in which labour unions and the Catholic Church played a significant role (Glasius et al, 2004; May and Milton, 2005). Since then, civil society has obtained a prominent place in Western democratization theory, as well as in neoliberal development policies. This in turn has sparked heated debates about the shape and functions of civil society, especially in non-Western countries and places where similar democratization processes have not occurred (Lewis, 2001). Alagappa (2004) for example argues that the Asian region has remained underrepresented in research on civil society, social movements and political activism, despite a number of significant popular uprisings since the 1980s. He defines civil society in Asia as a 'distinct public sphere of organization, communication and reflective discourse, and governance among individuals and groups that take collective action deploying civil means to influence the state and its policies but not capture state power, and whose activities are not motivated by profit' (Alagappa, 2004: 9).

Within this definition, the following types of civil society organizations (CSOs) are identified: churches, labour unions, farmers' organizations, academic and student groups, debating societies and reading groups, non-state media, non-governmental organizations (NGOs), occupational associations, business federations, and sports and leisure groups. In addition to more and less formal organizations, Alagappa's definition includes loosely structured social movements such as transnational activists and diaspora communities. This is important, as it implies that the realm of civil society should not be defined primarily based on visibility or formal organizational format. As we will see in Myanmar, the definition and recognition of CSOs has been contested throughout military rule. Many of the most influential organizations were outlawed by the military government and consequently worked underground or from exile. Although political parties tend to be excluded from definitions of civil society, these outlawed Myanmar groups in some cases consisted of elected politicians in exile, while some civil society actors conversely transformed themselves into political candidates in the 2015 elections.

Though strictly speaking all organizations outside the scope of the military in authoritarian Myanmar are non-governmental, the term NGO is typically reserved for more formal organizations that tend to be identified as potential partners for foreign donors and other external actors.[4] The Amsterdam-based Burma Center Netherlands and Transnational Institute were among the first to write about civil society in Myanmar. In an edited volume they published in 1999, Purcell refers to Korten's earlier classification of NGOs into four 'generations' ranging from less to more overtly political activities: (1) delivering services to improve social welfare; (2) developing capacity and empowering communities; (3) attempting to bring about systemic change by working with national agencies; and (4) facilitating social movements by mobilizing people for social change. This distinction is meant to serve as a classifying tool and not as a hierarchy, and many organizations combine various strategies. Other distinctions have been made between development or service delivery organizations and advocacy or human rights organizations (Van Tuijl, 1999; Banks et al, 2015). Despite the usefulness of these broad classifications, an exclusive focus on either overtly political or exclusively non-political activities risks overlooking the intended and unintended political effects of social activities that are characteristic of non-democratic and non-Western environments. Therefore, actors and organizations in this study are described in terms of the activities they engage in rather than their formal labels. Akman (2012) proposes studying civil society actors based on their 'social orientation' or behaviour in the public domain, which implies that 'uncivil components' could be included on the far end of the continuum. This is particularly relevant in light of the Buddhist nationalist groups that (re-)emerged in Myanmar during the political transition period. The debate around 'uncivil society', as well as the issues of professionalization and elitism, will be discussed in Chapters 2 and 3. First, the methodology and main respondents underlying this book are introduced.

## Respondents and methodology

This book centres on the experiences of a small section of Myanmar's vibrant and diverse civil society, mostly young, educated, urban citizens, as they sought to navigate the quickly changing political circumstances, carving out opportunities to contribute to social and political change. The civil society actors described here can be seen as intermediaries trying to balance local and international agendas while interacting with governmental and non-governmental stakeholders on the local, national and transnational level. The activists I encountered both in Thailand and in Myanmar, some of whom became my respondents for several years, were neither prominent political dissidents nor representative of the 'average' Myanmar citizen. Most spoke good English, and many had travelled or even conducted part of their education abroad. They were roughly between 25 and 40 years old at the time of my research, were active in some form of organized civil society, and seemed eager to take up new opportunities emerging in the political transition. While most of them sought to bring about social and political change (as described later in this introduction) by engaging in ostensibly non-political activities such as education or development, others were well-known dissidents who actively sought to stay out of reach of the military and its intelligence service.[5] Throughout my research, these respondents offered access and insight into a variety of views among activists about the preferred way forward in Myanmar, the role of the military and the political opposition, and the plight of the various ethnic and other minority groups in the country.

Data were collected through a combination of ethnographic fieldwork, interviews and desk research consisting of literature review and (social) media analysis. After a short preliminary visit to the Myanmar community in northern Thailand in early 2010, I conducted five months of fieldwork starting in July 2010, including a one-month visit to Myanmar, during which elections were announced for 7 November. The remainder of this time was spent predominantly with the participants of various civil society training courses in Chiang Mai, some of whom were based at exile organizations in Thailand, while others had come from Myanmar to attend the trainings. In 2010, it was still considered dangerous or difficult to openly conduct trainings or research activities inside the country. Many of the activities I was interested in took place on Thai soil and, consequently, so did most of the first phase of my research. This period also served as a mapping exercise to identify the various civil society actors and views that could be found inside and outside Myanmar.

My first interviews took place predominantly around a 'community development' training course in Thailand, which I was allowed to sit in on for three months. The participants in this training came from various parts of Myanmar and had come to Thailand just for the training. Some had been sent by their organizations, while others had taken a break from work but could reflect on previous activities in CSOs. This training provided a unique opportunity to meet with a variety of actors from all over the country with recent first-hand experience working in the local context. The fact that we were mostly in the same age range and that I was able to join them for an extensive period in a classroom setting allowed me to interact with them in a more informal manner than when visiting offices. Apart from providing a relatively stable environment to meet civil society actors, the trainings in themselves also provided important insights into the transfer of knowledge and values between foreign actors such as trainers and donor representatives and Myanmar civil society actors from various geographical, ethnic and religious backgrounds. I also interacted with participants in another training programme in Thailand, which was aimed explicitly at young democracy activists from Myanmar. I followed up with several of these participants during subsequent visits to Myanmar and encountered some of them in public platforms and conferences elsewhere in Asia and Europe.

During the second phase of my research in 2011, I spent two months in Thailand and two months in Myanmar. During one of these visits, I participated in a British civil society strengthening project aimed at non-state education providers in Myanmar. This provided further insights into the interaction between donors and CSOs, as well as deeper knowledge of the educational challenges in Myanmar (reported in Matelski, 2015). I also interviewed a number of donor representatives in Bangkok and Yangon. From 2012 to 2019, I returned for shorter visits. From then on, there were increased opportunities to join civil society activities, and I participated in several trainings throughout the country. These later stages of fieldwork also provided the opportunity to ask retrospective questions to some of my respondents on topics that had earlier been problematic to discuss, as well as follow-up questions on the evolving political situation. An overview of the main research activities and respondents is provided in Table 1.

The quotes used throughout this book result from interviews, focus group discussions and informal interactions during these fieldwork periods. I refer to my respondents anonymously and provide information on their age, gender, ethnic and geographical background where available. For ethnic

**Table 1:** Overview of research activities, respondents and locations

| Type of activities | Respondents, locations and timeframe |
| --- | --- |
| Interviews and participant observation | • Voluntary work with Burma Center Netherlands in Amsterdam (2004–6); ongoing contact with Myanmar community in the Netherlands.<br>• Interviews and participant observation with Buddhist, Christian, Muslim, non-religious and ethnicity-based organizations active mostly under the banner of education, women's rights and social development in Yangon (2010–19).<br>• Three-month community development training in Thailand with participants from social development organizations and various (I)NGOs in Myanmar – observations and informal conversation; nine interviews/focus group discussions with a total of 18 participants and alumni from various ethnic backgrounds: Burman, Dawei, Kachin, Karen, Kayan, Mon, Rakhine, Shan and Myanmar Muslim (2010); see the section 'States, regions and ethnicities in Myanmar' for an explanation of these identities.<br>• Interviews with democracy activists: one female representative of Burma Partnership – now Progressive Myanmar; male representatives of Human Rights Education Institute of Burma – now Equality Myanmar, Generation Wave and the Assistance Association for Political Prisoners (Burma), and three male representatives of The Best Friend Library – all of Burman ethnicity; attending their public events in Bangkok, Chiang Mai and Yangon (2010–19).<br>• Interviews and informal interaction with four alumni (two male Burmans, two women of Kayah and Shan ethnicity) of a training for young democracy activists from Myanmar in Thailand (2010–19).<br>• Participation in education project of Pyoe Pin, a civil society support initiative at the British Council; visits to non-state education providers; attending meeting on non-state education organized by UNICEF in Yangon (2011).<br>• Interacting with two Yangon-based civil society strengthening projects set up by INGOs: the Local Resource Centre and Paung Ku. Participant observation with a local organization set up under the umbrella of Paung Ku in Yangon, Mandalay and Shan State (2010–19).<br>• Participation in study trip to Delhi, India, with over 30 Myanmar representatives from civil society and political parties (2012).<br>• Attending public events organized in Yangon, including Chin National Day, charity events for Kachin war victims and lectures by American scholars James C. Scott and Joseph Stiglitz (2011–12). |

(continued)

**Table 1:** Overview of research activities, respondents and locations (continued)

| Type of activities | Respondents, locations and timeframe |
| --- | --- |
| Organizational visits | • Visit to 'Third Force' organizations Myanmar Egress in Yangon and Vahu Development Institute in Chiang Mai; interviews with three male Burman directors (2010 – organizations no longer operational).<br>• Visits to organizations active on land rights, civic participation and development in Myanmar (2010–19).<br>• Visits to a monastery in Mandalay, four non-state education initiatives, the Myanmar Peace Center, the 88 Generation Peace and Open Society office, an art gallery and a labour organization in Yangon, and two refugee camps in Thailand (2010–19). |
| Interviews with diplomats, INGO representatives and academic experts | • Interviews at embassies of the Netherlands, Denmark, Norway, United Kingdom, Canada, United States and Australia responsible for Myanmar in Bangkok and Yangon (2010–17).<br>• Interviews at INGOs with programmes on Myanmar in the Netherlands, Belgium, Australia, Thailand and Myanmar (2010–15).<br>• Interviews and discussions with academic experts in Europe and Australia (2009–11) and at various workshops and conferences. |
| Remote activities | • Interviews with 14 young women of 11 different ethnicities working for CSOs in Myanmar; conducted by co-researcher during COVID-19 (2020 – further details in Matelski and Nang May Noan, 2022).<br>• Attending online seminars and advocacy activities since COVID-19 (2020–23). |

background I rely on self-identification, as many respondents are in fact from mixed backgrounds.[6] For reasons of consistency and anonymity, I refrain from naming respondents except where I rely on information from published sources or public events. Despite my conscious attempts to bring in various views and voices, I do not claim to provide a representative sample of civil society, much less of Myanmar society as a whole. Indeed, this book intends to show that any such claims would be illusory.

## Local and global perceptions on social and political change

As stated, this book combines local and global perspectives on civil society. Looking beyond definitional questions, it explores what activities are undertaken under the banner of civil society in Myanmar and in exile at different points in time. Given the limited access to the country up to 2010, academic studies on Myanmar often focused on outside perceptions, such as legal positivist discussions on adherence to international human rights norms and the implications for foreign policy – primarily the question of engagement versus punitive action such as sanctions, and to a lesser extent, debates around humanitarian assistance.[7] Coming from a background in human rights and having been involved with the small advocacy organization Burma Center Netherlands, my interest in Myanmar primarily originated from a wish to analyse the severe human rights violations committed by the military government and the responses this prompted on the social and political level. However, human rights violations dominated Western reporting on contemporary Myanmar to such an extent that the experiences of those seeking to bring about social and political change remained underreported. By focusing on daily practices and dilemmas, rather than the ideals and statements of prominent political representatives such as Aung San Suu Kyi, this book seeks to provide insights into the way civil society actors in and from Myanmar manoeuvred in sometimes extremely harsh circumstances.

Similar to the discussion on civil society, the global human rights movement has been criticized for presenting Western political standards designed by states, academics and international NGOs as objective and simplistic depictions of good against evil, devoid of historical context or power analysis (Mutua, 2001; De Waal, 2003; Hopgood, 2013). In this light, the debate around depictions of Myanmar in Western writing has also intensified. While regional references to 'Asian values' as a basis to restrict civil and political rights in the 1990s have been largely refuted as self-serving arguments by political elites (Sen, 1997; Donnelly, 1999), those actors imposing Western political or economic models have come under equal scrutiny. Michael Aung-Thwin (2001), for example, a Myanmar-born historian who held academic positions in various countries, referred to depictions of Burmese democratic demands in the Western sense as 'parochial universalism', 'democracy jihad' and 'orientalism'. Similar arguments have been made regarding the use of annual freedom indices, which are presented as neutral but are in fact overly state-centric, particularly in authoritarian environments, and tend to prioritize civil and political rights over socio-economic rights (Brooten, 2013). Others have pointed out that actors in Myanmar do not necessarily share the same notion of concepts such as democracy and human rights. Political leaders such as Aung San Suu Kyi and other NLD representatives, for example, tend to prioritize responsibility and moral conduct over individual entitlements (Wells, 2021; Doffegnies and Wells, 2022; see also Houtman, 1999). As this book will demonstrate, the overt Western focus on civil rights and democratization was welcomed by democracy activists in need of assistance and support but sometimes came at the expense of the socio-economic needs of the larger population living under military rule, including a large number of refugees and internally displaced persons. The 2007 'Saffron Revolution' uprising, for example, brought large-scale international attention towards Myanmar for the first time, yet cyclone Nargis in 2008 had a more far-reaching impact on the livelihoods of local populations throughout the country. In order to make meaningful comparisons between the local and the global, and to incorporate both civil-political and socio-economic priorities, this book focuses on the terminology of social and political change rather than human rights and democracy. It seeks to provide insights into the way civil society actors striving for change during Myanmar's political transition period invoked foreign support in the form of moral, political and financial assistance to further their goals, but prioritizes local realities over foreign depictions.

This book takes as a starting point a social constructivist approach to human rights. From this perspective rights are given neither by birth nor by law but acquire meaning as a result of claim making by marginalized social groups (Stammers, 1999; Cowan et al, 2001). The civil society actors I interacted with in the field were clearly influenced by foreign entities as a result of globalization. With the increased availability of international media, communication and travel opportunities, they came across new ideas based on international human rights language, which they 'translated' into concerns and demands that are relevant to the local context (compare Merry, 2006). Rather than human rights constituting either a universal discourse or, contrarily, one with no local relevance, it is more likely that a process of 'friction' takes place, and that the local and the global interact in complex and sometimes unpredictable ways (Tsing, 2004). A social constructivist perspective is suitable when studying the daily activities of Myanmar activists and their interactions with foreign actors, as it allows for an exploration of the strategic way that certain rights claims are made and adjusted towards local and international audiences. Meanwhile, it leaves room for cultural factors that influence the conceptualization of human rights, not only on the country level, but also in more localized activities by different actors throughout the country.

## Burma or Myanmar?

The country now known as Myanmar has been referred to in English by two names: Burma and Myanmar. Although they are sometimes used interchangeably, each name carries significant connotations, and the decision to use one or the other therefore requires explanation (Dittmer, 2008; Metro, 2011). The British colonizers that took power at the end of the 19th century called the country Burma, a name closely related to the word for the majority ethnic group 'Bamar' but adapted to English pronunciation. Successive governments after independence in 1948 maintained the name Burma, but the military government changed it to Myanmar in 1989, reportedly to rid itself of connotations of British colonialism. The English names of various geographical places were also changed under the 1989 'Adaptation of Expressions Law': the name of Rangoon, for example, the country's former capital and main city, was changed to Yangon. However, the word Myanmar, although considered by some to be more inclusive of ethnic nationalities, in fact also refers to the dominant ethnic group: it is the older, literary version of the colloquial 'Bamar' (Houtman, 1999: 49). The political opposition, unhappy with the military rulers and their unilateral decision making, rejected the name change and continued to refer to the country as Burma. Many Western supporters followed this trend, while the United Nations and most Asian countries used the official name (the Republic of the Union of) Myanmar, a decision that critics saw as legitimizing the military rulers. Although reference to the country as Burma may signal disapproval of military rule, many Westerners (especially British) have habitually continued using Burma without any intended connotations.

Among my respondents, preferences for one name or the other differed widely, and some used the names interchangeably. For reasons of consistency, this book uses Myanmar to discuss the current situation, Burma to refer to the pre-1989 era, and Burmese to refer to the general population and the official language. When quoting respondents or written documents, I have maintained the name used by the original source. For names of cities and other places that have been changed by the military government, I use the name relevant to the time period discussed (for example, Rangoon pre-1989 and Yangon post-1989). Burmese personal names are written in full, as most Burmese people (with the exception of certain ethnic nationalities) do not use surnames.

## States, regions and ethnicities in Myanmar

Myanmar consists of fourteen administrative units: seven 'ethnic states' – Chin, Kachin, Kayah/Karenni, Karen/Kayin, Mon, Arakan/Rakhine and Shan; and seven regions, formerly called divisions – Ayeyarwady/Irrawaddy, Bago/Pegu, Magway, Mandalay, Sagaing, Tanintharyi/Tenasserim and Yangon/Rangoon.

The ethnic states are named after their largest ethnic group, but the actual ethnic composition is much more complex. Most of the Karen, for example, live outside Karen State, and many ethnic majority Burmans live in the urban areas of ethnic states (TNI, 2015). In this book, I mostly refer to ethnic minority groups as ethnic nationalities, which is the preferred term for their self-identification in Myanmar. Ethnic states refers to the seven states just mentioned, and EAOs refers to armed groups fighting on behalf of a (sub-)group of ethnic nationalities. This terminology is in line with common usage in and on Myanmar. I acknowledge that Burman/Bamar is an ethnicity too (see Walton, 2012b) and aim to avoid overlooking the various minorities within the ethnic states which do not have a state named after them, such as the Dawei who live mostly in Tanintharyi. Furthermore, this book refers to Muslims as both an ethnicity and a religion, as several respondents identify as Myanmar Muslim, a group different from the Rohingya that form another Muslim minority in Myanmar. Lastly, since this book targets an English language audience, all Burmese terms are written in romanized spelling.

# Conflict, Repression and Resistance from Colonialism to Military Rule

With the exception of 2011–20, Burma/Myanmar has the questionable honour of being the longest running military dictatorship in the world. The consecutive military governments that came to power in 1962 and 1988 were each known for their severe human rights violations, and the military leadership that took power in the 2021 coup has even surpassed their violent legacies. This chapter provides a brief historical overview, explaining how contestations over territory, political structures and ethnic minority rights have been recurring since before colonial independence and provided a motive for the military to continue its rule. Pre-existing tensions as a result of ethnic diversity had been exacerbated during British colonialism, which ended in 1948, and were far from solved when a military coup in 1962 brought an end to the recently established parliamentary democracy. Nationalist sentiments intensified as ethnic nationalities struggled for self-determination, while Buddhist nationalism also surfaced periodically, re-appearing in the course of the political transition period that started in 2010. Respective periods of nation building resulted in both extensive military rule and the search for a Burman Buddhist identity at the expense of indigenous minorities.

## British colonialism and nationalist resistance

Between 1824 and 1886, the British took control of the territory now known as Myanmar during three Anglo-Burmese wars and engaged in violent pacification campaigns towards the local population. The Burmans, in turn, had come to dominate the earlier inhabitants of the territory, including the Karen and the Mon (Harvey, 1925; Lieberman, 1984). Burma initially became part of British India and from 1937 was a separate colony. In their efforts to formally map territorial boundaries, the British brought together a number of previously unaffiliated ethnic and linguistic groups.

A division was created between the central area inhabited by the majority Burman population and the current ethnic states in the border areas, where bureaucratic rule by the British remained largely absent. The colonizers brought in staff for administrative positions from elsewhere and treated Burma as a less advanced and less profitable part of British India, which increasingly upset the Burmese population. In her book *Making Enemies*, Mary Callahan (2003) describes how the indigenous population was treated as an internal threat to colonial rule rather than inhabitants entitled to protection and inclusion in institution building. The British created territorial boundaries that had not previously existed as well as arbitrary divisions between ethnic identities, contributing to 'politicized violence along ethnic lines' (Callahan, 2003: 22). They succeeded in establishing good relationships with some of the ethnic nationalities (mainly the Chin and the Kachin), who accepted British rule in exchange for non-interference in local affairs such as taxation. Some of them were also actively recruited for the British army in Burma, which by the early 1940s consisted of only 12 per cent Burmans.[1]

Burman nationalist sentiments increased under colonial rule. Resistance was led by prominent Buddhist monks, while peasant populations also protested, particularly against detrimental economic policies (Taylor, 2009; Aung-Thwin, 2011). These groups joined forces in the Hsaya San Rebellion (referred to as the 'Burma Rebellion' by the British),[2] a two-year movement (1930–32) named after a rural Buddhist leader who sought attention for peasant grievances. This uprising, although violently suppressed, marked the start of a 'tradition of boycott and avoidance of the state' (Taylor, 2009: 196). The Burman resentment about ethnic nationalities collaborating with foreign entities continued to dominate their views on who should be considered part of Burmese society, and Burman activists set up several nationalist groups called *tats*. Rangoon University students set up the Dobama Asiayone ('We Burmans Association', also known as the Thakin Party) in the 1930s. After World War II, members of this group played a central role in the independence movement, and student groups continued to be politically active in the following decades. Meanwhile, ethnic nationalities also organized themselves to represent their distinct social, cultural and political interests, which strengthened their nationalist sentiments (Taylor, 2009: 181).[3]

Ethnic segregation was further fostered during World War II. While some minorities supported the Allies, Burman nationalists started the Burma Independence Army (BIA) led by General Aung San with assistance from the Japanese. The BIA would support the Japanese until 1945, while communist and Karen armed groups cooperated with the British to remove the Japanese from power (Taylor, 2009). In 1945, Aung San withdrew his support for the Japanese and sided with the British and various political allies, including ethnic nationalities, to liberate the country under the banner of the Anti-Fascist People's Freedom League (AFPFL). After the Japanese were defeated, Aung San led negotiations for independence from the British. He also negotiated with ethnic nationalities, resulting in the Panglong Agreement that was signed on 12 February 1947. This agreement, which arranged for the Chin, Kachin and Shan to join Burma in a federal union, has continued to be used as a source of legitimacy for ethnic self-determination struggles.[4] Although Aung San promised the ethnic nationalities equal treatment, they felt betrayed by the 1947 constitution, which laid the foundation for a centralized system (Callahan, 2003: 94). Aung San, perhaps the sole person on whom all parties had relied to bring inter-ethnic unity, was tragically assassinated by political rivals on 19 July 1947 before any of his promises could be realized. According to some scholars, the 'Panglong Spirit' has since become an ahistorical myth propagated by Burman-dominated governments proclaiming harmonious ethnic relations that never actually existed (Walton, 2008; Sadan, 2013: 304).

## Post-independence politics and the start of military rule

After Burma achieved formal independence on 4 January 1948, Aung San's AFPFL emerged as the leading party, with U Nu as the first elected prime minister. He would remain in that position intermittently until 1962.[5] U Nu's rule can be considered largely democratic, and elections were held in 1947, 1951–52, 1956 and 1960. Yet he was simply unable to undo all the disrupting effects of colonialism, World War II and the assassination of Aung San. The many weapons circulating after the war in combination with the simmering ethnic grievances and the geopolitical effects of the Cold War posed major challenges to his rule, and civil war soon erupted. The Communist Party of Burma (CPB), which had gone underground in its struggle against the British, soon launched its armed resistance against the newly independent state and would remain a popular political party in post-independence Burma (Lintner, 1990: 25).[6] Ethnic groups continued to demand federalism, autonomy and independence, and several of them took up arms against what they perceived as Burman domination, with the Karen National Union (KNU), created in 1947, posing a particularly serious threat (Charney, 2009: 75). During the Cold War, Chinese Kuomintang soldiers entered Burmese territory and joined forces with some of the ethnic insurgent groups in the border areas, creating fear of a Chinese invasion (Lintner, 1990: 29). Faced with these internal and external threats, the military quickly expanded its size and rule and came to consider itself a guardian needed to govern the country.[7] While it took on responsibility for everything from law enforcement to economic and political affairs, it proved unable to secure electoral support and increasingly came to see the domestic population as its enemy (Callahan, 2003). Worried that the new elections would lead to disturbances or other undesired outcomes, the military successfully suggested that U Nu stage a 'constitutional coup' (Callahan, 2003: 188). During this first period of military rule, which lasted from October 1958 to April 1960, General Ne Win served as the head of a 'Caretaker Government'.[8] This was a reasonably successful government which, given the politically chaotic democratic period, was 'not entirely unwelcome' to the Burmese public (Lintner, 1990: 14). Yet the army continued its repression of ethnic insurgents and relocated part of the population of Rangoon to new satellite towns in remote suburbs, which 'soon became breeding grounds for anti-army discontent' (Lintner, 1990: 35–6).

For reasons that can only be speculated on, the military organized elections in 1960. These elections, referred to as 'free and unfair', were again won by U Nu, contrary to the military's expectations (Callahan, 2003: 197). These were to be the last credible Burmese elections of the 20th century of which the results were honoured. With threats of instability remaining from the side of the communists, the Karen, the Shan and the newly founded Kachin Independence Army (KIA) in 1961, Ne Win worried about the political and economic prospects of the country. He staged another coup on 2 March 1962, which, contrary to the previous one, was 'entirely unconstitutional' (Holliday, 2011: 47). The army suspended the 1947 constitution, dissolved the parliament, the judiciary and other established institutions and took full and indefinite control of the country. Ne Win would remain in power for 26 years, although he hardly ever appeared in public (Taylor, 2009: 322). After the 1962 military coup, U Nu and other winners of the 1960 elections were imprisoned, and single-party rule was formally established with the creation of the Burma Socialist Programme Party (BSPP).[9] Military rule ended formally (but not de facto) in 1974, as Ne Win handed over power to the People's Assembly, which elected him as president. During this period, he built up the notorious Military Intelligence Service (Selth, 1998). Political dissidents and their supporters were arrested, imprisoned and sometimes tortured, and informers even infiltrated the growing Burmese community in exile (Lintner, 1990; Selth, 1998).

A new constitution was put in place in 1974 containing provisions for the single-party Socialist Republic of the Union of Burma. The country was divided into seven 'ethnic nationality states' (Arakan, Chin, Kachin, Karen, Kayah, Mon and Shan) and seven 'divisions' which were predominantly inhabited by Burmans.[10] In the borderlands, inhabited mostly by ethnic nationalities, over 20 ethnic armed organizations (EAOs) controlled their own territories and administrations (Smith, 1999: 16). The military implemented its infamous 'four cuts strategy', whereby the ethnic armies were cut off from recruits, food, finance and intelligence. A controversial Citizenship Act would follow in 1982, which distinguished between 'full citizens' (Burmans, plus other ethnic groups who could prove they were related to Burmese citizens before the Anglo-Burmese wars), 'associate citizens' (those who were born in Burma after 1823, such as many Indians and Chinese), and 'naturalized citizens' whose citizenship could be revoked if they were 'disloyal to the state'. Only the first group could vote, take on all political positions and participate in higher education (Steinberg, 2010: 72–3).

The BSPP proved particularly weak in economic governance, and the country's economy quickly collapsed. The government became completely isolationist, nationalized around 15,000 businesses, expelled many foreigners (predominantly Indians) from the country and hardly allowed any foreign visitors. Many educated Burmese became unemployed and decided to leave the country, while groups of ethnic nationalities fled the ongoing civil wars. BSPP rule, though 'nominally socialist', was in fact a 'deeply dysfunctional form of state capitalism' with nationalist and xenophobic features (Holliday, 2011: 51). The economic crisis of the 1980s caused further hardship, as poverty levels increased and Burma obtained least developed country status with the UN in 1987, which caused great shame among the population (Steinberg, 2001: 131). Students, who were also severely affected by this economic decline, openly showed their discontent in what would become a mass movement that brought an end to the BSPP era, but not to military rule.

## The 'four eights' uprising and continued military rule

A violent incident in a Rangoon teashop on 12 March 1988 involving the son of a local BSPP representative became the starting point of a large uprising. The man's preferential treatment invoked a demonstration by Rangoon University students, in which one person was shot and killed by the authorities (Lintner, 1990). His fellow students demanded justice, but the government denied responsibility. Protesting students were met with increased violence, including the killing of dozens of demonstrators at the 'White Bridge' in Rangoon (Skidmore, 2004: 89). After about 1,000 students had been arrested and imprisoned, the protestors were able to gather country-wide support. Ne Win attempted to de-escalate the situation by stepping down from his position in the BSPP and proposing a referendum on a multiparty system, a proposal that was rejected by congress (Charney, 2009: 151). This option, however, inspired the students to call for democracy, rather than merely protesting against the government's violent tactics as they had done before (Holliday, 2011: 55). Monks, dockworkers, civil servants, businesspeople and religious leaders joined in, resulting in a large strike and demonstrations. An estimated one million people from various ethnic and religious backgrounds were involved in Rangoon and Mandalay alone at the height of the demonstrations on 8 August 1988, which would become known as the Four Eights (or 8888) uprising. Although largely peaceful, some demonstrators targeted and even killed suspected government representatives, including policemen (Lintner, 1990: 102). The army's violent response resulted in many casualties, with numbers ranging from 440 according to official government statistics to eyewitness estimates of 1,000 to 3,000 or more (Lintner, 1990: 103; Brooten, 2004: 175; Fink, 2009: 52). Information on this demonstration hardly reached the international community, with the first report by Amnesty International only appearing in 1989 (Lintner, 1990). Over 10,000 dissidents left Rangoon, and some even fled the country. This would mark the start of the 'democracy movement' in exile (described in Chapter 2).

As the calls for democracy grew and spread throughout the country, Aung San's daughter Aung San Suu Kyi, who had returned from her home in the UK to visit her mother, decided to respond to appeals to get politically involved, a call that had been largely inspired by her father's reputation. On 15 August 1988, she signed a letter calling on the government to end the political crisis (Lintner, 1990: 108). The next week, martial law was suddenly lifted in Rangoon. After a number of prominent demonstrators had been released from prison, Aung San Suu Kyi gave a speech on 26 August at the famous Shwedagon Pagoda in Rangoon to an audience of over 500,000 people, in which she called for democracy and a 'second struggle for independence'. Her eloquence and reference to her father's legacy gained her much support and inspired people to turn against the government and resign from its organizations (Lintner, 1990: 116). On 18 September, a military group led by General Saw Maung announced that it would take control of the country to restore order and prepare for multiparty elections. By 26 September, the State Law and Order Restoration Council had been formed. Its acronym SLORC was 'seized upon for its Orwellian overtones by the foreign press and Western diplomats' (Taylor, 2009: 388).[11]

The post-1988 military government abandoned all ideology and pronounced 'law and order' to be its sole objective (Cheesman, 2015). The primary goal became the restoration of 'peace and tranquillity' and the suppression of 'destructive elements' in order to secure its own position (Lintner, 1990: 138). The 'three main national causes', which could be found in state media and on public billboards were non-disintegration of the union, non-disintegration of national solidarity and perpetuation of sovereignty. SLORC Martial Law Order 2/88 set limitations on public meetings of five or more persons, which could only be held with advance permission from the authorities, a provision that has remained in place since. Many dissidents were arrested and received long prison sentences. Senior General Than Shwe acted as head of the military, prime minister and defence minister for almost two decades. After taking power, the SLORC opened up the economy, and the military became increasingly involved in trade. A system of crony capitalism soon developed, to the advantage of military officers and their family members (Ford et al, 2015). The SLORC also significantly increased its use of forced labour to develop the country's infrastructure, particularly in the ethnic states. In 1989, it formally changed the country's name to (Union of) Myanmar. By the 1990s, Myanmar was reportedly among the poorest in the world (Babson in Steinberg, 2001: 168). While international business ties with other Asian countries (particularly China and Thailand) intensified, the population did not benefit. Large-scale extraction of natural resources generated profit mostly for the military and its business partners, while local populations suffered the consequences such as environmental degradation and forced relocation (Woods, 2011, 2017; Simpson, 2014; Kramer, 2015, 2021; Sekine, 2023).

Although the army continued to restrict civil liberties, it did proceed with the proposed multiparty elections and allowed political parties to register. Due to the increase in political freedoms, but also the material benefits granted to political parties such as telephone lines and petrol supplies, over 200 parties were formed. Some were considered 'merely fronts for the military', and the SLORC was accused of intentionally encouraging this proliferation: as long as the public was divided, it could use political stability as an argument to stay in power (Charney, 2009: 161). The most prominent party that emerged was the National League for Democracy (NLD), started by Aung San Suu Kyi and two former members of the military. Despite the apparent liberalization, Aung San Suu Kyi and other NLD members were harassed by the SLORC during their campaign tours (Lintner, 1990: 170–1). The military arrested between 2,000 and 6,000 NLD members, and Aung San Suu Kyi and Vice Chairman Tin U were placed under house arrest in July 1989 after being accused of subversive activities (Charney, 2009: 167). Although the military tried to ensure a favourable outcome and intimidated the opposition, it lost the elections of 27 May 1990. The NLD, with its leadership under house arrest, obtained 392 of the 447 seats it contested. Only ten seats went to the National Unity Party (NUP), the party representing the military. The rest of the seats were won by ethnic nationality parties such as the Shan and the Rakhine. Aung San Suu Kyi remained under house arrest (or 'protective custody' as the military called it), and the SLORC announced that it had no intention to transfer power to the winning parties.[12]

The military then started 'de-democratizing the country' by further cracking down on dissidents and the political opposition (Charney, 2009: 173). It suspended the 1974 constitution and took over all decision-making power.[13] When it became clear that power would not be transferred quickly, some elected members of the NLD and other opposition groups secretly set up a parallel government, the National Coalition Government of the Union of Burma (NCGUB), founded in Karen State in 1990. Its members then moved to Thailand and eventually the United States in order to lobby for their cause from exile. The NLD continued to claim the right to govern based on the 1990 election results, a position supported by the United States and other Western actors. Aung San Suu Kyi was released in 1995, then again placed under house arrest from 2000 to 2002. In 2003, she was nearly assassinated during an attack in Depayin, which many suspect was orchestrated by the military (Fink, 2009: 94). After surviving this incident, in which around 70 people died, she was again placed under 'protective custody' until 2010. Aung San Suu Kyi, who had gained both domestic and international popularity, refused offers to leave the country even when her husband in the UK was terminally ill. She was granted numerous international awards for her struggle for democratization, including the Nobel Peace Prize in 1991.[14] Meanwhile, the military leaders tried to weaken the NLD's position, while the party also fell subject to internal rivalries and debates about the desired approach towards the military.

Despite the military's long and intrusive rule, it continued to present itself as a transitional government. In 2003, then Prime Minister General Khin Nyunt announced the military government's 'Roadmap to Democracy'. This roadmap laid out seven steps that would result in a 'modern, developed, and democratic nation' (Fink, 2009: 94). As a first step, it reconvened the National Convention in 2004 with the intention to draw up a new constitution; this process would take until 2007. The NLD refused to participate in the National Convention as long as its leaders Aung San Suu Kyi and Tin Oo were imprisoned. In 2005, the military suddenly announced that it would move the country's capital from Yangon to the newly built city Naypyidaw ('Abode of Kings'). This move was reportedly a matter of prestige (in the past, influential kings had also established new capitals), but probably also an attempt to secure a more central location less vulnerable to foreign invasion (Farrelly, 2018).

## The 2007 'Saffron Revolution'

After a number of periodic popular uprisings in the 1990s (discussed in Chapter 2), the next large-scale protest took place in September 2007 with the so-called 'Saffron Revolution'.[15] After the government suddenly removed the subsidies on fuel and gas prices, resulting in a doubling of bus fares overnight, activists from the 88 generation (as the group became known) staged a demonstration which resulted in several arrests (Human Rights Watch, 2009). The next month, a small group of politically educated monks staged a peaceful demonstration that was met with violence by the authorities. On 10 September, the newly formed All Burma Monks' Alliance demanded a public apology from the military to the monks, along with a reduction of fuel prices, the release of all political prisoners and the start of a dialogue with the 'democratic forces for national reconciliation' (Fink, 2009: 102). The monks threatened to withhold their religious services from the SPDC leadership if their demands were not met within a week. After a week had passed, they took to the streets on 18 September and were soon joined by 88 Generation Students and some NLD members. On 22 September, they passed by the house of Aung San Suu Kyi, who made a brief appearance from behind her gate. By 24 September, an estimated 40,000–100,000 monks and laypeople took part in the protest (Kyaw Yin Hlaing, 2008: 132; Fink, 2009: 103).

After an initial non-violent episode, the government began hunting down the organizers. On 26 September, it opened fire on the demonstrators, including monks. The estimated number of casualties ranges from 15 (government count) to around 160 according to the opposition, and over 5,000 people were detained (Kyaw Yin Hlaing, 2008: 133; Min Zin, 2010a: 91; Cheesman, 2015). In contrast to 1988, this time some international observers were present, and local journalists managed to smuggle footage to the international media (as depicted in the Oscar-winning documentary *Burma VJ*). Although the number of casualties was much smaller than in 1988, the images of the shooting of unarmed Buddhist monks, as well as a Japanese journalist, caused international outrage. After the crackdown by the army, the situation went back to 'normal', although the monks remained under surveillance, and there were said to be many infiltrators in their midst. Members of the 88 Generation Students received prison sentences of up to 65 years (Fink, 2009: 105).[16] Other dissidents fled to the Thai border. Although political prisoners were occasionally released as part of military amnesties, hundreds died in prison due to torture and neglect, while others who were released had trouble reintegrating into society and developed severe physical and mental problems (Fink, 2009).[17] The 2007 uprising put the country in the international spotlight and showed both domestic and international observers that dissidents continued to resist the military government. The uprising did not, however, bring about regime change.

## A cyclone, a constitutional referendum and an election

Despite the NLD's refusal to take part in the National Convention, and undeterred by the 2007 uprising, the military continued to the next steps of its 'Roadmap to Democracy', which included the drafting of a new constitution that would have to be adopted through a national referendum. Yet on 2–3 May 2008, just days before the referendum was supposed to take place, lower Myanmar (the Irrawaddy delta and Yangon) was hit by a cyclone of great magnitude. An estimated 140,000 people died, and over two million were displaced or otherwise affected. The cyclone's severe consequences were compounded by the military's indifferent response. Just days after this natural disaster occurred, it went ahead with the referendum, in which 98 per cent of the population reportedly voted, with 92 per cent approving the draft constitution. The 2008 constitution, which remains in place to date, has been much criticized, not only because its drafting process lacked any form of democratic consultation, but notably for its undemocratic content. It grants 25 per cent of the seats in parliament to sitting military officers, leaves three influential ministries (Home Affairs, Defence, and Border Affairs) under full control of the military, and allows for a military coup in case of emergencies. It also bars anyone with family members abroad (such as Aung San Suu Kyi) from becoming president. Since amendments require over 75 per cent approval in parliament, the military can effectively block any constitutional changes.

In line with points 5 and 6 of the 'Roadmap to Democracy', the military organized elections on 7 November 2010. Opposition parties were again restricted. The NLD decided to boycott the elections and was subsequently deregistered (see Chapter 6 for a detailed discussion of the election boycott campaign). Restrictions were also imposed on parties representing people from conflict areas such as Kachin State (TNI, 2010). Of the 37 parties that were eventually approved, only two were able to organize national campaigns: the SPDC-affiliated Union Solidarity and Development Party (USDP) and the BSPP-successor, the NUP. Each had more candidates than the other 35 parties combined (Holliday, 2011: 84).[18] Neither the political opposition nor the international community considered the 2010 elections free or fair. Opposition parties had hardly been able to campaign, and voters felt pressured by the military to support the USDP, which also secured a suspiciously large number of advance votes (TNI, 2010). The results indicated a victory for the USDP, which reportedly received 77 per cent of the votes.[19] In February 2011, the parliament elected former military general and prime minister Thein Sein as president, while the vice-presidents and speakers of the lower and upper house also hailed from the USDP. Due to the undemocratic manner in which the USDP was able to win, and the continued role of both the military and its proxy party, the Thein Sein government is referred to by critics as quasi- or nominally civilian.

## The quasi-civilian USDP government

Unexpectedly, in the course of 2011 President Thein Sein's government started taking significant steps towards political reform by granting selective liberties to the political opposition and other dissidents. In May 2011, the government issued its first amnesty for thousands of prisoners, who were released or saw their sentences reduced, including 47 identified by activists as political prisoners. Hundreds more political prisoners were released as part of amnesties in October 2011 and January 2012. A secret blacklist with over 6,000 Burmese and foreign persons was revealed in 2012, and only some of these people were subsequently removed from the list (Holliday, 2013: 95; Duell, 2014: 121). By the end of 2013, a total of twelve amnesties had been issued, freeing an estimated 1,000 'prisoners of conscience' (UN General Assembly report in Cheesman, 2015: 128). It must be noted, however, that these amnesties were conditional, and that no former political prisoners were formally absolved from their 'crimes' (Cheesman, 2015: 130). Moreover, new laws were later invoked to detain dissidents for their activities on social media or in organized demonstrations. A National Human Rights Commission set up in 2011 was heavily criticized for its lack of independence and its slow functioning (Cheesman, 2015; Liljeblad, 2016, 2017). Various new laws were passed improving labour rights and the right to peaceful assembly, although restricting conditions remained in place. Of particular significance for civil society was the introduction of the Right to Peaceful Assembly and Peaceful Procession Act in December 2011. Although this law formally allowed demonstrations to take place, the condition that organizers had to apply for permission from the authorities at least five days in advance was widely viewed as an unnecessary restriction, which moreover granted the government with new legal tools for oppression in case of 'unlawful' or 'non-peaceful' processions. Media censorship was largely abolished in August 2012, although journalists could be accused of publishing false information retroactively. The government also sought consultation with critical opposition media and civil society organizations in drafting new laws, while dissidents and journalists who continued to criticize the government were subject to prosecution.

The most visible changes, however, took place on the political level, as Aung San Suu Kyi reached an agreement with President Thein Sein to re-register her NLD party in August 2011. In the highly symbolic by-elections that were held in April 2012, she won nearly all available seats and was able to take a seat in parliament (Lidauer, 2012). In response to the NLD's entry into the formal political sphere, the NCGUB was formally dissolved in September 2012. Another visible consequence of these political developments concerned the re-engagement of Western countries with both the government and non-state actors in the country. US Secretary of State Hillary Clinton paid a visit to Myanmar in 2011, followed by President Barack Obama in 2012. After these visits, the country witnessed a steady increase of Western tourists, businesspeople and politicians who were eager to reward the government for its democratic progress.[20] For the first time in

22 years, the United States appointed a full ambassador to Myanmar in July 2012 (Pedersen, 2014). Myanmar also hosted the World Economic Forum on East Asia and the Southeast Asian Games in Naypyidaw in 2013, and assumed chairmanship of the Association of Southeast Asian Nations in 2014 (Moe Thuzar, 2013). The following chapters will further explore how these developments were experienced by a variety of civil society actors based inside and outside the country and will cover the later stages of the political transition process, in which both domestic and international audiences were disappointed, although for different reasons.

## Conflict and peace talks in the ethnic states

From the BSPP era onwards, the military fostered divisions between ethnic groups, favouring some ethnic elites with formal political positions and lucrative business deals while excluding others. Although large sections of the population suffered from restricted civil liberties and poverty under military rule, the estimated 30 per cent ethnic nationalities, particularly those living in the border areas, have been the primary victims of military violence. Populations in the conflict areas frequently fell victim to forced labour, rape and forced displacement (Smith, 1991, 1999; Gravers, 2007). Ethnic post-independence struggles for equal rights and self-determination became entangled with the contest for control over natural resources, predominantly located in the border areas, which both the military and EAOs sought to regulate (Woods, 2011). Various armed insurgent groups and political elites capitalized upon the sense of deprivation among ethnic nationalities to nurture ethnic identities, foment hostility towards the Burman oppressors and legitimize the armed struggle (Sadan, 2013: 337). The total number of forces within the EAOs is estimated at around 72,000 persons, as opposed to 350,000 in the Myanmar military (Selth, 2015).[21]

General Khin Nyunt, head of intelligence services and later prime minister, initiated peace talks in the 1990s and managed to arrange ceasefires with most of the 21 'major anti-government forces' (Callahan, 2003: 215). Under these arrangements, EAOs were allowed to administer their own area, establish trade relations and keep their weapons until the new constitution was in place.[22] Kevin Woods (2011, 2017) argues that the military–private partnerships that resulted from some of these ceasefires, including with political elites from among the ethnic nationalities, led to new levels of exploitation of land and natural resources in the border regions, a process he refers to as 'ceasefire capitalism'. Despite the ceasefires, by the late 1990s at least 500,000 people had died during four decades of civil strife (Smith, 1999; Callahan, 2003: 210). Fighting in the various border areas resulted in millions of internally displaced people, as well as millions of refugees in neighbouring countries such as Thailand.

Although all fighting parties were suspected of involvement in human rights violations, accusations towards the Myanmar military were particularly serious, including rape, extrajudicial killings and even genocide (Matelski et al, 2022). After Thein Sein became president in 2011, he initiated new peace talks with a number of EAOs and managed to reach a ceasefire with the oldest ethnic insurgent group, the KNU, and several other parties in the first months of 2012. A formal 'Nationwide Ceasefire Agreement' was agreed on in October 2015 and presented to high-level international delegates, although eventually only three significant EAOs signed: the KNU, the Shan State Army (the armed wing of the Shan State Progress Party), and the Chin National Front (TNI, 2017).[23] The government received support from the Norwegian-backed Myanmar Peace Support Initiative and the Yangon-based Myanmar Peace Center, which will be discussed in Chapter 7. Meanwhile, in June 2011, the ceasefire reached with the KIA in the 1990s had broken down, resulting in a conflict that caused thousands of casualties and displaced over 100,000 people, just as the situation in central Myanmar was improving (TNI, 2013). The breakdown of ceasefires such as in Kachin State and other ethnic areas is attributed to the absence of lasting political settlements and the continued exploitation of populations in ceasefire areas (Woods, 2017; Kramer, 2021).

Under military rule, those groups not recognized in the 1982 Citizenship Act have been denied even the most basic rights, with the Rohingya as the best known example (Ferguson, 2015; Cheesman, 2017). Other ethnic and religious minorities, such as the Christian Chin, have also been subject to violence, discrimination or forced conversion to Buddhism (Sakhong, 2007: 223). The role of ethnic nationalities, their languages and their historical contributions were largely deleted from government textbooks, while ethnic organizations (described in Chapter 2) wrote their own history curricula, portraying Burmans as the enemy (Cheesman, 2003; Salem-Gervais and Metro, 2012). Many scholars regard 'the ethnic question' as one of the key issues to be resolved in the country (see, for example, Smith, 1991; Steinberg 2001; Gravers, 2007; South, 2008b). Others have argued the contrary, namely that the interests of ethnic nationalities have been over-represented in international platforms (Aung-Thwin and Aung-Thwin, 2012). It is generally acknowledged that the Burman majority has been the privileged ethnic group in the country (Walton, 2012b), although the role of class within ethnic groups has arguably been under-studied (McCarthy, 2019; Doi Ra and Khu Khu Ju, 2021; Campbell and Prasse-Freeman, 2022). A number of authors have therefore focused particularly on the plight of one or several of these ethnic groups and the development of social and political ethnic organizations in the border areas (for example, Smith, 1991, 1999; South, 2004, 2008a; Laungaramsri, 2006; Gravers, 2007; Thawnghmung, 2008; Brees, 2009; Woods, 2011; Brooten, 2013;

Sadan, 2013, and several publications by the Transnational Institute, or TNI). The plight of the Rohingya has also been covered extensively since 2015 (see Wade, 2017, for example, and several articles in human rights journals, including Matelski et al, 2022) and will be discussed in later chapters. The next two chapters further unpack the various identities of Myanmar's civil society actors, including the role of ethnicity.

2

# Constructing Civil Society in Myanmar

> For every two Burmese persons you need three organisations: one for each, plus an umbrella organisation.

This common joke refers to both political parties and civil society organizations (CSOs) in Myanmar.[1] It demonstrates the vibrancy of associational life but also points towards the internal divisions that have arguably played into the military's divide and rule tactics. This chapter explores what constitutes Burmese civil society over time, and what the various groups stand for. The concept of civil society is explored as it developed and became used in Myanmar after exposure to Western influences. Chapter 3 then introduces a number of fault lines in Myanmar society and analyses how they are reflected in civil society. Understanding diverse identities based on gender, age, class, education level and other characteristics is essential for the analysis of positions and contestations within civil society in the course of the political transition process. An additional factor discussed concerns the interaction between civil society actors based inside the country and those in exile. As with other factors, this 'inside–outside' division is not static, as activists moved in and out of the country in recent decades depending on the openness of political space over time. The way various civil society actors experienced and navigated this political space will be discussed in Chapter 4.

## Tracing the 'civil' in civil society

As previously mentioned, civil society is a much used, but also much contested and criticized concept. On the most general level, it can help interpret how social relations and collective action take shape over time (Edwards, 2011). For practitioners and scientists, the concept often serves as a blanket term to cover various organized non-state actors and activities, leading to a possible conflation of analytical and policy goals (Lewis, 2001).

The critical and systematic engagement with the theory and practice of civil society is complicated by overly simplistic expectations, based in Tocquevillian definitions and democracy promotion schemes. These concern civil society's presumed positive role in society, its ability to criticize or check on the role of the state, and its counter-hegemonic qualities (Chambers and Kymlicka, 2002; Edwards, 2009). In contrast, Gramscian theorists are more likely to regard civil society as a sphere of contestation, exploitation and hegemony (Hedman, 2006; Glasius, 2012). Chandhoke (2007: 608) laments the dominance of professionalized organizations, whereby the concept of civil society 'has been abstracted from all debates and contestations over its meaning, stripped of its ambiguities, its dark areas, and its oppressions, and presented to us in a sphere of solidarity, self-help, and goodwill'. As we will see in this chapter, the label 'civil society' is often first used by Western actors, before Southern actors adopt it as a term to self-identify. This does not necessarily imply that they become puppets of the West, as some critics argue; rather, it shows that the civil society discourse provides them with the necessary language to obtain international attention and assistance (Lewis, 2001). The risk, however, is that the concept may either become a tool for the imposition of Western interests or become so broadly defined that it is rendered almost meaningless. The purpose of this chapter is neither to provide definitional precision nor to declare the concept of civil society useless, but to analyse how these debates have played out within the specific context of Myanmar.

In response to what has been regarded as an overly positive depiction of civil society as a harmonious sphere where actors work towards democratic goals, some authors have advanced the concept of 'uncivil society' (May and Milton, 2005; Weiss and Hansson, 2023). This term refers to actors that are perceived to challenge liberal democratic values through the promotion of violence, exclusion or fundamentalism (Glasius, 2010). One such example covered in this chapter is MaBaTha, or the Organization for the Protection of Race and Religion, a movement of nationalist Buddhist monks that has promoted anti-Islamic sentiments in the public sphere. To simply distinguish between civil and uncivil society, however, would not do justice to the sometimes exclusivist practices within civil society groups that claim to pursue democratic goals. Moreover, movements that have come to be regarded as pursuing progressive goals are not necessarily internally democratic, nor do they all restrict themselves to non-violent means. Some therefore argue to do away with the label 'uncivil society', since it can simply be used to discredit actors whose goals or methods one disagrees with (Bob, 2011). In essence, both 'civil society' and 'uncivil society' can be seen as heuristic concepts that are used by academics, policy makers and practitioners to refer to certain demarcated groups.

This chapter focuses on a diverse group of actors that have come within the view and interest of Western donors but places them in perspective to other, more historical non-state actors that have influenced Myanmar's public sphere. Since the 1990s, Western donors have attempted to identify and support organizations in Southern countries that somehow mirror their own structures and values. Consequently, many organizations were set up in response to donor demands rather than local needs (Whaites, 1996; Hulme and Edwards, 1997). This pattern has also been observed in other countries in the region such as Cambodia (Hughes, 2009; Öjendal, 2014). In Bangladesh, the development of a strong 'indigenous' non-governmental organization (NGO) sector has been encouraged by the influx of foreign and international organizations since independence, and by the early 2000s 85 per cent of foreign funding appeared to be directed towards only ten large NGOs (Lewis, 2004). Myanmar civil society too has been criticized for its donor dependency (Rieffel and Fox, 2013; Bjarnegård, 2020), but the restrictive civic space and the relatively low overall levels of donor funding have resulted in different aid dynamics, as will be discussed in later chapters. Nevertheless, it should be acknowledged that religion-based groups and community-based organizations (CBOs), although not the subject of this book, have continued to play a vital role on the local level in Myanmar. Welfare organizations, referred to as *parahita* (literally: 'for the benefit of others'), have a long-established presence on the community level (Griffiths, 2019; McCarthy, 2019). Their societal importance has arguably been overlooked by foreign donors, although community-level religious and social activities are increasingly identified as having potential political impact (Walton, 2016). These organizations rely largely on domestic donations, which tend to be 'sporadic and arbitrary' (Prasse-Freeman and Phyo Win Latt, 2018: 412).

Some authors distinguish between these 'traditional' groups, which are characterized as informal and loosely structured, and the more specialized, modern 'professional' CSOs (Fink and Simpson, 2018). This book focuses on actors involved in the more informal section of modern-style CSOs. They are active in organizations which are neither community-based in the geographical sense, nor as professionalized as the large NGOs observed in Bangladesh and elsewhere. These mid-level organizations engage in service delivery, advocacy or a combination of the two, and thereby act as intermediaries between foreign donors and local populations. Although the diverse identities and preferences imply that civil society groups can only ever represent certain sub-groups in society, some groups make wider representation claims on behalf of the Myanmar population in order to influence local, national and transnational advocacy targets. Their diverse identities and the resulting fault lines will be discussed in Chapter 3.

## Civil society in the context of Myanmar

The term civil society is not indigenous to Myanmar but was adopted when transnational ties developed and foreign donors entered the country. By self-identifying explicitly as civil society, organizations make themselves eligible for financial and political support; hence, the term can be said to have become a 'currency' in contemporary Myanmar (Zarni, 2012: 291). The term civil society does not translate easily into Burmese language. Some use the Burmese term *lumu(yay) apwe asi* (social affairs organization), but this mostly refers to traditional organizations or those engaging in social welfare (*thayay nayay*). Respondents in this study indicated they were more likely to refer to the organizational composition, such as 'farmer association' or 'religious organization'. Yet in public events, I frequently heard participants use the English term 'civil society', indicating that they lack an adequate Burmese translation for this imported concept. Some organizations even used the English term CSO in their organizational name or slogan. Although respondents had trouble thinking of an adequate Burmese equivalent for civil society terminology, they stressed that the idea behind it was far from new: "We had organizations in every village and every quarter. Some have names and some do not. Now they call it CBO. These terms came from outside donors, and people in the civil society community decided to use them", according to one Yangon-based respondent interviewed in 2015. This chapter describes how some of these previously existing organizations merged into formats that made them identifiable to donors seeking to fund 'Western-style' CSOs. More traditional religion-based organizations, as well as most CBOs, continued to rely on local donations, although recognition of the importance of self-help groups and social welfare organizations, particularly in the ethnic areas, has increased among donors (Lorch, 2008; South, 2008a; Lall and South, 2014). These interactions will be further discussed in later chapters. First, we explore the history of associational life in Burma/Myanmar.

## Associational life in (post-)colonial Burma

Before the British invasion, the Burmese territory was ruled by local power holders through personalized patronage networks (Steinberg, 2010: 18; Harriden, 2012), while territories inhabited by other ethnic groups had their own forms of local governance (see Leach, 1954 on the Kachin). In these systems, community-based and faith-based organizations operated primarily on the village level (Steinberg, 2001: 105; Heidel, 2006: 4). Around the start of the 20th century, hundreds of Buddhist associations were created to deliver social and educational services and to collect food for the poor, a practice called *satuditha* (Turner, 2014). Although the activities of Burmans are best documented, ethnic Mon, Shan, Arakanese and Chinese also participated in these associations. In Buddhist-dominated areas, the *sangha* (Buddhist monkhood) played an important role, including in education (Cheesman, 2003). Yet the first religious organizations identified by scholars as CSOs were Christian: the Burma Baptist Convention started in 1865, and the Karen National Association started in 1881 (Heidel, 2006; Kramer, 2011). For most of these organizations, the political, social and religious goals were highly intertwined.

As stated earlier, the Burmese nationalist sentiments that increased under colonial rule laid the foundation for associational life in central Burma. The British ban on political activities resulted in a re-positioning of nationalist anti-colonial resistance into the realm of Buddhism (Maung Maung, 1980; Turner, 2014). The Young Men's Buddhist Association (YMBA) was established at Rangoon College in 1906 (with a possible predecessor in Arakan in 1902) to disseminate political views and oppose British colonial policies (Maung Maung, 1980: 2; Schober, 2011: 65), and the Young Women's Buddhist Association (YWBA) was started around the same time (Turner, 2014: 180 note 17). While initially functioning as a pro-colonial organization, the YMBA quickly took on a nationalist tone against the British rulers, protesting the wearing of shoes inside Buddhist temples and calling for a boycott of British goods (Schober, 2011; Turner, 2014). The slogan 'to be Burmese is to be Buddhist', often attributed to the YMBA, has continued to be used by subsequent Buddhist nationalist movements (Bechert in Turner, 2014: 194 note 9).

In 1918, a younger faction that sought more direct political confrontation split from the YMBA. It transformed into the General Council of Burmese Associations (GCBA) in 1920, an umbrella organization that went on to organize various student strikes and demonstrations against the British (Steinberg, 2010: 35).[2] U Ottama, a Buddhist monk inspired by the Indian independence movement, played an important role in combining Buddhist and political activities from the 1920s onwards. He founded the *wunthanu athins*, or patriotic societies, that sought to emancipate rural communities and other minorities such as women, who started their own Wunthanu Konmari Athin in 1919 (Aung-Thwin, 2011: 146; Harriden, 2012: 125). Their efforts to bridge the gap between rural and urban communities resulted in the 1930–32 Hsaya San Rebellion, discussed earlier. Like his predecessor U Wisara (who died as a result of a hunger strike in 1929), U Ottama was arrested by the British administration for 'seditious activities' and died in prison in 1939. Both monks have become heroes of the independence movement (Maung Maung, 1980; Walton, 2016). The GCBA and other organizations eventually became factionalized over the level and desirability of political involvement (Taylor, 2009: 183–4).

Not only Buddhist but also Christian, Muslim and Hindu organizations emerged under colonial rule. The Karen, Kachin, Shan, Mon, Kayah and

Rakhine engaged in political and social activities, which contributed to the development of their ethnic and political consciousness (South, 2003; Kyaw Yin Hlaing, 2007a). Many of the larger ethnic organizations were started towards the end of the colonial period. The Karen Central Organization, for example, later became the Karen National Union, while various early Baptist organizations in Kachin State later merged into the Kachin Baptist Convention. Likewise, the All Ramanya Mon Association turned into the influential Mon Literature and Culture Committee (South, 2003: 307). Taylor (2009: 181) concludes that 'different groups in Burmese society were mobilized for different reasons, but all did so under the cloak of nationalism'. Burman Buddhists sought to protect their country and religion from foreign influences, while ethnic nationalities developed organizations to represent their distinct social, cultural and political interests.

## Post-independence resistance movements

Several new associations and organizations were started after independence from the British, particularly in urban areas where civil war was absent. Associational life under the Anti-Fascist People's Freedom League (AFPFL) (the ruling party after independence, founded by Aung San) has been characterized as 'active and important' and 'semi-autonomous' (Steinberg, 2001: 99). Prime Minister U Nu encouraged the formation of social and business associations, and his own AFPFL started labour organizations as well as organizations for peasants, youth and women (Kyaw Yin Hlaing, 2007a: 150). The aftermath of World War II, moreover, saw an increasing involvement of women's organizations in the reconstruction of social services (Harriden, 2012: 141). Ethnic nationalities developed social, youth and educational organizations parallel to the political parties that emerged after World War II (Sadan, 2013: 278–9). The number of organizations associated with the political opposition, however, was much smaller than those associated with the AFPFL, which contributed to nepotism and strengthened the party's position (Kyaw Yin Hlaing, 2007a: 151). Social mobility was obtained either through AFPFL-affiliated organizations or through the military or the *sangha* (Steinberg, 1999: 6). Religious organizations functioned more independently from the government and were sometimes able to criticize it, particularly on its religious policies (Kyaw Yin Hlaing, 2007a: 152). Student unions were even more autonomous, although they 'often acted more like an opposition party than an independent organization' (Kyaw Yin Hlaing, 2007a: 153). In short, the line between political organizations and independent CSOs remained blurred.

While the (post-)colonial period saw the start of many social and political organizations, the Burma Socialist Programme Party (BSPP) era from 1962 onwards marked the end of the legal existence of independent associational life in Burma. David Steinberg (2001: 106) famously wrote that 'civil society died under the BSPP; perhaps, more accurately, it was murdered'. Independent organizations were identified as a source of political unrest, and the BSPP itself became the main 'mass organization', claiming to be supported by the people. The BSPP government started its own organizations, including the infamous Lanzin Youth Organization. Its members were expected to infiltrate youth movements, report on suspicious activities and trick students into 'sham antigovernment activities orchestrated by government agents' (Kyaw Yin Hlaing, 2004: 396). The Lanzin Youth Organization and several others served as preparation for full BSPP membership and claimed to have several million members (Lintner, 1990: 58).[3] Political opposition groups became illegal, and since the National Solidarity Act did not define 'political', the result was a general inclination among the population to stay away from politics outside the BSPP sphere (Kyaw Yin Hlaing, 2007a: 155). The military dismantled labour unions and imposed restrictions on the press and eventually also on the Buddhist *sangha*. Other independent organizations managed to survive, either because they were hardly visible, or because they were perceived as non-political, such as the YMBA and its Christian equivalents the YMCA and the YWCA. Thus, while Steinberg (1999: 9) rightly concludes that 'dissent was publicly eliminated', his next statement that 'civil society had disappeared' does not do justice to the social and even covert political activities that continued to take place.

Ardeth Maung Thawnghmung (2004: 169) notes a striking absence of peasant protests and rebellions since the start of the BSPP government, which contrasts with the 'periodic outbursts of peasant revolts' under British colonial rule. She attributes this absence to the repressive atmosphere under military rule but also to farmers' ambivalent attitudes towards authorities, and their tendency to employ various non-rebellious mechanisms to deal with their grievances (see Scott, 1985; Malseed, 2009). In contrast, students continued to play an important role in public resistance. Soon after the take-over in 1962, the Revolutionary Council took full control of the universities of Rangoon and Mandalay and imposed a curfew for students. On 7 July 1962, the students organized a demonstration, after which riot police took control of the student union. In the crackdown that followed, an unknown number of students were killed – the official count stands at 15, but eyewitnesses estimate the actual death count to be several hundred (Lintner, 1990: 39). The next morning, the army dynamited the historic Students' Union building in Rangoon, a highly symbolic act considering the role of students in the anti-colonial resistance. Students demonstrated periodically throughout the 1960s and 1970s and continued to face violent repression. They famously protested against the unceremonial treatment of former UN Secretary General U Thant when his deceased body was flown back from New York in December 1974. During his funeral, students took hold of

U Thant's coffin and carried it to the site of the former student union, where he was given an honorary burial with the help of Buddhist monks. The military recovered the coffin and reburied it elsewhere. Hundreds of students and monks were arrested, causing further demonstrations in Rangoon. In response, the military declared martial law on 11 December 1974. When protests continued, the army killed a number of students (nine according to the government, 300–400 according to the demonstrators) and arrested nearly 1,800 others (Lintner, 1990: 52).

Further demonstrations were held in 1974 and 1976. Each time, students were arrested and universities closed temporarily. As surveillance increased, anti-government protests became increasingly rare, until the mass student-initiated uprising of 1988 described earlier. The 1988 Law Relating to Forming of Organizations prohibited CSOs from operating without registration, a process which could easily take years and was not accessible for politically oriented groups (Fink and Simpson, 2018). Apart from these politically active groups, a number of non-political organizations engaged in social welfare were started as a result of ceasefires in the ethnic areas in the 1990s and early 2000s, which sometimes cooperated with, and sometimes competed for recruits with ethnic armed organizations (EAOs) (South, 2008b). These organizations worked primarily on health, education and humanitarian service provision (Lorch, 2008). More of these organizations emerged in the aftermath of cyclone Nargis in 2008. Some initiatives were temporary, while others continued to operate in the following years (Fink and Simpson, 2018).

From the 1988 uprising and its violent crackdown emerged the so-called 88 Generation Students, many of whom were imprisoned, while others fled to the border areas or to neighbouring countries, where they formed various 'democracy organizations' (Lintner, 1990).[4] Among the opposition movements that emerged during this period were various Buddhist organizations and the All Burma Federation of Student Unions, the successor of a student union formed in the 1950s that was revived by a student who called himself Min Ko Naing (Lintner, 1990: 122).[5] Labour unions, which had gone underground after having been outlawed in 1962, re-emerged in the course of the 1988 uprising and were subsequently repressed (Arnold and Campbell, 2017). New generations of students continued to resist military rule, with particularly prominent uprisings being organized in 1996, after which the main universities were closed for another three years (Liddell, 2001). When colleges and universities were slowly reopened, the government tried to discourage student organizing by dispersing campuses outside the city centres and encouraging distance education. Together with a lack of resources and heavy censorship of the curriculum, including the prohibition of political science and other potentially 'dangerous' subjects, these changes had a disastrous effect on the educational opportunities of young people inside the country, and those who could afford to do so continued their education abroad. For young people in some of the ethnic states, alternatives were available in the form of education systems run by ethnic nationality organizations, which were rolled out in parts of the ethnic states as well as in refugee camps on the Thai side of the border (Lall and South, 2014). Many young adults were directly impacted by the lack of (higher) education opportunities and considered government universities, especially those offering distance education, a waste of time. Eventually, the label 'student' in Myanmar became associated more with resistance than with the acquisition of knowledge. The next generations of protesters would emerge from the 2007 'Saffron Revolution', with student protests continuing under the later Union Solidarity and Development Party (USDP) and National League for Democracy (NLD) governments.

## The rise of the (pro-)democracy movement in the 1990s

Although 'waves of exit' from Burma can be traced back at least to the 1960s, the origins of the Burmese democracy movement (sometimes called 'pro-democracy movement') can be dated to 1988 (Lintner, 1990; Kyaw Yin Hlaing, 2007b). After the crackdown on the 1988 demonstrations, over 10,000 political activists crossed the Thai border in order to avoid arrest, while a few thousand others fled to China, India, Bangladesh or elsewhere (Zaw Oo, 2006: 236). By the early 2000s, the number of Burmese people living abroad was estimated at around 3 to 4 million (Egreteau, 2012; Duell, 2014). These included migrant workers and other people actively seeking economic and educational opportunities. Meanwhile, some of the '88 activists joined forces with other dissidents who had been fleeing the country since the military takeover of 1962 (Dale, 2011: 82). Several new activist groups emerged outside the country and in insurgent-controlled areas after 1988, such as the All Burma Students' Democratic Front (ABSDF), the National League for Democracy – Liberated Area,[6] the Forum for Democracy in Burma, and a group of ethnic minorities that in 2001 became known as the Ethnic Nationalities Council (Kyaw Yin Hlaing, 2004; Dale, 2011; Williams, 2012).[7] Various 'exile media organizations' were also founded, which sought to counter the propaganda issued by the Burmese state and distribute information on Myanmar to the outside world. The most prominent pan-ethnic media organizations to date are the Democratic Voice of Burma, The Irrawaddy and Mizzima News, but many smaller ones cater to various ethnic groups.[8]

Kyaw Yin Hlaing (2004: 408) writes that '[i]f the socialist period can be called the era of informal political groups, then the SLORC/SPDC period must be labeled the era of overseas Burmese prodemocracy groups' (though in fact, most of them were technically not 'overseas'). In the 1990s, over 40 such groups were formed in North America, Europe and Asia. Although Burmese democracy organizations in Western countries were relatively influential in international debates, most of the organizations in exile were based in Thailand (Duell, 2014: 130). By 1999, over 50 Burmese CSOs, including migrant organizations, were active in the Thai border area alone (Steinberg, 2001: 117). Taylor (2009: 430–1) counts nearly 70 'exile political organizations' worldwide in 2005, including thematic organizations, ethnic nationality organizations and umbrella organizations in which members of individual groups send representatives to work together on a particular topic, such as women's rights or the environment. As with Myanmar-based organizations, no authoritative registration numbers are available, and the actual number is likely to be higher.

While organizations such as the ABSDF and various EAOs took up arms against the military government, student activists in the 1990s particularly benefitted from the rise of global communication channels such as the internet. Many of them took up educational opportunities abroad while continuing to campaign against the military from exile (Zaw Oo, 2006: 232). The post-Cold War era, moreover, saw 'an ideological shift towards normative-idealist discourses of democracy, non-violence, human rights, and the rights of ethnic minorities and of women', which the Burmese democracy movement played into (Duell, 2014: 114). Organizations focusing on various human rights issues were started, such as the Federation of Trade Unions of Burma (FTUB), the Burma Lawyers Council, the Assistance Association for Political Prisoners-Burma and umbrella organizations such as the Network for Human Rights Documentation-Burma and the Burmese Women's Union.

Many ethnic nationalities developed their own human rights organizations, some of which became quite well known internationally, such as the Karen Human Rights Group, the Kachin Women's Association Thailand and the Shan Women's Action Network. Their close ties with EAOs sometimes limited these CSOs' ability to speak out against abuses committed by non-state actors, and the armed groups did not always welcome criticism from within their own ranks (South, 2008a).[9] Other organizations, including some of the exile-based media, were sufficiently independent to criticize both sides (Liddell, 2001: 172; Brooten, 2006; Kramer, 2011: 28). While ethnic groups in the Thai border areas such as the Karen were most prominent in their connections with the international community, other links were established with India (mainly the Chin) and Bangladesh (largely resulting from forced displacement of the Rohingya). Other groups joined international environmental networks, such as the Rakhine around the Shwe gas pipeline (Simpson, 2014). The relationship between Burmans and ethnic nationalities in the democracy movement will be discussed in more detail later on.

# Civil society during the early stages of political transition

The limited quantitative studies conducted on civil society in Myanmar under the State Peace and Development Council government point towards a steady increase in the number of organizations. A desk study conducted by an employee of an international organization in 2003–4 estimated the number of NGOs in the country to be at least 270, and the number of CBOs over 200,000 (Heidel, 2006). The Yangon-based Local Resource Centre published a directory of registered NGOs which rose from 62 in 2004 to 118 in 2012, the last year it was published online (see Dorning, 2006). The actual numbers were probably much higher, since politically oriented organizations were unable to register and presumably did not want to be listed in public directories. As political discussions were normalized and donor interest increased during the political transition period, Myanmar saw a rise in publicly visible CSOs. The 2021 military coup that disrupted the transition period sent most organizations back underground, as discussed in Chapter 8.

Although the USDP government that came to power after the 2010 elections was widely viewed as a proxy for the military, it quickly surprised both Burmese and international observers by opening up space for civil society to operate, particularly in the early years of its rule (Lall, 2016). In September 2011, President Thein Sein unexpectedly suspended the Myitsone Dam project, a project with Chinese investment which was already underway in Kachin State (Kirchherr, 2018; Kiik, 2020). He attributed this decision to civil society pressure, although critics argued that it could also be seen as a move to reduce the influence of Chinese investment in the country. In his State of the Union speech on 1 March 2012, President Thein Sein explicitly referred to CSOs as vital to democratization. In the course of that year, he actively reached out to critics of the military regime by inviting back prominent activists in exile, as well as several media groups. Many of the exiled organizations opened offices in Myanmar that year under a different banner, including the FTUB, which changed its name to Confederation of Trade Unions of Myanmar, and the Human Rights Education Institute of Burma, which changed its name to Equality Myanmar. An Association Registration Law was drafted in 2013 and approved after significant changes in 2014, whereby registration for CSOs was simplified and made mandatory only for those receiving foreign funding (Fink and Simpson, 2018).

As mentioned earlier, the USDP government sought out public consultation, including from civil society actors. It changed its formal handling of labour unions, demonstrations and free speech by drafting new laws, although not always in the direction desired by civil society (Arnold and Campbell, 2017; Brooten et al, 2019). While public gatherings were no longer prohibited and media censorship was relaxed, dissidents could still be arrested for 'unlawful processions' and online incitement or defamation. Some of the many changes in laws during the early stages of the political transition were therefore viewed as cosmetic changes in order to show democratization efforts to the outside world. It has also been argued that the whole transition process was in fact aimed at political stabilization rather than genuine democratization (Campbell, 2023). Where changes did take place, civil society actors were quick to make use of new opportunities, and citizen initiatives became both more frequent and more public. Occasional public displays of inter-ethnic solidarity started occurring around the campaign against the Myitsone Dam in 2011, and in 2012 when demonstrations protesting the resumed war in Kachin State were organized in Yangon. Discussions on politics and human rights became more prominent, and a Human Rights Human Dignity Festival was organized annually between 2013 and 2017 with support from Aung San Suu Kyi and Min Ko Naing. Although protest movements continued in the early USDP years, they were primarily organized in opposition to specific laws or policy plans, rather than challenging the military or the quasi-civilian government directly (Lall, 2016). Two new land laws were adopted in 2012 (the Farmland Law and the Vacant, Fallow and Virgin Land Law) that resulted in increased marketization of land and threatened customary land use and communal management of natural resources (Kramer, 2015).[10] As the country opened up to foreign business, protests increasingly focused on land rights and the rights of workers (Arnold and Campbell, 2017; Campbell and Prasse-Freeman, 2022; Sekine, 2023).

## The rise of Buddhist nationalism, hate speech and violence against Muslims

Under the Thein Sein government, non-state actors posed the main new threat to democratic rights and freedoms. In 2012, a number of violent incidents between Muslims and Buddhists occurred in Rakhine State, resulting in at least 200 casualties and 140,000 displaced persons (Walton and Hayward, 2014; Min Zin, 2015). In 2013 and 2014, violence spread to other parts of the country, including the central towns of Meiktila and Mandalay, and, to a lesser extent, Yangon. Some of the incidents occurred after the spread of false rumours, and several observers pointed towards active involvement in addition to a complete lack of protection on the part of the government (Human Rights Watch, 2013; Fortify Rights, 2015). There were also persistent rumours that President Thein Sein in 2012 had suggested the removal of most Rohingya from the country as the best solution (Walton and Hayward, 2014: 13).

In the course of these events, groups of Buddhist nationalists began to organize and distribute hate speech. First, a '969 movement' was started around calls to boycott Muslim businesses.[11] Next, Buddhist monks formed the organization MaBaTha in 2014. The monk Wirathu, who had earlier been imprisoned for his hate speech against Muslims, emerged as the most prominent leader. MaBaTha presented Muslims as a threat to the country's Buddhist identity, made use of hateful rhetoric and called for prohibitions on Islamic ceremonies. It played an influential role in convincing the government to refuse to include Rohingya as a category in the 2014 census and to revoke the temporary registration cards of over 1 million Rohingya and other minorities (Min Zin, 2015). It also actively promoted four draft laws restricting inter-religious marriage and regulating religious conversion, the so-called Protection of Race and Religion Laws (Walton and Hayward, 2014). Despite opposition by some politicians and civil society actors, these proposals were signed into law in 2015, while those objecting were threatened and labelled traitors (Min Zin, 2015). Protest by civil society groups against the Race and Religion Laws started early in 2014. In January 2015, 180 CSOs from a range of ethnic and religious backgrounds issued a public statement condemning the draft laws (Min Zin, 2015). Such protests, which were not without repercussions given the widespread nationalist support among the Buddhist population (including females), were primarily led by women's organizations and those taking an explicit human rights stance (Walton et al, 2015).

The rise of hate speech against Muslims coincided with increased access to social media in the early years of the political transition. When the telecom sector was liberalized in 2013, the price of sim cards dropped from thousands of dollars to just a few dollars, and a large section of the population gained access to mobile internet. Many smartphones were sold with Facebook already installed. The platform gained an enormous share in Myanmar, where internet access had been largely contained, and many users believed it to contain verified facts comparable to news outlets (Brooten, 2020). The number of Facebook users rose from one million in 2013 to an estimated 21 million users by 2020, which is over a third of the total population (Brooten, 2020).

Facebook also became widely used by senior government and military officials. These actors, including from the President's Office, played a significant role in promoting hate speech by posting degrading messages about perceived Rohingya terrorists and spreading rumours about imminent riots or large migration flows from Bangladesh intended to cause unrest and stir up prejudice against Muslims (Kyaw Zeyar Win, 2018; Brooten, 2020). Buddhist nationalists, who had distributed DVDs and pamphlets with anti-Muslim propaganda, also made use of Facebook to disseminate their views. Wirathu and other MaBaTha members posted fake rumours on rape by Muslim men on their Facebook page, which likely contributed to some of the riots (Walton and Hayward, 2014: 8). Those in Rakhine State suspected of trading or otherwise interacting with Muslims were publicly shamed online (Kyaw Zeyar Win, 2018). Given its own active role, the military leadership did not act against anti-Muslim hate speech and often protected the instigators. In 2013, it banned an issue of *Time Magazine* which depicted Wirathu with the title 'The face of Buddhist terror' on the cover (Min Zin, 2015). In 2017, Aung San Suu Kyi used her own Facebook page to discredit reports about rape of Rohingya women (Brooten, 2020).

As violence against Muslims escalated, Facebook (now renamed Meta) was accused by human rights activists of failing to prevent hate speech, fake accounts and fabricated news items on its pages (Stecklow, 2018). As early as 2012, local CSOs raised concerns about the potential for hate speech and misinformation to contribute to actual violence, while also seeking to counter this development (Brooten, 2020). In April 2014, a civil society group called Myanmar ICT for Development Organization launched an online Pan Zagar ('flower speech') campaign to promote co-existence, particularly among youth. In 2018, six local CSOs wrote a letter to Facebook CEO Mark Zuckerberg calling for increased transparency about the potential dangers of Facebook in Myanmar. Later in 2018, the UN Human Rights Council released a report that confirmed the accusations of hate speech on Facebook. As a result, Facebook removed the accounts of several senior officers, including Senior General Min Aung Hlaing. These developments also prompted Facebook to hire moderators for Burmese language content, something it had been reluctant to do in earlier years (Amnesty International, 2022). In 2015, the Burmese language team consisted of two people, and by 2017 this had increased to over 60 (Brooten, 2020). That same year, Rohingya activists sued Facebook for its failure to prevent hate speech and incitement against them.

Hate speech and discriminatory treatment by the government targeted several Muslim groups in Myanmar, including the Kaman Muslims in Rakhine State which are recognized as an ethnic group in the 1982 citizenship law (Min Zin, 2015). However, given their relative isolation and weak legal status, the Rohingya eventually faced the worst consequences. For decades, they were denied citizenship rights, severely discriminated against both in law and in practice, and increasingly referred to as illegal 'Bengali' (Wade, 2017). Violence and repression came from both state and non-state actors, and both Burmans and Rakhine. Many were forced to flee from Rakhine State as violence increased in the course of 2014, but the most severe military violence would occur under the NLD government in 2017, as detailed subsequently.

## The NLD's electoral victory in 2015

The rapid and unexpected political developments since 2011 culminated in the next national elections, which were held in November 2015. This time, the political opposition was well prepared and managed to campaign. Civil society activists provided extensive voter education, including through social media (Tin Maung Maung Than, 2016). They particularly aimed to target underrepresented groups such as rural populations and female voters and candidates by conducting visits on the village level, including in the ethnic areas (Matelski and Nang Muay Noan, 2022). The NLD achieved an overwhelming victory at the expense of both the military candidates and many ethnic parties that had gained seats in the 2010 elections (Thawnghmung and Saw Eh Htoo, 2022). Aung San Suu Kyi, being constitutionally barred from the presidency, took on the influential roles of 'state counsellor' and foreign minister, while her close aide U Htin Kyaw became the first civilian president in 53 years. U Htin Kyaw's public appearances remained limited, and Aung San Suu Kyi openly stated that she would be above the president in terms of de facto power relations. Military representative Myint Swe and Chin representative Henry Van Thio became the first and second vice-president. U Htin Kyaw resigned as president in 2018, presumably for health reasons. He was replaced by U Win Myint, who had been speaker of the Lower House since 2016. The 2015 elections in combination with the provisions for military involvement in politics and government effectively resulted in a 'two-headed government' in which the NLD and the military were forced to share power (Thawnghmung and Saw Eh Htoo, 2022). During its rule, the NLD made two attempts to change the constitution and reduce the role of the military, both of which failed.

In the early years, hopes were high that the NLD would capitalize on Thein Sein's reforms by working towards a fully democratic state. The party recruited several civil society members as members of parliament, including Phyo Zayar Thaw, well-known rapper and founder of youth movement Generation Wave (see Chapter 3), and Susanna Hla Hla Soe, former executive director of the Karen Women's Action Group. Yet despite their involvement, the NLD government proved remarkably repressive and dismissive towards independent civil society and other dissenting voices (Walton, 2018). Old and new laws were used to sentence students, farmers, journalists and lawyers for unlawful demonstrations, revealing state secrets, defamation or contempt of court.[12]

Unlike the USDP, the NLD did not consult civil society on new legal amendments. It even issued a directive ordering MPs to seek permission before participating in civil society activities (Bächtold, 2017). As early as 2013, when Aung San Suu Kyi had gained a seat in parliament after the 2012 by-elections, she headed a commission to investigate the violent repression of protesting farmers and monks at the Letpadaung copper mine in 2012, which ruled in favour of the government (Prasse-Freeman and Pyo Win Latt, 2018). Public protest continued to be repressed under NLD rule after 2015. The Peaceful Assembly and Peaceful Procession Law was adapted in 2018 and applied selectively: activists protesting against controversial government decisions were frequently arrested and sentenced, whereas demonstrations held in support of the military did not face similar repression. Authorities used violence during protests against a draft education law in the town of Letpadan in March 2015 and imprisoned over 70 students (Fink and Simpson, 2018; Campbell, 2023). By 2018, at least 43 journalists had been arrested (Brooten, 2020).

The NLD victory arguably resulted in 'unevenly restrictive conditions, including continued restricted access to basic democratic rights for much of the population especially outside the main urban areas', where armed conflict often continued (Doi Ra and Khu Khu Ju, 2021: 497). In the eyes of many ethnic nationalities, the NLD abandoned efforts to create a federal system, which remained a primary demand from the side of most ethnic parties, whereas the military continued to push for disarmament and securitization of the ethnic areas (Thawnghmung and Saw Eh Htoo, 2022). In an effort to continue peace talks that had been started under the USDP, the NLD government organized a '21st-century Panglong conference' in 2016, which yielded limited results (Callahan, 2018). In March 2020, the NLD gave in to military pressure to label EAOs which continued fighting, such as the Arakan Army, 'terrorist organizations' (Thawnghmung and Saw Eh Htoo, 2022). Armed conflict in Kachin State continued, and new conflicts flared up particularly in northern Shan State (Callahan, 2018). While the peace process continued in the early years of the NLD government with significant donor support, it was arguably used by the military to defer a durable agreement while continuing to fight individual groups, and thus sow further divisions between ethnic groups. The peace process will be further discussed in later chapters.

## Escalating military violence against the Rohingya

The marginalization of Rohingya and other Muslims continued under the NLD government. In its 2015 election campaign, the NLD responded to Buddhist nationalist influence by removing Muslim candidates from its lists (Kyaw Zeyar Win, 2018). Consequently, and in contrast to 2010, no Muslim representatives were elected into parliament in 2015.[13] At the insistence of Buddhist nationalist groups, moreover, around 500,000 Rohingya who had previously been able to vote lost their voting rights in the 2015 elections (Kyaw Zeyar Win, 2018: 268). The NLD victory in itself was a defeat for MaBaTha, which had campaigned vigorously for the military party USDP. Yet the NLD government did not bring the Muslim population any tangible benefits. Under international pressure, it appointed an Advisory Commission on Rakhine State in 2016 headed by former UN Secretary General Kofi Annan to investigate the treatment of Rohingya. In January 2017, a prominent Muslim lawyer and legal advisor to the NLD, U Ko

Ni, was murdered outside Yangon airport in what was presumably a hate crime. Despite their close relationship, Aung San Suu Kyi failed to respond publicly, while Wirathu and several army representatives showed support for the murder (Fink, 2018). Government institutes responsible for Buddhist matters banned Wirathu from giving speeches, but these restrictions were not strictly enforced, and anti-Muslim raids continued without any response from the authorities (Fink, 2018: 159). When MaBaTha was ordered by the state's religious body to stop operations in May 2017 the organization changed its name to Buddha Dhamma Parahita Foundation after which it seemed to lose most of its influential role.

When the Advisory Commission on Rakhine State shared its recommendations on ending forced segregation between Rakhine Buddhists and Rohingya Muslims on 24 August 2017, these were initially welcomed by the NLD government. The day after, however, a Rohingya resistance group called the Arakan Rohingya Salvation Army coordinated an attack on 30 police posts and army bases in northern Rakhine State and killed a number of soldiers. In an act of collective punishment, the military unleashed a 'security operation' on the Rohingya population in Rakhine State, which the UN High Commissioner for Human Rights later labelled "a textbook example of ethnic cleansing" (Simpson and Farrelly, 2020: 488). A mass flow of refugees fled to Bangladesh, which ended up receiving over 700,000 new Rohingya refugees, in addition to the existing numbers. In an effort to contain unrest and the spread of information about the events, the government imposed internet blackouts in several affected areas and restricted activities of journalists and aid workers in the region. In December 2017, two local Reuters journalists who had reported on one of the Rohingya massacres were invited to a police meeting and then arrested and prosecuted for possessing internal military documents under the Official Secrets Act (Callahan, 2018). Rohingya populations, both those remaining in Myanmar (often in prison or internally displaced) and in Bangladesh, have remained in dire conditions since, with no prospect of a durable solution.

The Independent International Fact-Finding Mission on Myanmar established by the UN (discussed in Chapter 7) concluded that the military violence against the Rohingya in August 2017, if proven, would amount to genocide (Renshaw, 2019). It explicitly called for Senior General Min Aung Hlaing and other generals to face genocide charges. Aung San Suu Kyi admitted to the disproportionality of the military's reaction but insisted it would be dealt with internally. When the Gambia filed a case at the International Court of Justice (ICJ) in 2019 accusing Myanmar of genocide, she travelled to The Hague to defend the government.[14] The violence against the Rohingya and especially the reaction of Aung San Suu Kyi, who was viewed internationally as an icon of human rights, caused widespread international indignation. It also influenced international perceptions of Buddhist monks, who had been largely viewed as peaceful (Arnold and Turner, 2019). The international responses and depictions of Myanmar since this so-called 'Rohingya crisis' will be discussed in Chapter 7. First, the following chapter lays out the identities and characteristics of various Burmese civil society actors.

3

# Diversity and Fault Lines
# in Burmese Civil Society

In order to analyse the activities and advocacy positions of various civil society groups (as covered in Chapters 4 to 6), it is important to establish the identity factors that influence people's lived experiences and help explain their stance towards the government and other actors. By employing this intersectional lens, moreover, we can explore how certain minority identities interact to create multiple forms of marginalization. The fault lines in Myanmar that are most relevant for analysing contemporary civil society are ethnicity and religion, generation and gender, and class, including poverty levels and the rural/urban divide. Furthermore, this chapter covers the division between independent and government-associated civil society organizations (CSOs), and between organizations inside and outside the country. Lastly, it will reflect on the elitist nature of some CSOs and their relationship with grassroots activism.

## Fault line 1: ethnicity and religion

As discussed earlier, religious organizations have historically played a key role in Burmese society, where around 90 per cent of the population is Theravada Buddhist. Buddhist monasteries have been providing social services such as schools and orphanages in central Myanmar since long before any of the 'Western type' non-governmental organizations (NGOs) appeared, and Christian organizations (consisting predominantly, but not exclusively of ethnic nationalities) have long been active in the ethnic states. In fact, a distinction between religious and secular organizations in the context of Myanmar would be rather artificial, as many actors working outside faith-based organizations nevertheless identify with a particular religious group.[1]

## The role of Buddhist monks

Buddhist monks (together with nuns referred to as *sangha*) have gained prominence in the Western imagination of Burmese civil society, especially since the 2007 uprising in which they played a significant and internationally visible role. The role of Buddhism as a force in contemporary Myanmar politics, however, continues to be subject to debate (Jordt, 2007). Aung-Thwin (2013), for example, argues that the Western scholarly and media emphasis on politically motivated monks is based on a misunderstanding of the nature of the *sangha*, which remains predominantly apolitical. According to Aung-Thwin, monks only made up 10 per cent of those involved in the 2007 uprising, and the uprising itself was heavily influenced by external (mainly American) funding. The military government made similar allegations about the opposition and democracy movement, as discussed in Chapter 7. These views can be contrasted with the work of scholars such as Schober (2011) and Walton (2016), who do see a significant role for politically inspired monks within the *sangha*. Walton introduces the concept of a 'moral universe' in which Buddhist monks deal with political issues in direct and indirect ways. He further argues that 'the discourse that separates "true Buddhists" from "traditional Buddhists" contains an implicit moral and intellectual critique that questions the moral capacity of most of the Buddhist population of the country' (Walton, 2012a: 170).

The All Burma Monks Alliance, which was founded in September 2007, can be viewed as an example of monks voicing public criticism towards the government (Walton, 2012a: 215). Founding members include the well-known monks U Gambira and Ashin Issariya, also known as 'King Zero'. The latter was also involved in setting up The Best Friend, an organization founded in 1999 by two monks attending university in Yangon.[2] The Best Friend was originally set up as a literature group and educational organization. Military Intelligence learned of their existence after they attempted to meet with Aung San Suu Kyi in 2000. When the government tried to stop their activities, they decided to stage a boycott by refusing to take university exams, after which they were expelled from university. The founders stayed temporarily in Europe, while others participated in the 2007 uprising. After this uprising, U Gambira was sentenced to over 60 years in prison. He would later be released as part of an amnesty issued by President Thein Sein, then briefly re-arrested in 2016. Other monks fled the country to avoid arrest and remained active educating Burmese migrant communities in Thailand. When asked whether monks should be involved in political affairs, one of The Best Friend founders answered: "You cannot separate politics from the Buddha's teaching ... When the monks are getting involved in politics, we are not seeking power ... We feel we are responsible to point out injustice." This is in line with Walton's (2015b: 520) observation that some monks consider it acceptable to take part in occasional political activities, as long as they do not view politics as a possible profession, for example by trying to start their own political parties. Despite their insistence on being non-partisan, the founders of The Best Friend were sympathetic to the National League for Democracy (NLD), and many of their friends were NLD members. U Gambira's brother, a local NLD law maker, was imprisoned after the coup in 2021. In other cases, strong relationships exist between Buddhist community leaders and more secular-oriented CSOs, which often use the monasteries of progressive monks as safe spaces to organize activities without interference from the authorities or other intruders such as members of MaBaTha.

Not only have some Buddhist monks in Myanmar become active in the political sphere (though outside the realm of political parties), but many have been further 'politicized' as a result of the military's oppressive and violent treatment of Buddhist monks. After the 2007 uprising, analysts even spoke of a 'new breed of monks' (Human Rights Watch, 2009: 105), citing the example of Sitagu Sayadaw, who was involved in both political uprisings and humanitarian aid deliveries (see also McCarthy, 2019) but was later criticized for his close association with the military after the 2021 coup (International Crisis Group, 2023a). Similarly, Walton (2012a: 153) argues that 'the rise of NGO activity as well as the increase in social donations (as opposed to purely religious donations) by Buddhists has expanded the discourse to include positive interpretations [of political actions], often justified through Buddhist teachings'. The discussion about Buddhist monks and politics suggests that we should neither dismiss the monks' self-stated interest in political affairs, nor automatically assume that their visible activities correspond to Western conceptualizations of human rights and democracy promotion.

## Minority religious and ethnic organizations

While Buddhist organizations form the vast majority of religious civil society in Myanmar, people from minority religions have long been forming associations too. As stated, one of the earliest NGO-style CSOs was founded by Baptists in the late 19th century (Heidel, 2006: 92; Kramer, 2011: 6). The Myanmar Baptist Convention, as it is now called, is headquartered in Yangon. Like other Christian associations such as the YMCA and YWCA, it has managed to establish significant international contacts (Kramer, 2011: 9). Christian leaders play a prominent role in Myanmar society, with Charles Maung Bo, for example, who became Myanmar's first cardinal in 2015, speaking out in support of peace and ethnic and religious minority rights.[3] In addition to Buddhist and Christian civil society, Hindus and Muslims in Myanmar have also set up welfare organizations that often reach beyond their own religious communities (Kramer, 2011). In a survey among 140 communities in Myanmar, Heidel (2006) found the number of Buddhist organizations to be proportionally lower (64 per cent), and the number of Christian NGOs higher (23 per cent) than the average population, while the number of Islamic (10 per cent) and Hindu (3 per cent) organizations was more proportionate to the general population. Islamic organizations faced significant threats around the start of the communal violence in 2012, whereas inter-religious peacebuilding efforts were also started by leaders from the Buddhist and Muslim communities (Walton and Hayward, 2014).

Similar to religion, ethnicity is another, related identity marker in Burmese society. Ethnic identity forms the basis around which many civil society groups organize themselves, particularly in the ethnic states. Kramer (2011: 7) describes the Karen National Association that was formed in 1881 as 'the first formal ethnic nationality organisation in Burma'. While Christian organizations were among the earliest identified as civil society, the ceasefires that were reached between the military government and several armed ethnic armed organizations (EAOs) in the 1990s marked a new phase in the development of ethnic organizations in the country (Smith, 1991, 1999; South, 2008a). In particular, the ceasefires gave ethnic CSOs (including many faith-based groups) the opportunity to take on the role of mediators and peace builders on the local level, while significant relief activities across the border with Thailand also developed (South, 2004; Kramer, 2011). Conversely, the position of certain Burman organizations which continued to oppose the government arguably weakened as a result of the ceasefires reached with their former allies among the ethnic nationalities (Kyaw Yin Hlaing, 2007b: 24).

Two of Myanmar's best known CSOs developed after the Kachin Independence Organization (KIO) reached a ceasefire with the military government in 1994 (South, 2008a; Fink, 2009; Kramer, 2011). Metta Development Foundation was founded in 1998 by a former KIO officer in order to promote development in the post-ceasefire areas. It operates in several ethnic states as well as in the Irrawaddy delta and works primarily on sustainable agriculture. The Shalom (Nyein) Foundation was started by a former leader of the Kachin Baptist Convention (KBC) in 2000, in order to promote peace and reconciliation in several (post-)conflict areas. Both organizations started locally but have grown into nationally operating NGOs, assisting people of various ethnic backgrounds in the development of participatory action and development management skills.

Similarly, Karen organizations were started and expanded as a result of a temporary ceasefire between the military and the Karen National Union (KNU), the country's oldest ethnic armed group, in which they had been allowed to play the role of mediators (Kramer, 2011: 26). Organizations that aimed to preserve the cultural identity of ethnic nationalities, such as the Mon and Shan literary and culture committees, also saw their role expanding in the 1990s (South, 2003, 2008a; Michio, 2007: 195). Other ethnicity-based organizations that play a prominent role in the ethnic states include the KBC, and various organizations in Karen and Mon states that are often connected to EAOs and thereby hold significant power over everyday life in the areas under their control (Kramer, 2011; Lall and South, 2014). Ethnic human rights organizations such as the Karen Human Rights Group founded in 1992 aim to operate more independently but are still often restricted in their reporting on violations conducted by EAOs (MacLean, 2022; Matelski et al, 2022).

The 1990s ceasefires thus had a significant influence on the development of civil society in the ethnic states. Populations in other areas were less able to benefit from this development, as the military intensified repression in non-ceasefire areas (Lall, 2016).[4] Moreover, the ceasefires contributed to the exploitation of natural resources in ethnic areas, in which ethnic elites were often complicit (Woods, 2011; McCarthy and Farrelly, 2020). The Union Solidarity and Development Party (USDP) government initiated new peace talks, resulting in the Nationwide Ceasefire Agreement (NCA) signed in 2015 between the government, the military and a number of EAOs, in which some provisions for a future federalist system were included.[5] The peace talks have generally been characterized by unequal relations between the military and the EAOs, however, and the agreements reached earlier were violated after the 2021 military coup (Vrieze, 2023). Kramer (2021) argues that the peace process since 2011 has had no significant transformative effect and, together with economic reforms, has led to further loss of land and natural resources for populations in the ethnic states.[6] Meanwhile, the peace negotiations invited the emergence of a Myanmar peace industry, in which old and new CSOs benefitted from significant donor investment (Bächtold, 2015). The international involvement in Myanmar's peace process will be further discussed in Chapter 7.

## Inter-ethnic relations and intra-ethnic diversity

In contrast to traditional nationalist organizations, more contemporary CSOs do not present themselves explicitly as Burman. Where Burman members dominate, this is largely implicit, whereas organizations with members from minority groups tend to be more explicit about their ethnic origins. The privileged position of Burmans in Myanmar society has been widely acknowledged. Walton (2012b) refers to the 'wages of Burman-ness', which he argues became more apparent during the political transition. Burman activists were generally able to benefit more from the transition than activists in the border regions such as Kachin State, which were subjected to increased military violence. Combined with intensified resource extraction in ethnic areas, and the discrimination and violence experienced by the Rohingya and other Muslim groups, the overall outcome of the political transition has been detrimental to ethnic nationalities. The military violence inflicted on all sections of the population, including Burman activists, has in some cases fostered a dynamic of 'competitive victimhood' in which groups find it difficult to acknowledge each other's victimization (MacLean, 2022; see also Walton, 2012b).

Fault lines and tensions occur not only between various ethnic and religious minority groups, but also among ostensibly homogenous groups. Significant religious, linguistic and cultural divisions exist among the Karen, for example, the second largest minority group in Myanmar (Thawnghmung, 2008). While the Christian Sgaw Karen have the strongest transnational profile and are probably Myanmar's best known minority group abroad (at least until the violence against the Rohingya made international headlines), there are in fact around 20 Karen subgroups, most of which are Buddhist. Less than 25 per cent of the Karen, moreover, actually live in Karen State, and those living in the lower and/or delta areas of Myanmar are much more likely to interact with Burmans and have Burmese, not Karen, as their first language (Thawnghmung, 2008: 4). Sadan (2013) makes a similar argument regarding the separate identities of various Kachin groups, and criticizes the emphasis on Christianity in the outward portrayal of a pan-Kachin identity, while Michio (2007: 192) uses the term 'Shanization' to refer to 'the hypothetical formation of collective identity in contrast with other groups' among the Shan, Myanmar's largest ethnic minority group. Likewise, Chin State actually houses over 20–30 ethnic sub-groups who speak mutually unintelligible languages, making it difficult to develop activities for the Chin as a whole.

These divisions between ostensibly homogenous ethnic groups illustrate the complexity in ensuring adequate representation of minorities, as no single person or group can be expected to cater to these multiple identities. Ethnic minorities within ethnic states, moreover, such as the Danu, Pa-O and the Wa, fear that their interests may be overruled by larger ethnic groups. Together with the other identity factors discussed here, these divisions explain the large number of CSOs with an ethnic orientation that can be found in contemporary Myanmar. The military government attempted to draw arbitrary lines between ethnic groups from the 1982 citizenship law to the contested 2014 census process (Ferguson, 2015). However, since these categories often do not correspond to self-identification, they have limited relevance for the study of contemporary civil society dynamics.

Myanmar's ethnic diversity also complicates the position of ethnic nationalities within the democracy movement. Although some of the Burman leaders of the '88 uprising joined forces with the EAOs that had been operating in the border areas, distrust frequently surfaced, and the leaders of both groups disagreed on issues such as leadership positions and the permissibility of violence and armed resistance. Those suspected of infiltration were executed in rebel camps (Kyaw Yin Hlaing, 2004, 2007b). The ethnic nationalities' demands for federalism and self-determination, moreover, were not always included in the work of the opposition movement, as the Burman democracy groups, at least until recently, did not necessarily support the creation of a federalist state (Brooten, 2004; South, 2004; Brees, 2009; Kramer, 2011: 67). Egreteau (2012: 133) writes that the 'failed attempts to unify the Myanmar-focused transnational networks under a pro-democracy flag (often Burman-led)' encouraged the 'ethnicization of Burmese exile politics' in the 2000s, and thus led to an emphasis on ethnic minority rights in a context of Burman domination. This sentiment was apparent even among ethnic nationalities who had grown up in central Myanmar around Burmans, without first-hand experience of armed conflict. Respondents of ethnic nationality background frequently tried to explain how 'pro-democracy' and 'pro-federalist' were in fact very different. Ideological splits also occurred within ethnic nationalities regarding the prioritization of ethnic federalism, ceasefires or national democracy promotion (Thawnghmung, 2008; Brees, 2009: 34; Lall, 2016). Moreover, political elites on all sides are said to have actively magnified the differences between ethnic groups while downplaying shared historical and social experiences (Sadan, 2013: 455). Inter-ethnic advocacy efforts seem most successful for causes of mutual concern, such as the struggle for land rights, women's rights and environmental rights (Harriden, 2012: 285; Simpson, 2014; Doi Ra and Khu Khu Ju, 2021). Chapter 8 will discuss new forms of inter-ethnic advocacy in response to the 2021 military coup.

## Fault line 2: generation and gender

Apart from ethnicity and religion, generation and gender play a significant role in the identity of civil society actors in Myanmar. Women represent about 52 per cent of the total Myanmar population (estimated to be between 51 and 55 million people), and almost a third of the population is between 10 and 24 years old (UNFPA, 2017). Yet neither women nor youth are particularly well represented in Myanmar, either in civil society, in politics or in general public life. Rather than age, which is not a static factor, this section focuses on generations defined as groups of actors who grew up in a particular era, which influences their self-identification as activists. The various stages of military rule and the periodic protests had a large impact on the country's younger generations of activists, as did the occurrence of cyclone Nargis in 2008. One respondent even concluded that "Burma is a strange country, not divided by politics but by generations."

### *Generations of student activists*

Myanmar's landscape of student activists, the backbone of the country's democracy movement, can be categorized into a number of generations, based on events in the country with which they started their social and political activities. Although resistance to military rule dates back to the 1960s, the most contemporary activist experiences emerged from the student movement of 1988, a group later referred to as the 88 generation. While this group was temporarily weakened after the crackdown of 1988 and continued much of its opposition from exile, prison time for others strengthened their convictions ('university of life', as some of them called it), as well as their connections to new generations of activists. With the universities closed for several years after 1988, the student unions re-emerged in 1994. A large student demonstration in 1996 was followed by a severe crackdown, resulting in some activists self-identifying as 'the '96 generation', many of whom were also imprisoned or had to flee. Further demonstrations took place between 1996 and 1998. In 2000, a group of former political prisoners founded the Assistance Association for Political Prisoners-Burma (AAPP, or AAPP[B]), an organization initially based in Thailand which monitors the number and treatment of political prisoners at various points in time, advocates for their cause in national and international platforms and takes care of their needs and those of their families during and after prison time. In the following decades, it would take up a leading role in documenting violations of civil liberties in Myanmar, including cases of torture, unlawful detainment and arbitrary arrest (Matelski et al, 2022).

A group of activists released from prison in 2005 regrouped under the banner 88 Generation Students. Some of their members were again arrested after the 2007 uprising, while others re-established the historical All Burma Federation of Student Unions (ABFSU) in the aftermath of this uprising. Many student activists were released during one of President Thein Sein's mass amnesties in January 2012, and some 88 generation activists started the '88 Generation Peace and Open Society Group', a civil society group with political aspirations led by ABFSU-leader Min Ko Naing. This group started engaging in more direct advocacy towards the USDP government, while taking up the plight of farmers, workers and other local communities. Although some politicians viewed them as competition, they pledged support to Aung San Suu Kyi. They spoke out in favour of NLD policies towards constitutional amendments and the treatment of the Rohingya people, but opposed the activities of MaBaTha (Min Zin, 2015).

Another significant organization that emerged out of the 2007 demonstrations is Generation Wave, a youth movement founded by a new generation of student activists involved in the 2007 demonstrations.[7] Like AAPP, Generation Wave initially had to operate from a secret location in Thailand, while members continued to operate in Myanmar. Their non-violent guerrilla tactics consisted of distributing leaflets, writing graffiti messages and mobilizing people inside the country through social media. Generation Wave was particularly active around the 2008 constitution and the 2010 election boycott campaign, as discussed in Chapter 6. During the political transition, they experienced a period of increased freedoms, for some even resulting in a political career. One of the co-founders, hip-hop artist Phyo Zayar Thaw, successfully ran as an NLD candidate in the 2015 elections and became a popular member of parliament. This popularity, including his personal connection to Aung San Suu Kyi, would cost him his life in the aftermath of the 2021 military coup.[8] New generations of student activists emerged during and after NLD rule.

*The post-Nargis generation*

While a new generation of student activists emerged out of the 2007 demonstrations, many of the less politically vocal actors started their civil society involvement in 2008. Cyclone Nargis struck the south-east part of the country on 2 and 3 May 2008, resulting in at least 140,000 casualties (Human Rights Watch, 2010). Around 2.4 million people's livelihoods were also affected, due to the limited availability of infrastructure, housing and facilities such as clean water (Fink, 2009: 108). The military government's inadequate response to the cyclone severely aggravated the catastrophe. Not only did it lack the equipment, capacity and willingness to respond to humanitarian needs, but it also initially rejected the international assistance that was being offered from several sides (Fink, 2009; Larkin, 2010). Only after UN General Secretary Ban Ki-Moon paid a personal visit to the country three weeks later did military leader Than Shwe allow limited amounts of foreign assistance.

This lacuna resulting from the military's ill-treatment of the disaster paradoxically opened up new roles for local and international actors. On the international level, the Association of Southeast Asian Nations (ASEAN) was instrumental in establishing a Tripartite Core Group, in which representatives from the government, ASEAN and the UN took equal part. The Tripartite Core Group was intended as 'a sort of humanitarian broker' that prevented the military government from losing face while accepting international assistance (Larkin, 2010). In the meantime, news of the devastating effects of the cyclone had reached people around the country, who started operating their own small-scale relief efforts despite active discouragement from the government. High-profile activists such as comedian Zarganar, who had previously been imprisoned for criticizing the government, organized relief efforts. Zarganar was subsequently arrested and imprisoned together with 20 other relief workers (Human Rights Watch, 2010).

Yet these prominent activists were not the only ones who intervened in the aftermath of the cyclone. For many young social activists, especially in central and southern Myanmar, their post-Nargis involvement in relief efforts turned out to be a benchmark in their personal and professional lives.[9] Many young people who had been active in local educational and training institutions joined forces by starting ad hoc organizations or joining existing ones and taking on challenging tasks such as removing dead bodies from the river. Some became active in the Nargis Action Group, an ad-hoc organization set up by Myanmar Egress (discussed later in this chapter), while others were hired by ASEAN to coordinate relief efforts. Urban-based civil society actors in particular gained the opportunity to learn about life in the rural areas by engaging directly with the cyclone-affected farmers. Solidarity increased among youth from better-off families, who learned about the social problems in the country and became passionate about what some respondents described as a 'community spirit'. Meanwhile, young people dared to question some of the patterns of the older generation of activists, whom they saw as overly traditional and hierarchical. Cyclone Nargis also marked the first reported instance of large-scale relief efforts being conducted by Buddhist monks, who in many cases were the first to reach out to affected populations well before NGO workers gained access (Jaquet and Walton, 2013). The cyclone, moreover, brought about increased involvement of Western donors with local civil society actors, as will be discussed in Chapter 7.

## The role of women

As in many Southeast Asian countries, Myanmar society is characterized by persistent gender inequalities, attributable to a complex interplay of cultural practices, religious (mostly Buddhist) values and marginalization under military rule (Walton et al, 2015).[10] Despite the prominent role of Aung San Suu Kyi, who grew up outside the country, not many women feature prominently in Myanmar's political landscape. Where women are involved in public platforms, they are often from an elite background, or operate under the influence of military leadership (Harriden, 2012). On the face of it, Myanmar's contemporary civil society forms a positive exception. Women have been relatively visible, especially in exile groups and transnational platforms. Women also play a prominent role in ethnic civil society, and even in some EAOs. Yet organizations that do not focus explicitly on women or youth continue to be dominated by middle-aged men.[11] Although the Karen, Kachin, Shan and other groups established prominent women's rights organizations, ethnic women too continue to struggle for equal rights, not only with men but also with older women who challenged the younger generation's deviance from traditional norms. Female respondents experience a 'glass ceiling' and complain about the absence of female leaders in virtually every aspect of society: "In politics, among the armed groups, CBOs [community-based organizations], religious [organizations], the administrative structures, the village headmen, are all men."[12] Research demonstrates, moreover, that many people in Myanmar, including women, disapprove of women taking on political roles (Shwe Shwe Sein Latt et al, 2017). Young women aspiring to leadership roles, consequently, experience both a lack of support and a lack of role models. This is attributed to conservative cultural norms, although these differ across contexts and circumstances, and to a lack of willingness among older leaders, including women, to delegate responsibilities to younger co-workers (Matelski and Nang Muay Noan, 2022). Although this applies equally to women of Burman and ethnic nationality backgrounds, the latter face the extra burden of living in economically marginalized areas which are underdeveloped in terms of educational opportunities and infrastructure, and often face conflict-related security risks.

Prominent examples of women's organizations in Myanmar are the Burmese Women's Union, founded by members of the All Burma Students' Democratic Front in 1995, and the Women's League of Burma (WLB) founded in 2000, both originating from the Thai border area. WLB was started by 12 ethnic women's organizations that were concerned about ethnic rights being made subordinate to the larger women's rights agenda. It explicitly seeks to combine women's rights and ethnic rights (Hedström, 2016; Pepper, 2018). One of the rare female spokespersons of a democracy organization described how her career as an activist of the 88 generation contributed to the emancipation of Burmese women. She explained that politics in Myanmar was seen as a man's affair, and that even her mother told her to "back out".[13] On her position in the democracy movement, she commented:

> Even though we were working shoulder to shoulder on the street, when it comes to organization in the jungle, then the decision-making positions are with men. They see women as a burden to the movement. ... We are fighting together for this cause. But of course from the cultural point of view women are fragile, so you should be protecting them.

She conveyed how her study in the United States as a political refugee had made her aware of gender differences within the democracy movement, which she later used for her resistance activities in Thailand: "We are no longer keeping silent about our gender norms, and we try to apply that in our democracy movement. It is like a movement within a movement."

Research has shown that transnational activism may offer opportunities for emancipation of marginalized groups, as they get to interact with international human rights activists and supporters. The Shan Women's Action Network, for example, has provided opportunities for female Shan activists in Thailand to build up a reputation through contacts with the international women's rights movement. Their 2002 report 'License to rape' was particularly influential in putting sexual violence against ethnic women on the international agenda while increasing the profile of women within Shan politics (Laungaramsri, 2006). Chua and Gilbert (2015) describe a similar effect for members of sexual minority groups who drew attention to LGBT(IQ+) rights by engaging in organization, training and advocacy activities in Thailand, thereby challenging dominant sexual norms in Myanmar. These examples demonstrate the intersectional effects of identity factors such as gender, sexuality, generation and ethnicity. Other factors that influence civil society actors' activities and room to manoeuvre are their level of independence from the government and their location inside or outside the country.

## Fault line 3: government-organized and independent NGOs

Independence from government is one of the key defining characteristics in Western conceptualizations of civil society. For civil society under authoritarian rule, the question arises to what extent organizations can operate completely independent from the government, a question that will be further explored in Chapter 4. Whereas mass organizations in countries such as Vietnam were considered suitable partners for international NGOs (Salemink, 2006: 118), such organizations in Myanmar were mostly considered to be government-organized NGOs (GONGOs) subject to undesirable influence by the military. While some CSOs under military rule were certainly co-opted by the government, research on civil society in authoritarian environments calls for a more nuanced approach to the criterion of independence. This section covers the role of GONGOs, while later sections focus on a number of high-profile organizations that insisted on their independence but were nevertheless accused by critics of being closely affiliated with, or supported by, the military government.

In 1993, the State Law and Order Restoration Council (SLORC) government started its own mass organization, the Union Solidarity and Development Association (USDA), intended to gather support for military policies and to mobilize youth. Its five stated objectives were 'nondisintegration of the Union, nondisintegration of national solidarity, perpetuation of sovereignty, promotion of national pride, and the emergence of a prosperous and peaceful nation'. Although formally a non-political organization, the USDA was led by the SLORC chairman and senior ministers, and presumably financed largely by military leaders and their various business undertakings (Steinberg, 2001: 112; Taylor, 2009: 446). USDA membership reportedly rose rapidly from 5 million in 1996 to 11 million in 1999 and over 22 million in 2005 (Steinberg, 2001: 111; Taylor,

2009: 446; Holliday, 2011: 72). Since this comprises over a third of the total estimated population (including ethnic nationalities and children), critics have dismissed this number as exaggerated. It seems beyond doubt, though, that the organization managed to attract a large membership. Some members joined because they felt coerced (membership was nearly compulsory for civil servants, and highly encouraged for university students), while others hoped to benefit from membership privileges such as access to government officials (Kyaw Yin Hlaing, 2007a: 162).

The USDA increasingly became known for its mass rallies, some of which brought together over 100,000 people (Steinberg, 2001: 113). Orchestrated mass events were often directed explicitly against the NLD and other dissidents, including the 2003 Depayin attack on Aung San Suu Kyi described in Chapter 1. A few years later, the government admitted the existence of a civilian security force, the Swan Arr Shin ('masters of force'), that operated parallel to official security services and appeared irregularly and unannounced at public gatherings (Fink, 2009: 102; Cheesman, 2015: 205–6). This group was also accused of involvement in the crackdown on the 2007 uprising (Human Rights Watch, 2009), as well as in later violence directed against student demonstrations during NLD rule. The USDA always maintained close connections to the military and was transformed into a military-backed party, the USDP, in advance of the 2010 elections. Although the extent to which it can be considered civil society, let alone an independent organization, is questionable, the USDA undeniably had a large impact on the country's social environment and is often mentioned in reports on Burmese civil society (for example, South, 2008ab; Kramer, 2011; Petry and South, 2013). Other organizations that maintained strong links with the military include the Myanmar Maternal and Child Welfare Association (MMCWA) (with a reported membership of between 1 and 5 million), the Myanmar Women's Affairs Federation, the Myanmar Red Cross Society, and the Myanmar Anti-Narcotic Association, whose activities consisted of a combination of social service provision, community organizing and 'pro-regime rallies' (Taylor, 2009: 447). These groups were usually led by wives of high-ranking military government officials, who were replaced whenever their husbands changed position (Harriden, 2012).

In some cases, organizations affiliated with the military tried to compete with, or take over, independent welfare providers. The MMCWA reportedly tried to co-opt the Byamaso Organization, an independent organization that provides cheap or free funeral services for the poor; the organizers had turned down offers of financial assistance as well as board members suggested by the MMCWA (Kyaw Yin Hlaing, 2004, 2007a). The Free Funeral Service Society, a similar organization that was started by famous film actor Kyaw Thu, encountered government harassment as a result of its widespread popularity but nevertheless managed to stay independent (Kyaw Yin Hlaing,

2004: 407; South, 2008b: 197). Other social welfare organizations such as the Myanmar Women Entrepreneurs Association were effectively turned into GONGOs (Fink, 2009: 149–50).

While the undeniable presence of government-led social organizations does not rule out the possibility of the existence of more independent CSOs in Myanmar, until 2008 many of them operated outside the view of the international community. A critical report on humanitarian aid that was published in Thailand in 2002 identified 'only 2 legitimate independent civil society organisations' inside the country, namely Metta Development Foundation and Shalom Foundation (ALTSEAN-Burma, 2002). Around 2010, the dominant international impression remained that few to no independent CSOs organizations could exist inside the country, as opposed to the politically oriented organizations in exile. The question of independence from the military was thus viewed as directly related to an organization's location inside or outside the country, a distinction that proved overly simplistic.

## Fault line 4: 'inside' and 'outside' Myanmar

Under the SLORC/State Peace and Development Council government between 1988 and 2010, the international profile of civil society was largely determined by organizations in exile. Representatives of these organizations constituted the public face of Burmese resistance, speaking at public events and receiving international recognition for their work. As civil society spokespersons, they had a much stronger influence on international perceptions of the situation in Myanmar than actors based inside the country who operated under daily repression. Among Burmese activists and their foreign supporters, this distinction became known as 'inside' versus 'outside'. This polarized debate was even reflected in the way people spoke about the country: 'Have you been "inside" Burma (never "to")?' (Liddell, 2001: 134). Activists in exile were more openly critical of the military government, while many local organizations tried to maintain working relations with the authorities; the distinction between 'inside' and 'outside' was therefore often equated to differences in ideology, strategy and knowledge. Yet in order to maintain credibility as representatives of the Myanmar population, exile organizations often emphasized their frequent interactions with people based inside the country.

Activists based outside the country, moreover, were constantly reminded of their country's pariah status and encouraged to express their disapproval, while civil society actors based inside the country, especially those who were reliant on the authorities to conduct their activities, were less likely to speak out against military rule. This way, the ideological distinction between organizations based inside and outside the country was amplified by the different roles they took on in each environment. Moreover, some organizations that were initially based in exile shifted part or all of their activities inside the country as the political transition gained pace, while they later had to go underground again, or flee. The 'inside–outside' distinction therefore is based mostly on geographical location and physical proximity to the Myanmar government at particular points in time, rather than on individual ideological positions.

## Transnational aspects of the Burmese democracy movement

The Burmese democracy movement described earlier shows characteristics of what sociologists identify as transnational social movements or advocacy networks: international networks of activists that can influence the re-distribution of resources, provide alternative sources of information and create a common discourse with the goal of bringing about social change (Keck and Sikkink, 1998; Dale, 2011). Members of the democracy movement use online platforms, address an international audience and adopt international human rights discourse in their campaigns, a process which has been referred to as 'vernacularization' (Levitt and Merry, 2009). They frequently call on the UN to take action, condemn the government for its failure to live up to international obligations and make use of international commemoration days to draw attention to their struggle. The rise of the internet and of international human rights discourse in the 1990s helped Burmese activists in exile to advocate for their cause abroad (Zaw Oo, 2006).

It was only at the end of the 1980s that international human rights networks started taking up the plight of the Burmese people. The first international report on human rights in Burma was published by Amnesty International after a fieldtrip to the Thai border areas in May 1988, around the same time that ethnic nationality representatives started a modest international lobby (Liddell, 2001: 163). In the aftermath of the 1988 uprising, international solidarity really took off, and the democracy movement became transnational not only in its networks and discourse, but also in its activities. Burma solidarity groups (which rarely used the name Myanmar) were started by 'young, idealistic and enthusiastic Westerners fired up by a moral indignation at such a clear injustice', in response to increased contacts with Burmese people during their travels to Thailand, and the growing availability of Western donor funding (Liddell, 2001: 163). Well known solidarity groups, run largely by foreigners and a few prominent exiled activists, include Burma Campaign UK (founded in 1991), the Alternative ASEAN Network on Burma (founded in 1996), and the Free Burma Coalition (FBC, founded in 1995).[14] FBC, co-founded by prominent activist Maung Zarni, was formed as a network for democracy activists in exile and in the border areas to share information through the internet and initially campaigned for US-based and other companies to withdraw from the country (Dale, 2011). From 2003 onwards, the US Campaign for Burma took over this advocacy role, as Maung Zarni no longer favoured a sanctions policy. Regional organizations often joined forces, for example in ASEAN meetings, and when making submissions to UN bodies. At the Human Rights Council's Universal Periodic Review, NGOs are invited to submit shadow reports. Networking among these organizations takes place on several levels. European 'Burma groups' cooperate in a European Burma Network, while many democracy organizations operating within Southeast Asia are members of the network organization Progressive Voice (formerly named the Asia-Pacific Peoples' Partnership on Burma and Burma Partnership, respectively).

Burma Partnership/Progressive Voice, a network established in 2006, is one of the most prominent Burmese-led organizations in exile. Its spokespersons appear regularly at public events, first in Thailand, later also in Myanmar, and increasingly online. The civil society career of the organization's leader is exemplary for a democracy activist trajectory, although she is one of the few leading women within the movement.[15] As a student activist, she fled to the border areas after the crackdown of 1988 and co-founded the organizations Burma Partnership and WLB. She was granted refugee status in the United States in 1990, completed her studies and campaigned on Burma for several American human rights organizations, before returning to the region in the late 1990s. She served as chairperson for the Network for Human Rights Documentation-Burma and Burma Partnership (now Progressive Voice) and has continued to make frequent public appearances as a spokesperson on human rights in Myanmar. The time spent in the Thai border area put her in touch with EAOs and made her aware of their struggle. After spending time with the 'armed resistance in the jungle', different groups started organizing around various causes, including the rights of youth and women. The Human Rights Education Institute of Burma (later transformed into Equality Myanmar) was founded in 2000 by another human rights activist, who is her close friend.

While Burma Partnership initially focused mostly on populations in the refugee camps and in exile as the most easily targeted populations, over time the focus shifted to include audiences inside the country. Up to the political transition, human rights training programmes run by democracy organizations mostly took place in Thailand, where these issues could be discussed more openly. Organizations inside the country faced restrictions in terms of the content of their trainings and interference by authorities. Those trained in Thailand were expected to transfer knowledge to populations inside the country, especially in the ethnic border areas, where they contributed to awareness raising on human rights and education systems that ran parallel to the government. The coordinator of Burma Partnership explained with foresight in 2011: "Even let's say for whatever reasons you are able to change the regime, you still need these people at last to become empowered, knowing their rights and being able to stand for their rights. You have the possibility of another regime who will become another dictator." As Chapter 8 will demonstrate, the impact of such rights-based organizations inside and outside the country became clearly visible in the aftermath of the 2021 military coup.

Throughout the 1990s and early 2000s, democracy organizations based outside the country tried to bridge local concerns and international human rights agendas. Yet there were both apparent and actual discrepancies between advocacy and training activities taking place inside and outside the country. Cross-border activities were particularly hazardous for actors based inside the country, who could be put at risk if associated with democracy activists who spoke out publicly against the military outside the country (Matelski, 2014). Exile organizations, particularly in Thailand and other neighbouring countries, received most information from the conflict areas in the bordering states. Consequently, they were often less aware of the sometimes positive developments in central Myanmar and dismissed organizations working in Myanmar as 'junta collaborators' (Lall, 2016: 24).

This discrepancy also led to accusations of democracy activists in exile becoming detached from the needs and experiences of people who continued to live under military rule (Callahan, 2010: 71; Egreteau, 2012: 117). While opposition members in exile had learned to address international audiences, critics wondered, 'can they still make equally convincing speeches to people on the streets of Rangoon or in Burma's villages?' (Liddell, 2001: 171). Similarly, Prasse-Freeman (2012: 385) concludes that 'the opposition's true constituents are not those who live and struggle in Burma, but rather reside in Western parliaments, think tanks, and NGOs', and that the political messages they bring across may become 'illegible' to the Burmese masses.

Although it is difficult for outsiders to get an adequate sense of the priorities of people in remote locations or otherwise marginalized positions, a 2007 'Open Heart Campaign' organized by a group of 88 Generation Students indicated that people were primarily concerned with socio-economic rights. They did not phrase their concerns (such as forced labour) in terms of human rights violations, but in terms of distribution and economic survival (Prasse-Freeman, 2012). Similar observations regarding the focus on daily survival have been noted in studies on rural Myanmar (Thawnghmung, 2004; Malseed, 2009; Doi Ra and Khu Khu Ju, 2021). These examples raise important questions about the views and tactics of civil society spokespersons and their ability to represent the larger population.

## Fault line 5: class, elites and grassroots

Class is an often overlooked identity marker in Myanmar, but it can also be difficult to define. Given the pervasive influence of the military since 1962, social mobility to a large extent has depended on economic or political relations with the military (Kyaw Yin Hlaing, 2007b; Woods, 2011; Ford et al, 2015). One possible indicator of class differences is between urban and rural. About 70 per cent of Myanmar's population lives in rural areas with limited access to infrastructure and social services such as electricity, health care or education (Thawnghmung, 2018). In the course of the political transition, while the country's gross domestic product (GDP) grew, rural populations who were dependent on subsistence farming were unable to benefit equally from economic progress, as the poverty gap between urban and rural populations increased (Warr, 2020). In some respects, rural populations were worse off than before. Commercial interest in their land increased, and many fell victim to legal or illegal land grabs (Prasse-Freeman and Phyo Win Latt, 2018; Doi Ra and Khu Khu Ju, 2021). The urban–rural division cannot be taken as a substitute for class, though, as the struggle over land rights has led to increased rural–urban migration, and a large number of urbanites work in low-paying jobs in urban manufacturing areas such as the Yangon township of Hlaing Thar Yar (Forbes, 2019; Kyed, 2019).[16] As more companies moved their operations to Myanmar during the political transition, labour opportunities in the urban areas increased, but workers continued to face restrictions and lacked adequate government protection, both under USDP and under NLD rule. The NLD government from 2016 onwards chose to prioritize foreign investment and privatization of state services and accepted significant contributions from business elites, some of whom had previously sided with the military (McCarthy, 2019). Meanwhile, the increase in urban populations and foreign investment led to rising rents in cities such as Yangon (Prasse-Freeman and Phyo Win Latt, 2018; Forbes, 2019).

Before the 2021 coup, the government's estimated spending on social safety was only 0.01 per cent of the country's GDP (Prasse-Freeman and Phyo Win Latt, 2018: 411). Measured purely by income, it was estimated in 2013 that 7.5 per cent of the Myanmar population belonged to the middle class, defined as earning a per capita income of over $120 per month, while the average salary for nurses and teachers was about $50 per month (Shein Thu Aung, 2013 in Prasse-Freeman & Phyo Win Latt, 2018). By 2020, this percentage had increased to an estimated 20 per cent, but reliable figures since the COVID-19 pandemic and the 2021 coup have been absent. The majority of the middle classes, moreover, are ethnic Burmans living in urban centres such as Yangon and, to a lesser extent, Mandalay and Naypyidaw.

Some authors warn that in the struggle over ethnic rights, the exploitative role of Burman elites over the Burman working class tends to be overlooked (Campbell and Prasse-Freeman, 2022). Moreover, it must be kept in mind that much of the country's potential middle class has left the country, fleeing from continuous repression and seeking better economic and educational opportunities elsewhere (Zarni, 2012: 306).

In this study, respondents are considered urban educational elites rather than middle class to emphasize their education level and their urban and international orientation, rather than their socio-economic position. Within social movement theory, such persons have also been referred to as 'popular intellectuals': leaders with formal or informal education levels who 'aim to understand society in order to change it', and mobilize others through activist frames and demands towards outside supporters (Baud and Rutten, 2004: 2). Although it is questionable to what extent Burmese civil society can be considered a coherent movement, a group of spokespersons did obtain prominent roles as they were consulted by international donors, media and researchers, and thus became gatekeepers to the outside world.

Respondents came from various family backgrounds, with parents' occupations ranging from farmers and small entrepreneurs to mid-level positions in government (with salaries well under $100 a month), or even the military. They had often received training outside the state curriculum, for example at English language schools in the American Center or British Council in Yangon. Some had participated in private courses on a semi-academic level tailored to upcoming youth leaders and other civil society actors inside Myanmar, such as the Myanmar Institute of Theology or Myanmar Egress (discussed later in the chapter), or in Thailand, for example at Chiang Mai University. Many had set up their own voluntary organizations and were providing low-profile educational or humanitarian services. Some subsequently became involved with more established (I)NGOs, UN agencies or think tanks during the transition, from which they could make a living. Respondents showed concern about the increasing brain drain away from local communities as a result of this increased professionalization of civil society in Myanmar: "[S]ince Nargis we were able to get many scholarships for our participants. We are building capacity and then they go away, it is hard to persuade them to stay involved."[17] The influx of foreign actors in the course of the political transition provided new opportunities to a small but emerging group of civil society actors. While in some cases this indeed contributed to a brain drain on the community level, trainees often returned to their places of origin to share their newly acquired skills with fellow community members. Many of those I had met at training activities in Thailand later showed up in the civil society scene in Myanmar.

## The professionalization of civil society

Within research on development and civil society, concerns are often expressed about the ability of professional organizational representatives to convey the needs of 'the grassroots' who form their intended beneficiaries (Chambers, 1997; Mercer, 2002). Some critics consider the role of donors particularly harmful to domestic civil society, as they focus primarily on organizations that mirror professionalized NGOs similar to Western organizations and tend to overlook community-based activities. Chandhoke (2007: 613) decries the 'tragedy that has befallen proponents of the concept: people struggling against authoritarian regimes had demanded civil society; what they got instead was NGOs!' She argues that 'even though most countries of the developing world are primarily rural, it is the urban middle-class agenda that is best secured by the invocation of civil society'. Those civil society actors chosen as legitimate representatives by foreign donors subsequently have to divide their time between local concerns and donor reporting requirements, a dilemma in which different actors set different priorities.

In Myanmar, an increase in international involvement in the civil society sector and the corresponding opportunities for education, funding and networking during the transition allowed CSOs to grow and expand their activities but also resulted in additional challenges to their legitimacy. One respondent was particularly critical of people working for NGOs:

> You know in our country working with NGOs is just like, let the hungry tiger deliver the fresh meat ... Most of the NGO workers work just for their own surviving, just an earning. Others are just for their writing proposals ... then they cut out 30, 40% for their own, and then they deliver to the society ... You know the NGO salary is the most highest in our country.[18]

Similarly, it has been argued that some of Myanmar's larger labour unions are dominated by a few leaders who are 'defined by their capacity to maintain good relations with international NGOs and trade unions through conference participation, research and report writing and other, largely English language-based activities, which facilitate expansion of organizational budgets' (Arnold and Campbell, 2017: 809). Yet it is important to distinguish between different types of CSOs, particularly in a context such as Myanmar where resources are generally scarce. Research among young ethnic women active in CSOs indicated that most NGO workers could live off their salaries, while most CBO workers could not (Matelski and Nang Muay Noan, 2022). Many of the local civil society actors are strongly driven by ideology, ethnic nationalism and genuine concerns for their communities, as they have little material benefits to gain from their involvement; on the contrary, they may face security risks and stigmatization in their personal environment.

Some respondents showed introspection regarding their role as civil society leaders. They often felt that their status was related to education. The few respondents who did not finish high school, for example, found it difficult to take on leadership roles, a challenge that some organizations tried to counter with leadership trainings and other types of non-formal education (Matelski and Nang Muay Noan, 2022). One respondent commented on his heightened status because he had studied abroad: "If someone studies in the UK, or the US, or Europe, Burmese people are very proud ... I got the trust from the people of Burma after coming back from England."[19] Another civil society leader criticized the activities of urban-based organizations such as his own: "Civil society in Yangon is very strong, especially when discussing in hotels. ... We call this NATO: no action, talk only."[20] Some respondents reported having turned down opportunities for promotion within their organization because they did not want to spend more time in the office: "I chose the fieldwork that enables me to meet with the people" (Matelski and Nang Muay Noan, 2022: 109). Another activist commented: "We should be reluctant to become a public figure, of becoming a one man show. Most organizations are just known for their leader. Then you refer only to one person and his ideas, not what the whole organization does. This is a problem. Civil society is a collective work."[21] He attributed this tendency towards 'one man shows' partly to the influence of international organizations, which only tend to invite leaders to consultative meetings, a responsibility which he argued should be equally divided.

Yet these male former student activists also struggled with their relatively privileged backgrounds to represent the views and needs of the rural population, despite their increased involvement in rural areas since cyclone Nargis. Some even described themselves as "not real civil society" but "more of an intellectual elite". They then referred me to others, usually founders of less professionalized groups who were considered more genuine representatives of civil society, though some later also acquired significant donor funding and became professionalized as a result. When travelling the country, respondents sometimes observed behaviour among local communities that they felt was not in their best interest, such as voting for the military party USDP after having been promised short-term economic benefits. Their aim, according to this organizational representative, was to "decentralize resistance beyond the educated people". Contrarily, they also sometimes dressed and acted in manners that made them stand out from rural populations, for example by wearing (khaki) trousers instead of the traditional *longyi*, using modern mobile phones, and taking pictures of the surroundings.

The establishment of civil society trainings with support from Western organizations has played an important role in the professionalization of the local civil society sector. In order to support the growth and effectiveness of local organizations, international organizations set up civil society consortiums and knowledge centres such as the Capacity Building Initiative (CBI),[22] the Local Resource Centre,[23] Paung Ku,[24] and Pyoe Pin[25] with the aim of channelling donor support to local organizations (Kramer, 2011: 38). Despite their solid reputation with both Western donors and local NGOs, some of my respondents were less positive about the growing influence of these consortiums, which put them in a powerful position in relation to local activists. Some accused them of "sitting on the money", "monopolizing their empire" and determining the priorities for local communities through their power to distribute funding obtained from INGOs. Others saw them as useful platforms for networking among previously unconnected organizations.

## *The rise of the 'Third Force'*

A section of civil society that was particularly accused of elitism during the political transition was the newly emerging 'Third Force'. This movement, initiated around 2006, was led by prominent Burman intellectuals who claimed to be affiliated neither to the military government nor to the political opposition (Kyaw Yin Hlaing, 2014; Lall, 2016; Mullen, 2016; Mon Mon Myat, 2023). By 2010, two main Third Force organizations were active: the Thai-based Vahu Development Institute, and the Yangon-based organization Myanmar Egress. Vahu was set up in 2005 by former student activists from the 88 generation who wanted to explore other avenues towards change than the isolationist policies proposed by the government in exile and the NLD.[26] The founders were all educated abroad and were sometimes referred to as the 'Harvard Mafia', after the university they had studied at before becoming active in the US-based 'pro-democracy think tank' the Burma Fund (see Zaw Oo, 2006 for a personal account of this experience). They became impatient with border-based attempts towards democratization and noticed that funding for these types of activities had diminished, so they decided to redirect their focus to developments inside the country. With Thai academic support and Western funding, they initiated capacity building projects in Thailand for various Myanmar-based actors such as social workers and Buddhist monks. Vahu also conducted policy-oriented research with the aim of providing both the Myanmar government and the international community with political and economic analysis. While critics questioned their mandate to offer policy advice, their approach won them much interest and funding from Western donors who were also growing tired with the lack of results obtained by the democracy movement (Duell, 2014).

The second main Third Force organization, Myanmar Egress, was established in 2006 by a group of businessmen and intellectuals. Myanmar

Egress soon gained a prominent place in Yangon's civil society scene. It initiated a wide variety of activities, from post-Nargis relief efforts to short-term courses in political science, leadership skills and social entrepreneurship.[27] Apart from humanitarian assistance, the organization consisted of a think tank, a media section (publishing the popular newspapers *Living Colour* and *The Voice*), another 'capacity development' training centre, and a network for alumni activities (Lall, 2016). Focused on student-aged youth, they explicitly played into educational gaps in Myanmar and the large demand for such 'donor-friendly' activities (Décobert and Wells, 2020). With their professionally looking office and their English proficiency, they stood out from most Myanmar organizations as resembling Western-style mid-scale NGOs. The organization's leaders, however, were publicly associated with prominent persons in the military government (through business and sometimes also family relations), and the organization was criticized for lending public support to the military's 'Roadmap to Democracy', including the contentious 2008 constitution. They were also criticized for being elitist and for misleading international donors by presenting themselves as more politically moderate than in trainings for local participants. These controversies indicate the complexity around elitism in civil society, as well as the sensitivity of condoning (or not publicly dismissing) military policies during the political transition period. The following chapter zooms in on the tactics and strategies employed by civil society actors towards the military government.

4

# Room to Manoeuvre
# under Authoritarian Rule

In Myanmar, if you want to change policy, you clash with authority ...
But we can do many things despite the military government. We can
make a change starting from a small, non-sensitive issue. Changing the
policy is important, but we cannot wait for the structure to change.[1]

This chapter centres on the notion of 'space', or room to manoeuvre, for civil
society under authoritarian rule. Under the State Peace and Development
Council (SPDC) government, Myanmar civil society actors operated in
a very restricted political space. Many of them adapted to working under
the radar of the government, while others refused to make concessions and
faced regular repression, imprisonment and threats to their lives. In the
course of the political transition, new opportunities opened up for civil
society to get involved in politics and contribute to policy development.
For others, including ethnic nationalities and vocal dissidents, room to
manoeuvre remained limited, or even diminished. This created tensions
within civil society over the nature of this new space, and the question
of the extent to which civil society in transitional Myanmar could really
operate independently from the government. This chapter and the next
illustrate both sides of the debate. They show how the space experienced by
various actors was determined by a number of factors including individual
background and strategies to mobilize support, the location and timing of
activities, and the language in which they were phrased.

While the whole military-led 'Roadmap to Democracy' was contentious,
particular contestations emerged around the 2008 constitution and the
referendum held in the days after cyclone Nargis, as well as the local and
international humanitarian responses to the cyclone. Heated debates arose
once elections were announced for 2010. The main political opposition
decided to boycott the elections due to their unfair nature and the obstructions
it faced to meaningful electoral participation. Others, particularly those

affiliated with the previously mentioned Third Force, saw the elections as a unique opportunity to create political platforms outside the influence of the military. This chapter discusses the ruptures that occurred within Myanmar civil society as space opened up for some but closed down for others. The following chapters focus on the way these discussions were portrayed towards outside observers, with the 2010 elections as a specific case study.

Despite increasing academic arguments for a deconstruction of 'the state' and an emphasis on civil society as potentially hegemonic (Hedman, 2006; Chandhoke, 2007), populations under authoritarian rule experience state power in very real ways. Myanmar's military is known for its pervasive influence on people's everyday lives, as well as its influence in the formal political sphere, from law making to international relations. This is not to say that the government necessarily forms a single entity; in fact, as this chapter demonstrates, people often rely on personal relationships in order to obtain privileges or increase their room to manoeuvre. Many families, moreover, have connections with both the military and the opposition, and a decision to become active in the military is often based on economic or other practical considerations (Fink, 2009: 4, 129). In terms of formal space for civil society, however, the military has had a decisively negative influence by repressing civic associations both in law and in practice. Due to its violent and extortive practices, the military is distrusted by the general population, particularly since the latest military coup in 2021, which took away many of people's recently acquired liberties and opportunities. This chapter describes how Myanmar's military and affiliated authorities managed to exert power over the population and regulate society, while civil society actors simultaneously attempted to carve out space for their activities, sometimes in opposition to, and sometimes in tactical interaction with the authorities. It starts with an exploration of the growing body of literature on civil society in authoritarian environments and demonstrates that a sole focus on overtly political activities does not do justice to the subtle ways that many local actors find to contribute to social or political change under repressive circumstances.

## Civil society under authoritarian rule

Academic literature on civil society has largely focused on bridging the gap between state and citizens in established democracies, or on the ability to overthrow a government deemed illegitimate in regions where democratization processes occurred, such as Latin America and Eastern Europe in the 1970s and '80s (Foley and Edwards, 1996; Glasius et al, 2004; May and Milton, 2005). The much scarcer literature on civil society under durable authoritarian circumstances displays a more flexible understanding of the shape civil society may take, and its ambiguous relationship with state authorities (Howell, 2007; Hsu, 2010; Spires, 2011; Wells-Dang, 2012). The dominant focus among outside observers on public protest in Myanmar in the 1990s and 2000s provided relevant insights into contestations of military rule. However, it also resulted in a one-sided view of civil society actors as politically vocal activists, ignoring the many others who tried to find room to act independently from, or even through cooperation with state actors.

As Alagappa (2004: 5) reminds us, 'mass movements and rallies are not the everyday expression of civil society. They erupt at moments of crisis and opportunity when a number of organizations combine efforts to mobilize public opinion.' James Scott (1985) showed that people in rural areas are more likely to engage in smaller forms of everyday resistance, rather than large protests and public dissent; the same has been argued in relation to Myanmar, where rural areas are often occupied by people of minority backgrounds and/or in economically marginalized positions (Thawnghmung, 2004; Karen Human Rights Group, 2008; Fink, 2009; Malseed, 2009; Prasse-Freeman, 2012). Many civil society activities, moreover, fall somewhere between public protest and everyday resistance. Under previous episodes of military rule, activists in Myanmar had become particularly skilled at tactics intended to have a societal impact while avoiding overtly political messages that might endanger the continuity of their activities or the personal safety of those involved. Contrarily, a smaller number of overtly political actors refused to adapt their actions or messages to the repressive environment. This way, they were able to test the boundaries of military rule, but they also risked continuous threats to their freedom and safety.

The interaction between space provided to and opportunities created by civil society actors themselves can be analysed in terms of the debate on structure and agency. Structuration theory holds that both individual behaviour and social, political and economic structures determine people's room to manoeuvre (Giddens, 1986). This analysis can even be applied to highly repressive circumstances, as people still have the ability to bring about change through individual actions, although the possibilities may be more limited, and the stakes can be very high. All civil society actors in authoritarian Myanmar have to operate within an unpredictable political and economic climate, where structural factors such as repression, poverty and conflict affect their own lives and the lives of people around them. As this chapter demonstrates, they have become particularly skilled at 'navigating' this uncertain and unstable environment (see Vigh, 2009).

## Restrictions on public speech

I came all the way to Thailand because I have a toothache.
Do you not have dentists in your country?
Yes, but in Burma we are not allowed to open our mouths.

This joke is attributed to the Moustache Brothers, a comedy act that performed for small groups of tourists in Mandalay during the SPDC era. It sums up the sense of repression in Myanmar under authoritarian rule. Of the many restrictions imposed by the military government, the lack of freedom of speech had perhaps the most noticeable effect on Burmese society. After the 2007 demonstrations and the aftermath of cyclone Nargis and before the 2010 elections, over 2,100 persons were imprisoned for their political beliefs, protest activities or criticism of the government (Human Rights Watch 2010). As previously discussed, the State Law and Order Restoration Council (SLORC, later SPDC), which took power in 1988, abolished the 1974 constitution and ruled largely by decree. It frequently invoked the 1950 Emergency Provisions Act to sentence journalists, opposition members and other dissidents for voicing criticism of the government.

The military government applied its rule of law in unpredictable and inconsistent ways, whereby anyone who was 'flawed politically' could become a 'public enemy' stripped of the right to judicial remedy or political participation. Those accused of ordinary crimes had the right to defend themselves or could attempt to buy off judges, while such options were not available to 'public enemies' prosecuted for their political views or actions (Cheesman, 2015). Some of the laws used against these persons, such as the Official Secrets Act and the Unlawful Associations Act, stem from the colonial period. In the early 2000s, dissidents and 'assorted troublemakers' complaining about state failure were increasingly criminalized, as were their lawyers (Cheesman and Kyaw Min San, 2013; Cheesman, 2015). The effect of imprisoning people for their dissenting beliefs or non-violent actions goes beyond the immediate repercussions for the individuals involved. Family members and friends of those detained are often harassed or watched by the authorities, and former political prisoners feel shunned and stigmatized in their communities, which limits their opportunity to participate in future activities. Experiences of repression also deter other potential dissidents from engaging in politically 'dangerous' activities such as demonstrations. As a result, many prominent activists felt forced to leave the country if they wanted to criticize the military government without fear of repercussions.

Working under the banner of a civil society organization (CSO) could provide protection to individuals, but it could also lead to new forms of prosecution. The Unlawful Associations Act, established by the British in 1908 and revised in 1957, criminalizes membership of, or support for, illegal organizations, and limits freedom of association. It has been used strategically to obstruct student organizations, religious organizations, political opposition groups and ethnic nationality organizations. In conflict areas, men could arbitrarily be accused of assisting ethnic armed organizations. Research in China and Vietnam has shown that registration can be used strategically by authorities to control the activities of non-governmental organizations (NGOs) (Howell, 2007; Hsu, 2010; Spires, 2011; Wells-Dang, 2012). Registered organizations draw more attention from the government, have to meet certain reporting requirements and risk losing registration if they displease the authorities. On the other hand, registration with the government can increase organizations' room to manoeuvre, as they no longer have to operate secretly and have more opportunities to take up office space and open a bank account.

Myanmar's military governments are particularly notorious for controlling and obstructing civic initiatives, contributing to a wariness among organizations to register with that same government for fear of arbitrary application of regulations. In response to the student uprising in 1988, the SLORC issued the Law Relating to the Forming of Organizations that requires NGOs to register with the Ministry of Home Affairs and prohibits organizations which may disrupt law and order or 'the regularity of state machinery' from registering. In order to avoid scrutiny as well as high registration costs, many of the smaller organizations working under military rule chose not to register.[2] Others were refused registration or were sent from one ministry to the next. Some registered as a business or education facility or tried to obtain a Memorandum of Understanding (MOU) with the government, in order to be allowed to conduct social, environmental or humanitarian activities. When they did not succeed in obtaining an MOU, they sometimes worked under a different banner such as religion, or in a larger network. As one respondent explained:

> The government does not allow registration, but we can work because we got an MOU. Sometimes we work with environmental groups, sometimes we make an MOU with the Ministry of Agriculture or the Ministry of Social Work, and sometimes when we do education, we need an MOU with the Ministry of Education.[3]

I asked another respondent whether they could work without registration, to which he replied:

> Actually, we are doing without. We work with other organizations … Even if we work in the community, we don't use the name of the organization. We just perform our programme, like child development programme. *M: right, no larger organization.* No. So if one programme ends … *They don't know about the others, ah ok.*[4]

These are examples of various forms of civil society agency despite highly restrictive administrative structures. Respondents also encountered more direct forms of surveillance.

## Dealing with surveillance

Although the Military Intelligence Service (MIS) had largely been dismantled with the removal from power of General Khin Nyunt in 2004, informers continued to operate on every level. Respondents detailed how they suspected spies were attending their meetings in supposedly safe spaces, such as the American Center in Yangon. These rumours were shared among friends and meeting participants and contributed to a widespread fear of informers, as well as many creative ways to evade them, often with the help of befriended local authorities. Respondents were also skilled at solving problems by personally lobbying local authorities, offering 'tea money' (small bribes) or giving them an honorary role in public events, in the hope of placating them and being allowed to continue with their activities. Such tactics only worked in certain cases and were mostly unavailable to well-known critics of the government (Cheesman, 2015).

One of the new rules imposed by the SLORC in 1988 was a ban on public gatherings of five or more people (SLORC order 2/88[b]). Although this rule was reportedly not frequently invoked, many civil society actors considered it a limitation on their community activities. Combined with the fear of infiltration by informers, it made people reluctant to speak their minds in the presence of strangers or people they otherwise distrusted. This also affected the environment in which researchers inside the country had to operate: respondents would occasionally joke that certain activities could lead to 'free housing' or 'free transportation' – meaning arrest or deportation (Matelski, 2014: 64). Respondents also expressed concern about speaking out in front of other people, who could potentially be spies. Some said they refused to answer political questions unless they were outside the country. Speaking about politics or views about the military required familiarity and trust. For this reason, much research before the political transition period, including part of the research underlying this book, took place with respondents outside the country.

Apart from secret informers, the SPDC government also maintained a strict hierarchy of state officials reporting from the very local level upwards (Fink, 2009: 135), generally referred to as the 'ten household' model. One respondent conveyed how he encountered a township administrative officer while trying to conduct social work in his area:

> I went to a small township, providing medical health service to the elder people, with doctors. And I was at the first house talking to an over 80 year old woman. She was very happy to talk with us, she was very poor, no guests in her house, like this. At that time the township administrative officer phoned to me: "Who are you? Why are you doing such kind of activities in my administrative area? Will you come

to me or should I come to you?" [laughs] "Oh sorry sir, I am going to come to you!" [laughs]

*M: How did he get your phone number?* Because you know as soon as I arrive in this area, I go and meet with the ten household administrative leader. I say I come from my organization to do medical care for elder people in your area, my name is … and that is my phone number. And he put it to the township administration officer, here are some strangers, working like this. So I halted my activities. *Did they tell you to stop?* Yes. They [the local authorities] asked, if I want to do such kind of activities, you better try to get an MOU with the government. See? This means, you better do [this] in next life. [all laugh][5]

The laughter of this respondent and others present at the focus group discussion illustrates the absurdity of the situation he described: for the seemingly harmless activity of caring for the elderly, he was not only checked on extensively, but also threatened and effectively prevented from carrying on. Although the consequences of conducting such non-sensitive activities were limited, this example demonstrates the pervasiveness of the authorities in people's everyday social lives, as well as the direct and unpredictable control over their activities. As one (male) respondent phrased it: "The government is like a mad woman. Hard to understand them. One thing good, one thing not."

As detailed by Selth (2013), the task of gathering domestic political intelligence under the Union Solidarity and Development Party (USDP) government was split between the Special Branch of the Myanmar Police Force, which falls under the command of the Ministry of Home Affairs, and the MIS, which comes under direct command of the armed forces. In practice, their tasks often overlap, and there is a continued risk of duplication and competition. One respondent conveyed how various branches of the government, from military intelligence to police or village chiefs, all asked the same questions while competing for information, sometimes without a clear idea what should happen with such information. This frequent obligation to provide personal information and explanation about activities contributed to feelings of arbitrariness and insecurity on the side of those under surveillance, but also resulted in a population skilled in evasion. Civil society actors were very careful, for example, not to refer to politics in any of their meetings, even if they dealt directly with political matters such as responses to the 2010 elections. Human rights matters were discussed in covert terms, such as 'development'. One respondent described his organization's activities as follows: "We have programmes on livelihood, environment, shelter, disaster risk reduction and protection. Protection means … [laughs] … Protection is like a hide [that is, a cover-up]. We can't mention human rights, or women's rights, very sensitive in Myanmar. That's why our strategy is, we change to protection."[6] Another respondent similarly explained how he managed to talk about human rights: "I use other names, not human rights. We are now, you know, 'studying law', something like that you know, now we are doing 'copyright' here ... We can also include business law in my curriculum, and social entrepreneurship. With these names, we can include human rights issues."[7] These examples show the semantic creativity civil society actors had become accustomed to in order to carry out their activities without drawing unwanted attention from the government. In some cases, however, civil society actors actively sought cooperation with state authorities in order to further their goals.

## 'Contingent symbiosis' between state and civil society

Research on Vietnam and China has shown that civil society actors in authoritarian environments do not always strive for maximum autonomy from the state (Spires, 2011; Wells-Dang, 2012; Salmenkari, 2013; Waibel, 2014). Instead, a complex interaction takes place in which both state and civil society actors simultaneously seek to benefit from each other while trying to avoid unwanted interference. Wells-Dang (2012) describes how civil society actors in China and Vietnam organize flexibly in order to maximize their influence and rely on informal structures and personal connections with state actors when necessary. Similarly, Spires (2011: 2) uses the concept of 'contingent symbiosis' to describe the 'mutual suspicion and mutual need that permeates the NGO–government relationship' in contemporary China, which implies that the relationship between authoritarian governments and civil society goes beyond a one-way system of control. In many cases, particularly in China, researchers find that civil society actors value the financial and operational ability to have societal impact, display solidarity and engage in networking as more important than the opportunity to criticize the government (Hsu, 2010; Salmenkari, 2013). Such studies indicate that civil society does not need to (openly) oppose the state in order to have a societal impact. In environments where the potential risks of political activities are high, many organizations and individuals try to disguise their politically sensitive activities by hiding them from the authorities, while others choose to stay away from such activities altogether.

While antagonistic organizations in repressive circumstances may be forced to hide their activities, flee or stay silent, less threatening civil society activities might actually be beneficial to authoritarian regimes, as Spires (2011) observed in China. The appearance of an independent civil society can legitimize the ruling government, as well as complement its socio-economic work, although organizations may lack the access and resources to do so on a larger scale. Wells-Dang (2012) therefore refers to civil society networks in China and Vietnam as 'informal pathbreakers in health and the environment'. Such activities may result in government endorsement, but they may also cause local authorities to view civil society actors as competitors. In Myanmar, some respondents reported being obstructed from carrying out social services such as education or humanitarian assistance because the authorities themselves wanted to be seen to provide such assistance. Other respondents reported better personal relationships, as a result of which they were allowed to conduct their activities. One respondent explained:

> Ground level staff, township level staff, they understand the situation … From the top level they are not interested in what happens. But in the township level, they also feel [the effects of] … water shortage, they also get the same feeling with the community. They understand and they like to help.[8]

While most respondents found local authorities to be more attentive to community needs than higher officials, some conversely made use of personal contacts higher up when local authorities proved difficult to work with. Civil society actors used their contacts in relevant ministries or within the military in order to obtain permission for their social activities, if local authorities would not cooperate. However, such avenues were only available to those who had established these personal connections and usually not to well-known dissidents.

In addition to making use of existing contacts, another way to obtain cooperation is to actively foster personal relationships. Representatives of CSOs would invite government officials to their ceremonies, pay regular visits to inform them about the organization's work, and give them tokens of appreciation in order to show respect and ensure smooth collaboration. Such tactics may be referred to as 'clientelism', which according to Kyaw Yin Hlaing (2007c) has characterized state–society relations in post-colonial Burma. Respondents also conveyed contrary dynamics, such as being asked to donate to state schools which lacked sufficient government funding (Matelski, 2015: 209). Another frequent practice described by respondents was giving authorities the opportunity to 'look the other way'. Although they might privately support certain civil society activities, authorities want to avoid being held responsible by giving formal approval. For this reason, they often refused to give their permission in writing, relying instead on informal understandings. Consequently, activities that officially would be illegal could often still take place, but permission was highly dependent on individual contacts and could be withdrawn at any time. Moreover, there were severe restrictions on openly addressing the main causes of many societal problems. As one respondent explained:

For example youth groups start talking about environmental issues, like don't use plastic bags, don't cut the trees. But if you look at government projects, huge projects, they are cutting the whole forest down but we cannot start pulling that issue. If we point out the poor man cutting the tree, we have to also point out the government cutting all the trees … [It is] putting medicine in the wrong place.[9]

The opportunity to influence authorities and obtain room to manoeuvre depends not only on the individual representative, but also on the nature of the activity and the persons conducting the activity. The more public a certain activity, the more difficult it is for local officials to look the other way. Moreover, as detailed later on, prominent civil society actors are more likely to mobilize people and draw attention from the authorities than lower-ranking civil society actors. As the next section will show, temporal and geographical aspects also determine how much 'space' civil society actors experience under authoritarian rule.

## The contested notion of 'space' for civil society in the run-up to the 2010 elections

The elections announced for 2010 elicited varying reactions in Myanmar. Despite some excitement about being able to vote for the first time, especially among younger generations (since the last elections were held in 1990), there were few indications that the outcome would be credible. The military had entrenched its continued power in the contested 2008 constitution, the main opposition party the National League for Democracy (NLD) called for an election boycott, and its leader Aung San Suu Kyi remained under house arrest. While the most outspoken political activists used the elections as a rallying point in their transnational campaigns against the military government (as covered in Chapter 6), many other civil society actors had started looking for more subtle ways to bring about social and political change on the ground, especially in the humanitarian space created after cyclone Nargis. Non-political civil society actors sensed a change in state–society relations from which they could potentially benefit.

This positive depiction of the early years of the transition was highly contested among both civil society actors and outside observers. Optimistic respondents said they wanted to use and expand the available space to conduct their activities, even if it meant not criticizing problematic aspects of the government's roadmap, such as the 2008 constitution. They also commented that government officials would have to grant increased civic space for the 2010 election process to appear credible. Moreover, for the first time in 20 years, state authorities would have an external incentive to satisfy their constituencies or risk losing power. The idea of available space, and civil society's ability to expand this space provided by the government, formed a key point of contention between optimists and pessimists about the political transition. Optimists were willing to put aside their objections in the hope of achieving durable societal change, whereas those with a more pessimistic view or principled objections were unwilling to make such concessions. They pointed out, for example, that the military would dominate the post-2010 landscape, both through the 25 per cent of parliament reserved for the military in the 2008 constitution and through the remaining 75 per cent which the military-led USDP was expected to dominate. One respondent commented cynically: "Some say there is more space after the elections. Which space?! There is more space for the government's friends, but not much for the rest of us."[10] Others expressed hope that a new government would expand the space available to civil society, which turned out to be the case in the early years of the post-2010 Thein Sein government.

The ability to make use of this increased space, however, proved highly dependent on individual characteristics, connections and reputations. Being located in central Myanmar or one of the ethnic states, for example, resulted in completely different experiences regarding the space granted by the military. Not only did ethnic nationalities encounter discrimination in a range of fields including social services and employment opportunities, but a significant number of them also experienced the direct consequences of armed conflict. It is in these ethnic areas that the worst human rights violations have been documented, with populations being exposed to forced labour, rape and extrajudicial killings. Populations in the ethnic states also face higher levels of poverty, ranging from land confiscation to a lack of infrastructure and facilities such as schools or hospitals. The threat of armed conflict before and during the political transition not only raised suspicion between the central authorities and ethnic nationalities, but also made people living in conflict areas more reluctant to engage in durable community activities. A respondent from Kachin State explained:

> Kachin people are very afraid of civil war. If they build a big house, it can all be destroyed in a civil war. So they don't want to build anything nice, plan long-term projects. This is a big challenge, because if the policy of our country changes, they get nothing.[11]

This comment, made in 2010, proved painfully accurate when conflict in Kachin State resumed in June 2011. Unsurprisingly, people living in ethnic areas were less likely to seek cooperation with the military or affiliated authorities. People living in the border areas generally tend to have stronger ties with their Thai, Indian, Bangladeshi or Chinese neighbours and with cross-border activist groups than with Burman people or state authorities from central Myanmar. Apart from ethnic areas, heightened surveillance has also been noted for Nargis-affected areas in south-east Myanmar and areas known to have high numbers of NLD supporters. Prominent civil society leaders are particularly likely to come under scrutiny. The Free Funeral Service Society led by film actor and director Kyaw Thu, for example, encountered frequent government harassment as a result of its societal influence. Popular comedians such as Zarganar and the Moustache Brothers were also subject to regular surveillance and imprisonment, because they had the potential to mobilize the masses through their jokes and performances. After the 2021 coup, the military again targeted celebrities who spoke out against their practices. For this reason, other civil society actors explicitly chose to operate 'under the radar', despite them having a smaller reach and being unable to take public credit for their activities. Risk taking remained part of their daily reality, which civil society actors learned to cope with; as one respondent explained: "If we [are] afraid too much, we can't do anything. We are always at risk here. [It is] everyday life. So if we can't deal with that risk, we can't do anything."[12]

Representatives of the democracy movement took a more principled stance on the risks and benefits of speaking out against the government, but many showed understanding for other activists who preferred to keep a low profile. They were less lenient, however, towards members of the Third Force (introduced earlier) who were openly involved with high-level officials and military leaders. Myanmar Egress was the most public supporter of the 'space discourse', as their slogan was 'creating space and engaging civil society'. The organization was criticized for its close relations with government officials, yet credited for contributing to the public sphere in the form of political trainings and development of media outlets and a think tank, all with Western donor support. In their trainings and publications, members of Myanmar Egress frequently expressed the view that the political opposition should accept the government's roadmap and participate in the 2010 elections. They also 'explained how the constitution should be understood and how the upcoming elections could open up the political space for ethnic minority groups' (Kyaw Yin Hlaing, 2014: 36). The organization's founder and frequent contributor of political analyses for *The Voice* newspaper, Nay Win Maung, had called for the opposition to let the military win the 2010 elections as the only way towards a political reform process. Many people had come to suspect that Egress was able to engage in openly political activities in return for supporting the military's reform process. Representatives of the democracy movement argued that the ambiguity around the relationship between Myanmar Egress and the military government could lead to popular distrust, as one prominent democracy leader explained in 2011: "In a country like Burma, you really need the public trust. Unfortunately when you are still supported by the authorities, you lose the public trust and confidence."

At the same time, Myanmar Egress was also credited for reaching out to young people and ethnic nationalities and for talking openly about politics. Several respondents had participated in its political education activities, which were generally considered of relatively high quality. Some were rather mild on the privileges obtained by the organization: "Because they agree with the government, the government gives them a chance, that is natural. Because if I am that organization, I will also take that chance too, that is no problem. If I am jealous or something maybe I am not mature enough."[13] Others were more critical, saying "Egress is not creating space, but a barrier. They are sitting on the fence, and then when one side is powerful, they change to that ... I think it's totally bad, potentially." Another respondent and Egress alumnus was positioned somewhere in between: "To make a dialogue, they have to make trust between the military leaders, because they have absolute power. They are trying to make a channel between the government and themselves ... It makes lots of sense to me. We cannot just wipe out the generals tomorrow."[14] In short, many people in Myanmar considered high-level civil society achievements to be the result of benefits provided by the authorities, rather than entitlements that they themselves could also claim. Some Third Force members perceived a culture in Myanmar in which it was easier to criticize than to give credit. When services were provided to certain communities, people were quick to point out how these initiatives discriminated against other groups, contributed to elitism or were conducted with selfish motives. We will now look at the implications of these different approaches in Myanmar for the broader discussion on civil society in repressive environments.

## Civil society beyond the overtly political

In repressive environments, civil society activities that are not overtly political may well be overlooked by outside observers. Foley and Edwards (1996: 48), for example, assert that

> [w]here the state is unresponsive, its institutions are undemocratic, or its democracy is ill designed to recognize and respond to citizen demands, the character of collective action will be decidedly different than under a strong and democratic system. Citizens will find their efforts to organize for civil ends frustrated by state policy – at some times actively repressed, at others simply ignored. Increasingly aggressive forms of civil association will spring up, and more and more ordinary citizens will be driven into either active militancy against the state or self-protective apathy.

This illustrates the frequent depiction of civil society and mass mobilization as dichotomies: civil society existing continuously but largely inactive due to repressive circumstances, and mass mobilizers being more vibrant but only occasionally visible in large-scale public protests. In his work on civil society and political change in Asia, Alagappa (2004: 5) warns that '[a]n undue focus on mass rallies and protests may overstate the strength and consequence of civil society ... [and] obscure the more mundane and less visible functions of civil society in normal times, functions that may be just as crucial as its actions in moments of crisis'. Some researchers writing on civil society in military-ruled Myanmar emphasize its political role. Hewison and Prager Nyein (2010: 13), for example, wrote during the early years of the political transition process: 'For all of this enthusiasm about the recent efflorescence of community-based organisations and NGOs ... we see the political space available for civil society as remaining remarkably constrained.' They oppose a broader definition of civil society 'in favour of a focus on civil society organisation that is political', as 'these are organisations that seek to establish and expand the political space available for non-state actors' (Hewison and Prager Nyein, 2010: 16). In other words, they suggest a hierarchy in civil society activities, whereby social welfare organizations can only function independently after (and to the extent that) political civil society has paved the way for their political freedom.

Other researchers writing on state–society relations present a more diverse picture of forms of contention. In his overview of methods of 'non-compliance' among Karen populations, Malseed (2009) distinguishes covert, semi-covert and overt resistance against central authorities and argues that most resistance in Myanmar in the late 2000s took the form of 'the covert and everyday'. Thawnghmung (2004) comes to a similar assessment regarding rural populations' daily survival strategies. These patterns of covert resistance or non-compliance are augmented among civil society actors, who tend to come under more scrutiny from the authorities than other people due to their organized form and potential popular influence. One respondent explained in 2011: "[M]any of us want political change, but because of the situation, we have to call it social change" (Matelski, 2014: 67). As the political space opened up in the early years of the USDP government, however, many activists and organizations that had previously worked under the banner of education or humanitarian work became more explicitly involved in political affairs, such as civic education around the upcoming elections.

While this growing body of research on authoritarian environments contributes to our understanding of civil society's strategic avoidance of overtly political matters, the definitions of civil society used by academics and practitioners should not become fully dependent on the political space allowed by the state. Narrow definitions of civil society as non-political may inadvertently legitimize boundaries set by repressive states that determine the types of activities allowed under their watch. There is a risk of undermining the position of dissidents who feel forced to leave the country and continue their antagonistic activities from abroad, as these voices are ignored by researchers focusing exclusively on forms of civil society that are visible inside authoritarian states. Salemink (2006), for example, notes that Vietnamese organizations that dare to bring up 'politicized' topics such as ethnic minority rights frequently run into problems with the authorities. Researchers and practitioners focusing on antagonistic activities tend to pay more attention to the views of civil society actors in exile, as they are considered to be in a better position to voice criticism towards the state. This discrepancy can help explain why researchers working on the local level inside authoritarian states find civil society there to be much more vibrant and diverse than researchers engaging in comparative work on the (trans)national level.

Although it is safe to assume that political activities are less acceptable to an authoritarian government than socio-economic activities, it does not follow automatically that political organizations should necessarily pave the way for community-based organizations to be able to function, or that they always seek to do so. If anything, the data on Myanmar point towards an opposite sequence: while demands on the military government to step down only resulted in more repression, the influx of development organizations after cyclone Nargis gradually resulted in an enlargement of political space that was both demanded from, and reluctantly granted by the authorities. This does not mean that political civil society has no role to play; rather, it suggests that political and non-political goals may be sought after simultaneously and are highlighted or downplayed strategically depending on the situation and the individuals involved. One respondent explicitly referred to the diverse civil society goals in Myanmar as a strength:

> So many people in Myanmar are working to strengthen civil society ... Most of the NGOs are just working in the humanitarian sector, and some are very eager to change [to a] positive political situation ... Small or big, no matter, I only care what they are doing for civil society.[15]

These data show that the presence and relevance of civil society should not be determined primarily by people's ability to engage in overt political action, but instead by their ability to raise issues that resonate with everyday experiences, which are mostly expressed as socio-economic needs but often carry political undertones.

## Testing the waters during the transition

This book focuses on the early years of the political transition period in Myanmar, from the 2010 elections to the unexpected liberalization and increased civic space under the USDP government. As discussed earlier, President Thein Sein explicitly called for civil society involvement in policy debates and invited exiled dissidents back to the country. Many respondents reacted to these invitations. Members of the youth organization Generation Wave were among the first to move their activities from Thailand back inside the country. Looking back in 2014, they described their decision to return in December 2011 as follows: "The situation was not so stable yet. We decided to celebrate our anniversary and challenge our freedom. The government said the country is changing, in transition, so we tested our freedom. If they come and arrest us, it will show that the country is not changing."[16] Similarly, a representative of The Best Friend commented in 2012, after one of its foreign associates was deported for distributing stickers with peace messages: "The junta claims to want peace … We have to test if they really mean this … Are they serious about their calls for democracy? Then why do they arrest people who call for exactly the same?"[17] Although Generation Wave activists were able to hold their anniversary celebration, they were followed closely by Military Intelligence and frequently had to move office, as their landlords were intimidated by the authorities. Despite remaining unregistered, they soon became involved in a dialogue with the government on issues such as the NGO Registration Law. They were also one of the lead organizations in the Association of Southeast Asian Nations (ASEAN) Youth Forum which took place in Yangon during Myanmar's ASEAN chairmanship in 2014.

Other dissidents in exile, including members of the Third Force, were similarly quick to take up the president's invitation to return to the country. The founders of Vahu, who despite their willingness to cooperate with the government had remained outside the country, paid preliminary visits in 2011, as did the director of the Euro-Burma Office, Harn Yawnghwe. The arrest in August 2012 of a returning former lawyer for the NLD showed how fragile the security of returning exiles really was (Duell, 2014: 121; Cheesman, 2015: 127). The exiled director of the Human Rights Education Institute of Burma (HREIB) was invited in 2011 to observe the situation and was reunited with his relatives after more than 20 years. Although he was reluctant to move his organization inside Myanmar, given the relative safety of their activities in Thailand, by 2014 he had managed to open branches in various Myanmar cities, albeit under a different organizational name: Equality Myanmar. He was later appointed minister in the National Unity Government, as described in Chapter 8.

Several respondents referred to a door which had been opened by the government in 2011, and which they had to push gently in order not to lose momentum. Returning exiles often had trouble getting their residency and their organizations legalized. The director of HREIB commented in 2014 that "the country is good at kicking people out, but not at bringing them back in". In March 2014, his and other former exile organizations played a prominent role in organizing the ASEAN Peoples' Forum that took place in Yangon. Nevertheless, he considered the situation "not really open yet", as most changes had come from the top, while local authorities were slow to change their attitudes towards NGOs and other activists. While the civil society sector was visibly growing, he commented that they were merely "testing the water". Representatives of more openly critical organizations such as Burma Partnership and the Assistance Association for Political Prisoners also returned to the country but reported continuous pressure from the authorities, and even threats to their security if they did not stop talking to the media and the international community about human rights violations.

Civil society actors who had remained in Myanmar also took up the invitation to contribute to policy discussions and political debates. Many felt encouraged by President Thein Sein's State of the Union speech on 1 March 2012, in which he emphasized the importance of civil society. Several organizations rolled out new activities or expanded to new locations. Activists from the 1990s student uprisings, who had operated semi-covertly under military rule, set up the Yangon School of Political Science and the Myanmar Institute for Democracy. By 2014, they could instruct people how to lobby political representatives who had taken office after the elections and hold them accountable, something which had been impossible under military rule. When politically oriented activities were organized outside Yangon, however, military surveillance was still very tangible. As organizations had trouble registering with the authorities, they remained unsure about what they were able to get away with. As Buddhist nationalism grew and the Rohingya were increasingly targeted by the military, moreover, Muslim organizations experienced increased threats from Buddhist non-state actors such as MaBaTha, as described in Chapter 2. Meanwhile, some splits occurred within other organizations whose leaders or membership held varying views on the plight of Muslim minorities.

One consequence of the increased space for large sections of civil society during the political transition was the fast professionalization of civil society leaders. As mentioned, some of them entered the arena of formal politics. Others used their experience and education, often obtained through training abroad, to contribute to policy making and capacity building for civil servants. One respondent encountered how this created embarrassment among some government officials:

> Almost all government staff is afraid of CSOs and ashamed to deal with them because their [own] education is lower [than from the CSO leaders]. They try to hide this by giving very rude responses to the community and CSOs. And the big CSOs look down on government staff. People from the government sector feel angry and easily misuse

their power. It's a big problem to build trust among CSOs, Political Parties, Army, Government Sectors.[18]

Civil society actors inside the country, including returning exiles, also had to learn to engage in dialogue rather than just criticize the authorities, as some had done before. Those entering politics, moreover, became subject to the same criticism they had previously issued to other power holders. One civil society leader commented in 2012 about the lack of experience among new parliamentarians: "It is the blind leading the blind. They need expertise, but they do not trust outsiders." This was illustrated during a study trip to Delhi in 2012, where Indian academics would meet with civil society actors and new politicians from Myanmar (both opposition and USDP). While the civil society participants were experienced in such study trips, some of the political representatives had never left the country and had to be closely supervised, particularly at the airport, where some of them missed their flight. These increased interactions between 'inside' and 'outside' groups in advocacy platforms and other public fora during the transition will be explored in the next chapter.

5

# Transnational Advocacy Strategies and Pathways to Change

While the previous chapter focused on room to manoeuvre for civil society under authoritarian rule, the following chapters describe how Myanmar civil society actors framed their advocacy messages towards an international audience in their search for political, moral and financial support. In contrast to the volatile 'under the radar' activities described earlier, the transnational advocacy activities of the democracy movement called for a clear and simple message concerning the social and political problems in Myanmar and the question of who was responsible and how such problems could be addressed. Social movement theory holds that human rights advocacy messages are only partly determined by factual situations and feasible solutions. Other factors, such as the susceptibility of the target audience to certain messages, also play a role.

In contrast to many actors working under the radar during Myanmar's early years of transition, as well as the more open engagement attempts of the Third Force towards the military, representatives of the democracy movement continued to openly oppose the government. The distinction between proponents and opponents of engaging the government, moreover, became more pronounced as the political transition unfolded. The occurrence of cyclone Nargis in 2008 not only led to a gradual emancipation of civil society actors based inside the country, but also resulted in the emergence of contrasting 'frames' about the benefits of distributing local aid. These frames became even more noticeable after elections had been announced for 2010, which further polarized both the political and the civil society landscape. Parallel to developments in the political sphere, those affiliated with the Third Force chose to call for participation in the elections, while those affiliated with the democracy movement boycotted the elections. This dichotomy was accentuated as both proponents and opponents of the elections attempted to reach out to the international community to influence foreign positions towards the Myanmar government. The contestations around the 2010 elections will be discussed in Chapter 6.

Although the elections formed the focal point of the disagreement over the government's 'Roadmap to Democracy', some of the varying frames had already become visible in earlier debates. These include the question of economic sanctions, the evaluation of the 2008 constitution and the distribution of aid in the aftermath of cyclone Nargis. Apart from exile media, which largely served as a platform for the democracy movement at the time, Burma Partnership emerged as the primary public advocate of the election boycott campaign outside the country. Meanwhile, Generation Wave took the lead in organizing an election boycott campaign inside Myanmar, as well as contributing to advocacy abroad. The public statements and events organized by these two organizations form the basis of Chapter 6. In contrast, Myanmar Egress came to be seen by respondents as the most public proponent of engagement in the elections, although they were not the only actors who viewed the elections as an opportunity for change. The following two chapters are based on interviews with representatives and alumni of these organizations, as well as media analysis and observations at civil society trainings and public events. I bring in theory on transnational advocacy networks in order to analyse the strategies of the democracy movement and other civil society actors involved in transnational campaigns.

## Framing and marketing in transnational advocacy campaigns

Transnational advocacy networks are defined as 'an international cooperation of activists which can influence the re-distribution of resources, provide alternative sources of information and create a common discourse' (Keck and Sikkink, 1998: ix). The Burmese democracy movement can be considered such a network, as it seeks to facilitate access to international supporters (including foreign governments, activists and intergovernmental organizations) and 'make international resources available to new actors in domestic political and social struggles' (Keck and Sikkink, 1998: 1). Democracy activists make use of the 'boomerang pattern', an attempt to indirectly influence their own government's domestic policies through international involvement when direct influence has proven impossible or ineffective (Keck and Sikkink, 1998: 12). The presence of significant numbers of Myanmar political activists in exile after 1988, combined with increased opportunities for international networking, travel and communication, led to the democracy movement's transformation into an influential transnational advocacy network, particularly since the late 1990s and early 2000s (Zaw Oo, 2006). This loose network of organizations uses and produces information on Myanmar strategically in order to pressure international organizations and governments and influence their policies.

Members of transnational advocacy networks lobby international actors in order to put across their viewpoints and motivate their audiences to take the desired action. Research has shown that domestic social movements often adapt their activities once they take on a transnational advocacy component. In this process of adjustment towards an international audience, three steps can be distinguished. First, a campaign becomes transnational as activists look beyond their own borders for assistance and support (Keck and Sikkink, 1998). Second, the activists' message and call for action must be 'marketed' to an international platform, where it competes with other causes that require international attention (Bob, 2005). Third, the activists' portrayal of the problem and the proposed solutions must be formulated in such a way that international supporters become susceptible to it and feel compelled to take action, a process which is referred to as 'framing' (Snow and Benford, 1988).

In his book *The marketing of rebellion*, Clifford Bob (2005: 4) describes how activists frame situations and formulate messages in ways that are likely to lead to international attention and support: 'In this global morality market, challengers must publicize their plights, portray their conflicts as righteous struggles, and craft their messages to resonate abroad.' Only a small number of potentially worthy causes will ever be picked up by international non-governmental organizations (INGOs), governments and donors, and so Myanmar activists lobbying abroad have to make sure they strike the right tone. Bob (2005: 5) argues that success in gaining international influence is determined more by a movement's 'promotional strategies' than by the content of its message or the legitimacy of its claims. This means that the movement's message must be constructed in a way that resonates with existing international frameworks and priorities. In order to tap into international interests, for example, land disputes might be rephrased as environmental issues, while poverty and ethnic minority concerns might be phrased in the language of human rights (Bob, 2005: 31). For activists campaigning against Myanmar's military dictatorship for several decades, moreover, it was a challenge to continue phrasing their messages in ways that ensured prolonged international attention for their problems and proposed solutions. As the current and next chapters show, the occurrence of cyclone Nargis in 2008 and the announcement of elections in 2010 provided a welcome new angle to existing democracy campaigns.

## Strategic framing efforts

According to theory on 'collective action frames', the way social movements mobilize around certain issues is determined not only by the content itself – the grievance, injustice or cause identified as requiring social change – but also by the characteristics and preferences of the individual actors that form the movement (Snow and Benford, 1988). Transnational activists engage in 'collective processes of interpretation, attribution, and social construction that mediate between opportunity, organization and action' (McAdam et al, 1996: 2), thereby constructing a certain depiction of reality (Benford and Snow, 2000: 614). While Myanmar activists found the structure of military rule difficult to change from within, they had more agency in determining how the situation in Myanmar was portrayed towards international audiences and in deciding how to frame their demands and proposed solutions.

Collective action frames often call for a simplification of reality, in order to bring forward a uniform advocacy message (Benford and Snow, 2000). Similarly, the Burmese democracy movement chose to highlight particular human rights abuses inside the country, allocate blame exclusively to the military government and its associates ('diagnostic' or 'adversarial framing'), and call for international condemnation and pressure to bring about a change in government ('prognostic framing'). In this process, exile organizations worked together with activists inside the country who sought to discredit the Myanmar government domestically. However, their depiction of the situation ran counter to the efforts of other domestic civil society organizations (CSOs) that sought to bring about gradual change by engaging with the government. In their efforts to identify culprits, moreover, democracy activists sometimes turned against other non-governmental actors whose interpretation of the root causes and preferred solutions in Myanmar differed from their own. These included local and international businessmen accused of supporting the military government financially, as well as foreign academics and local civil society actors who were accused of misrepresenting the situation in Myanmar under military rule (see Metro, 2011). Using vocabulary such as 'cronies' or 'apologists', these actors were accused of promoting their own self-interest, whereas democracy activists were portrayed as acting out of ideology or altruism. Research shows that in reality, situations such as conflict, poverty or repression often result in a combination of altruism and self-interest, ideology and calculated moves (Bob, 2005: 27).

Social movements tend to make use of generic 'master frames' that can be applied to multiple circumstances and thus can mobilize larger groups of people, such as the 'injustice frame' or the 'return to democracy frame' (Snow and Benford, 1992; Benford and Snow, 2000: 618). A human rights frame, for example, 'takes a particular story and makes it general, targeting the state as the responsible agent and source of redress', so that transnational alliances and coalitions can be built (Merry, 2006: 216). Since Myanmar's conflict and repressive government had little cross-border consequences in terms of regional instability or foreign (at least Western) economic interests, activists continuously had to compete for attention with other causes in the 'global morality market', resulting in strategic 'branding' of their cause (Bob, 2005). Internal divisions within civil society, consequently, did not contribute to the single message required to successfully compete with other human rights causes in international platforms. Some civil society actors who could not connect to the traditional democracy movement, such as ethnic nationalities, therefore chose to link up with other 'master frames', such as the indigenous rights movement or the women's rights movement.

Where social movements disagree on the interpretation or proposed solution of a human rights issue, 'framing contests' or 'frame disputes' may occur (Benford and Snow, 2000: 626). This was the case in post-Nargis Myanmar, where newly emerging civil society actors inside the country who called for strategic engagement with the government provided a counterframe to the democracy movement's calls for disengagement. In response, democracy activists felt compelled to oppose the engagement narrative by emphasizing the distinction between actors inside and outside the country as a proxy for the pro- or anti-engagement position. This 'framing contest' further intensified after the announcement of the 2010 elections, which provided a concrete action perspective for those inside and outside the country to accept or reject participation in the military government's 'Roadmap to Democracy'.

In reaction to the foundational work of various social movement scholars, others have stressed the need to focus not purely on mechanisms and motivations for collective action frames, but to bring back into the discussion the matter of content, particularly ideology (Oliver and Johnston, 2000; Walder, 2009). A framing analysis does not deny that historical patterns and country-specific characteristics, such as the level of diversity and the long history of repression, inspired the activities undertaken by Myanmar advocacy networks to a large extent. A framing analysis, however, focuses on portrayal towards external actors rather than an assessment of individual motivations. Although most actors described in this book would have liked to see the military removed from power, they often chose smaller, more attainable objectives in order to increase the likelihood of campaign success. All of them saw themselves (or were seen by others) as representing civil society, but they attributed blame differently, turned to disparate actors for solutions and proposed contrasting alternative visions for change. These observations counter the idea that the field of CSOs trying to bring about change in Myanmar consists only of single-minded actors with a clear, altruistic goal in mind. To ignore the influence of strategic decision making would falsely objectify the way campaigns on Myanmar have emerged and evolved in the transnational context. As Bob (2005: xi) argues, '[i]t is not enough to extol [transnational movements and NGOs] as "moral" forces while refusing to scrutinize their interactions with each other and the public'. From this perspective, transnational activists operate in an inherently competitive market in which they must first gain a voice before they can actually influence international debates.

## Encounters between civil society from exile and from inside the country

Throughout the 1990s and early 2000s, much of Myanmar activism against the military took place from abroad. These activities from exile influenced the conflicts taking place inside Myanmar in various ways (Brees, 2009). Activists residing outside the country were in a better position to challenge the government and expose human rights violations, due to their relatively safe environment, the opportunity for education and training, and the availability of their transnational communication channels. On the other hand, some argued that the privileged position of activists in exile detached them from realities inside the country, as discussed in Chapter 3. Moreover, the Myanmar diaspora in some cases may have prolonged conflict by providing financial and political support to ethnic armed groups and by 'holding on to strident, uncompromising rhetoric', for example by refusing to support ceasefire talks (Brees, 2009: 40).

For international human rights organizations, Myanmar activists in exile provided a channel through which information from inside the country was conveyed. People living inside the country, however, argued that activists in exile sometimes distorted information to suit their advocacy priorities, emphasizing the damaging role of the military government while downplaying the role of actors such as non-state armed groups (South, 2008b). Some authors argue that it is 'artificial and arbitrary' to separate external from internal activism, as these are fluent categories that mutually influence each other (Dudley, 2003). The power relations between actors inside and outside the country, however, tend to be unequal. With reference to Anderson's concept of 'long-distance nationalism', Dudley (2003: 22) argues that 'the "long-distance nationalist" ... in exile from Burma has both little impact on what happens inside the nation and little price to pay for the possible effects of his or her actions'. Similarly, South (2008b: 110) explains how a focus on exile agendas 'serves to reinforce the position of often unaccountable groups and individuals who – although they may be experts in fund-raising and rhetoric – are often quite marginal to the actual situation on the ground, inside Burma'.

An early example of diverging views and strategies that played out in the 1990s concerned the debate about economic sanctions and a tourism boycott on Myanmar (Pedersen, 2007; Mullen, 2016). These campaigns provided a clear action perspective to Westerners in relation to Myanmar and therefore received significant international attention over the years (Dale, 2011; Simpson, 2014). After Aung San Suu Kyi called for sanctions from inside the country, this issue was taken up by Myanmar advocacy groups in exile, who actively lobbied Western companies and governments to disengage with Myanmar. While lobbyists outside the country claimed to represent Myanmar people who could not speak out from within the country, critics argued that sanctions and boycotts were advocacy tools for foreign-based activists (both Myanmar and Western), which were of little use, or even damaging, to people living inside the country (Pedersen, 2007). While Western academics and prominent local activists debated the desirability of sanctions and the supposed effects on the Myanmar population, those expected to be directly affected by the sanctions lacked access to the international community and were therefore hardly heard. Internationally, these sanctions became of great symbolic value in signalling disapproval of the military government, and some observers commented that they could not be lifted with any credibility unless significant improvements were made on a number of publicly set benchmarks. In other words, it should be the Myanmar government's actions that would cause a shift in Western sanctions policies, rather than a change of mind on behalf of those imposing the sanctions. Nevertheless, some prominent activists who had earlier campaigned for sanctions publicly changed their minds and began opposing the sanctions campaign, leading to a split in the Free Burma Coalition and the start of the US Campaign for Burma (see Zarni, 2006 for a personal account of this decision).

A similar shift from foreign-based activism to supporting local organizations occurred among European Burma organizations, including Burma Center Netherlands (BCN) and the Brussels-based Euro-Burma Office (EBO), both of which had initially been supporting the campaigns of the democracy movement. During the time that I volunteered with BCN (2004–6), the organization had already changed position on the tourism boycott that it initially called for. This meant that the posters of Aung San Suu Kyi which were frequently used in public events had to be folded one by one, so that the phrase 'please don't come to Burma' was no longer visible. While previously BCN had focused largely on international advocacy directed against the Myanmar government and supporting democracy activists in exile, after Nargis it started engaging more with locally based activists, as mentioned on its website:

> From 2008 onwards, BCN moved towards more actively engaging political actors and citizens in the political process, in response to requests from key organizations in its civil society program. In 2010, BCN chose to support the democratic political actors and parties that decided to participate in the elections, through trainings and capacity strengthening, and from 2011 continued its program to support democratic forces in the changing political landscape of Burma/ Myanmar.[1]

According to a former staff member, most other Burma solidarity organizations in Europe continued the more activist stance, and BCN was asked to leave the Euro-Burma Platform.[2] EBO too was informed by the European Burma Network in 2010 that its observer status had been revoked, because its actions were 'no longer consistent with the "mandate of Burma's elected leaders and ethnic leadership"'.[3] In response, EBO's executive director (Harn Yawnghwe, himself a prominent activist in exile) wrote a letter in which he argued that

> [o]ver the years, the Burmese democracy movement has expanded to include many more voices from Burma ... there now exists in Burma a wide and diverse civil society, ethnic leaders from the ceasefire groups, and new political parties who are also working for democracy ... [whose] views and opinions need to be taken into account. To not acknowledge them is to ignore the majority of the people in Burma who are taking enormous risks to bring democracy.[4]

This exchange was exemplary of a growing disparity between organizations that emphasized change in Myanmar and those that focused on existing problems, which meant that some Burma support groups could no longer work together. A similar division between proponents and opponents of engagement with the government played out among foreign (mostly Western) academics. In 2005, democracy activists had severely criticized the European Commission for the composition of its 'Burma Day' held on 5 April. Burma Campaign UK, the National Coalition Government of the Union of Burma and EBO (before its aforementioned change in position) released statements in which they accused the Commission of being undemocratic by banning pro-democracy groups and 'the Burmese community' from participating, in contrast to the Burma Day of 2003, in which they had apparently participated. ALTSEAN-Burma also criticized the 'independent report' that had been written for the occasion by two Western scholars, whom they perceived to be anti-sanctions and pro-engagement. Burma Campaign UK (2005) accused the European Commission of 'pursuing an anti-sanctions agenda in direct contradiction to EU member states' policy'.

The scholars who had written the report were depicted not only as anti-sanctions, but also as 'regular visitors to Rangoon', which was apparently seen as a disqualification for speaking at a Burma meeting. At later events, including academic conferences I attended between 2010 and 2014, there were public and private complaints by democracy activists that pro-engagement scholars were given too much of a platform. These scholars in turn contended that the democracy movement was actually having a considerable influence on foreign policy towards Myanmar, whereas actors inside the country had less opportunity to speak out publicly about their experiences (Pedersen, 2012: 272). Metro (2011) refers to this debate in the context of the elections as 'the divided field of Burma studies', where 'Burmaphiles' (supporters of the democracy movement, often based in exile and highly idealistic or radical) and 'Myanmarites' (those who lived inside the country or visited frequently and whose views and actions were less radical and more conservative) competed for the legitimacy to voice the needs of Myanmar people, whereas fence-sitters refused to take sides (see Décobert, 2014).

Throughout the early 2000s, foreign, outside, academic and Burman voices were generally privileged over native, inside, activist and ethnic nationality voices (Metro, 2011). The relationship between 'outside' and 'inside' slowly started changing in the late 2000s, particularly after cyclone Nargis, which in some ways opened the country up to the outside world. Up to the start of the political transition, activists inside and outside the country had limited opportunity to interact. As the country started opening up to outside influences, and some of the European Burma support groups changed position, activists from inside the country were increasingly in contact with the democracy movement in exile. One respondent from Yangon was invited to Brussels by EBO in 2010, where he publicly addressed the European Parliament about his experiences inside the country. His encounter with activists from exile during this visit proved somewhat surprising to him, as he conveyed the year after:

> In Brussels, during lunchtime, I met with one exile group ... they are looking with a very strange eye, you know. Because they think we are a partner of the government ... We are inside here so we did a lot. So, according to their perception, if we get many things in Burma, we have a good relationship, good connection with the military generals. I don't know why they come with that idea.[5]

This activist felt that he was being perceived as a government collaborator, simply because he was able to conduct his activities inside the country without encountering severe difficulties. The conversation took an even stranger turn when he tried to make conversation on what turned out to be a shared place of origin in Yangon:

> And I ask them, oh, brother, where are you coming from in Burma, where is your place? They told me: "I am coming from, you know, rebel area." So I said, what rebel area? [he replied] "You don't know the rebel area!?" Haha! So [I asked] which place, in Rangoon? "Yeah, in Rangoon, Bahan [township]." Oh, Bahan, they call it a rebel area. So I told him, I am coming as a rebel in your rebel area. Ha!

Bahan township in Yangon may have been known to some as a 'rebel area' due to the presence of the National League for Democracy's offices and a restaurant known for hosting politically sensitive events. However, this respondent saw the reference 'rebel area' for a location where he had been working openly for years as slightly exaggerated and decided to make a joke about it. Finally, when he politely offered to stay in touch, the exile-based activist had responded: "Do you want to go to jail? If you contact me, you will spend seven years in prison."[6] Asked whether this could be true, the respondent answered: "Maybe sometimes it is true. But he thinks of himself as a very big guy, you know, and inside we didn't do anything. That is their perception." Such views were in line with existing advocacy positions among democracy activists at the time, who viewed local civil society as 'minimally effective at promoting the kind of reform they demand' (Callahan, 2010: 73). Comparable tensions were reported after exiled labour organizations returned to Myanmar in 2012 (Arnold and Campbell, 2017). During a community development training in Thailand in 2010, several respondents similarly indicated that they understood and valued the work of democracy activists and media in exile but objected to depictions of people inside the country as mere puppets of the military government who could not think or speak for themselves. In some cases, activists from inside the country who were taken to joint activist meetings in Thailand were indeed concerned about their security, fearing public attention through reports in exile media. Organizers of these early public events around 2010 had to carefully select participants from inside and outside the country, as exile activists were generally more experienced in advocacy events and often spoke better English, which could easily lead to a power imbalance. In other cases, older activists in exile relied on younger activists inside the country to update them on the changing situation in Myanmar after they had left the country. Eventually, these interactions resulted in more contact between activists inside and outside the country, which proved useful when exiled activists increasingly started returning in the course of the political transition.

## Post-Nargis counter-voices to the democracy movement

A concrete example of diverging portrayals of the situation and desired responses occurred in the aftermath of cyclone Nargis. In 2009, an American university and a Thai-based democracy organization that claimed to be active inside Myanmar issued a report on the lack of aid effectiveness after cyclone Nargis, called 'After the storm' (EAT/JHU CPHHR, 2009a). This report prompted a rare statement by 21 INGOs working inside the country, criticizing the way the research had been conducted. The American university and the Thai-based Burma organization had accused the government of obstructing development assistance, imprisoning locals involved in the provision of aid and making use of forced labour in its post-disaster reconstruction efforts. In response, the 21 INGOs involved in humanitarian assistance wrote an open letter, accusing the report's authors of ignoring the INGOs' activities on the ground and of neglecting the opinions and experiences of the 'courageous and resilient survivors of Cyclone Nargis' (Action Aid et al, 2009).

The open letter claimed that the 33 relief workers and 57 cyclone survivors surveyed by the researchers of the American university and the Thai-based Burma organization did not adequately represent the experiences of 'over two million cyclone survivors' (Action Aid et al, 2009: 2). It was argued that local organizations had conducted more transparent research on a much wider scale, which contradicted the findings of the 'After the storm' report. The accusations of 'theft and confiscation of relief supplies by authorities' as well as the use of forced labourers by the government mentioned in the report were dismissed as anecdotal and out of context: 'International and local relief groups did not hand over relief supplies to the Government. We were able to deliver relief supplies directly to cyclone survivors in virtually all circumstances.' The 21 INGOs also accused the authors of the report of undermining the continuation of aid distribution in Myanmar by calling for restrictions in aid delivery until the human rights conditions improve: '[T]he consistent "voice" of all the people in the Delta, in direct contradiction to the report, is "Please, don't abandon us."'

The authors of the 'After the storm' report reacted to these accusations as follows (EAT/JHU CPHHR, 2009b):

> We recognize that international organizations working under Memoranda of Understanding (MOUs) with ... the ruling military junta in Burma, both operate in a constrained environment and are motivated by real concern for the welfare of the peoples of the country. We understand why it would be difficult for these agencies and their thousands of local staff to report in an uncensored manner on cyclone relief aid problems, as well as issues of forced labor and other human rights violations. We suspect that many of these agencies would join us in calling for the immediate and unconditional release of humanitarian relief workers and those reporting on the situation now imprisoned by the SPDC [State Peace and Development Council] ... but understand why they cannot. We also recognize their inability to investigate and report incidences of human rights violations such as forced labor.

The report's authors thus refused to take the response of the 21 INGOs seriously, instead challenging the ability of the INGOs to openly express their views due to their position inside the country. They contrasted the INGOs' position with their own research, for which 'truly independent community members' had conducted interviews 'in settings of anonymity and maximum protection from the SPDC, USDA [Union Solidarity and Development Association], and other junta-related entities', allowing witnesses to freely speak their mind. They further brought up safety concerns for both researchers and humanitarian aid workers as a reason to refrain from openly contacting more locally based organizations for their research, although they did report conducting 'under the radar' interviews with some humanitarian aid workers.

This claim that organizations working inside the country were less independent and unable to create a safe environment for research, however, raises the question of why these 21 INGOs would voluntarily choose to issue a public statement in the first place. It seems more likely that they spoke on behalf of their local partners, who might indeed have been reluctant to publicly share their views on either the post-Nargis situation or the 'After the storm' report. In any case, the authors of the report asserted that the criticism of their report was 'based on a fundamental misunderstanding of the premise', since it was intended as a human rights investigation rather than a critique of humanitarian assistance. Clearly, the 'human rights master frame' of the democracy movement was so powerful that the report's authors instantly dismissed other, more nuanced framings of the post-Nargis humanitarian situation.

This example shows how different advocacy goals can lead to various, sometimes opposing ways to frame the situation in Myanmar. As described in previous chapters, for organizations working inside the country the aftermath of cyclone Nargis provided an important opportunity to expand their room to manoeuvre within the government's restrictive framework. A report that directly challenged this 'space after Nargis' discourse therefore ran counter to their attempts to gradually expand this space by building up durable relationships with the authorities. International organizations, moreover, were increasingly prepared to publish positive assessments. Organizations such as Human Rights Watch (2010) and the Centre for Peace and Conflict Studies (2009) had taken the opportunity after cyclone Nargis to draw attention to the agency and resilience of local communities and organizations. Human Rights Watch, a well-known human rights advocacy group, was especially praised by people working inside the country for pointing out opportunities, not just restrictions under military rule.

Many respondents from the democracy movement did not deny that the occurrence of cyclone Nargis had had certain long-term positive societal effects in Myanmar but were more inclined to see these effects as part of a larger process of raising criticism against the authorities, which had been re-invigorated during the 2007 demonstrations. Moreover, they were hesitant to connect these developments to their own activities inside the country, as they feared that public connections between them and local organizations could result in further repression. The result, however, was a somewhat one-sided portrayal of civil society in Myanmar, which made the debate about the post–Nargis situation appear more polarized than it might have been on the ground.

Cyclone Nargis certainly marked a turning point for the balance between information coming from inside and outside the country. Organizations such as the Cambodian-based Centre for Peace and Conflict Studies published a series of reports under the title 'Voices from inside', arguing that the voices of 'ordinary citizens' in Myanmar should be heard. While the democracy movement aimed to speak with a unified voice, the organizations promoting voices from inside the country were more diverse in composition and goals, and less focused on international advocacy. As a result, many of them emphasized diversity rather than consistency of opinions inside the country, which could be seen as a deliberate counter-strategy against the democracy movement's inclination to create the impression of a unanimous voice of the people. As international attention began to shift from a focus on exile activism to developments inside the country, locally based activists gained prominence in determining the narrative on Myanmar, eventually prompting adaptations and a diversification in transnational advocacy priorities.

6

# Competing Frames around
# the 2010 Elections

As part of the military's 'Roadmap to Democracy', elections were scheduled for 2010. Once the date of 7 November was announced in August that year, a framing contest around the elections took off. Those who saw the elections as an opportunity made a strategic decision to emphasize the political and societal changes inside the country, while opponents chose to emphasize the lack of significant political change and the need to maintain pressure on the government. Both camps drew selectively on 'marketing strategies' to emphasize their points and steer developments in the desired direction. Moreover, both parties claimed to act for the larger good of the country in advancing their preferred strategies towards democratization. For foreigners, too, the 'in-between' position became 'both more appealing and less tenable amid the polarization surrounding the 2010 elections' (Metro, 2011: 10). Those who were optimistic about the increased space granted by the government were not alone in their expectation that the elections would bring about further change: research on Malaysia two years earlier, for example, shows that elections may offer unique opportunities for political engagement by civil society in repressive environments, and may lead to a re-assessment of relationships between politicians, the state and the people (Lee et al, 2010). For many people in Myanmar, the 2010 elections would be the first time they could vote at all, thus providing an opportunity to discuss politics more openly in the context of voter education (Lidauer, 2012).

Yet the 2010 elections and the surrounding controversies also provided a unique opportunity for those opposing the military government to campaign against its political framework. In the course of 2010, a large election boycott campaign emerged consisting of two elements: a domestic component, calling on people inside the country not to vote (though there was some confusion as to the actual goal of the campaign, as discussed subsequently), and an international component, calling on other governments not to acknowledge the election results as legitimate. Although an election boycott by opposition parties is not uncommon in politically restrictive environments (Kagwanja, 2005; Beaulieu, 2006), the campaign in Myanmar was additionally characterized by a high level of involvement by civil society organizations (CSOs) that took the opportunity to publicize their goals. Public statements on the campaign were mainly issued by Burma Partnership, which openly called for an election boycott, and were directed at 'Burmese communities and organizations in exile and Burma solidarity groups around the world.'[1] An election boycott campaign might seem somewhat surprising coming from a movement that calls itself a *democracy* movement and that had long called for the previous election results (of 1990, won by the National League for Democracy [NLD]) to be acknowledged. Yet the 2010 election boycott stands in a long tradition of opposition to authoritarian rule. In the 1920s, the General Council of Burmese Associations sought to delegitimize colonial rule by boycotting various elections organized by the British, resulting in very low voter turnouts (Taylor, 2009: 185). More recently, the NLD and various democracy activists inside and outside the country had initiated a 'vote no' campaign in response to the government-imposed constitutional referendum in 2008, although this was technically a voting suggestion and not a boycott.

Many democracy activists as well as most foreign observers condemned the 2010 elections because they were designed in line with the military's own rules. The State Peace and Development Council was late to announce the exact election date, leaving non-military parties little time to register and campaign. Once they were allowed to enter the process, it became clear that prisoners, including many NLD members and Aung San Suu Kyi (who was under house arrest at the time), would not be able to contest the elections. The 2008 constitution, moreover, automatically allocated 25 per cent of the seats in parliament to the military. The military proxy-party the Union Solidarity and Development Party (USDP), with its strong influence and its near absence of female contestants, had a clear advantage running for the remaining 75 per cent. In response to what Burma Partnership referred to as 'systematic steps to destroy the opposition', the NLD refused to re-register as a political party due to unfair election rules, resulting in a de facto boycott (Win Tin, 2010). As an activist and academic explained in 2010, "in Burmese we have a saying: you don't decorate a corpse. And the Burmese see the elections as a corpse."[2]

Few people expected that the elections would result in anything other than a consolidation of military power. After the election laws had been published, Burma Partnership formally launched a 'Global Campaign on Burma's 2010 Military Elections' on 19 March 2010, signed by 150 Burma-related organizations from around the world, including many ethnic nationalities.[3] The campaign condemned the upcoming elections 'as shutting the door to any prospects for genuine democracy and national reconciliation'. Burma Partnership also issued statements on behalf of 'ten leading alliances of Burma's democracy and ethnic rights movement', representing 'the most broad-based and multi-ethnic cooperation of political and civil society organizations from inside and in exile working for national reconciliation, peace, and freedom in Burma'.[4] Although 150 organizations from a single country working on a single campaign seems impressive, such claims also demonstrate the democracy movement's attempt to show strength in numbers. Other advocacy groups, including many foreign solidarity groups, also started critical campaigns around the 2010 elections, although it remained unclear which sections of the population they claimed to represent.[5] On 2 November 2010, five days before the elections were scheduled to take place, Burma Partnership and Generation Wave organized a press conference in Bangkok to reiterate their objections to the elections.[6] The Burma Partnership representative argued that the elections were seen by some as a window of opportunity, because soldiers would change into civilian politicians:

> Those key responsible for Depayin [the attack on Aung San Suu Kyi's convoy in 2003] and other attacks are now running in the elections. They got promoted after the massacre. Fraud and human rights violations were conducted in the [2008 constitution] referendum. The NLD youth were arrested for flyering. People have been instructed to "vote correctly" and "motivate people", even though parties are not allowed to campaign on election day. The USDP and other junta-allied parties make up about 75% of the candidates, plus 25% military seats is nearly 100 … Our message is: no more wait and see.

The spokesperson of Generation Wave made a similar claim:

> The youth are against the elections, because they [the military] are lying all the time. Why did they not do anything for people over the last 20 years? Have they been sleeping? Asking our people to join the resistance movement and not to vote is a small opportunity for action. To the international community we say: don't recognize the elections, and pressure the regime to release political prisoners immediately and unconditionally.

As this quote shows, their calls were directed not only towards the people of Myanmar, but also towards the international community, and the campaigners frequently addressed the Association of Southeast Asian Nations and other international actors. Inside Myanmar, the youth activists of Generation Wave used stickers and posters to inform people of their right not to vote in the 2010 elections, although the messages reportedly also mentioned the 'right to vote' (Ko Htwe, 2010; Lakshmibai, 2010). Other tactics included holding secret trainings, composing anti-election songs and buying disposable SIM cards to send anonymous text messages to strangers without being traced. According to one activist from Generation Wave, the text messages generated a range of responses. Some people were supportive, but others were afraid and asked them not to send messages like that again. Other sources mentioned messages from the All Burma Federation of Student Unions that were more overtly opposed to military rule, including 'If you vote the USDP, monks and people will be killed again' and 'the 2008 constitution and elections guarantee that military rule will be prolonged' (Wai Moe, 2010a). Several student activists were arrested for distributing leaflets at a university in Yangon, and it was reported that disruption of the elections could result in prison terms of up to 20 years. Activists campaigning for the election boycott consistently referred to the elections as 'sham elections', 'fake elections' or 'military selection' that would further entrench military rule, and campaign activities were organized around the slogan 'this is not democracy'.[7] Such attempts to amplify certain frames through 'movement slogans' are arguably at least as important for a successful campaign as the content itself (Benford and Snow, 2000: 623). The election boycott campaign could in some ways be viewed as a campaign topic around which to frame broader opposition to the military government, as a failed or boycotted election in itself would not provide a solution to military rule.

## The elections-as-opportunity counterframe

As boycotts and strikes have been a common way of protest in Burma since colonial times, the election boycott frame could be said to 'resonate' with local political activists, although not necessarily with the large section of the population who had become accustomed to obeying the government. However, the boycott was not the only response emerging from Myanmar civil society. Indeed, for the first time democracy activists were met with a significant counter-narrative not only from the military government, but also from other actors inside the country, who in their communication with domestic and international actors presented a so-called 'counterframe' to the democracy movement's election boycott message (see Benford and Snow, 2000: 626). A number of ethnic nationality organizations as well as members of the Third Force saw the elections as a unique, albeit limited opportunity to take part in domestic political affairs without risking severe repression. It was the military itself that had announced the elections. Therefore, activities such as forming political parties or providing voter education were no longer off limits in the months preceding 7 November 2010. Such activities would increase the chances of influencing the course of politics in Myanmar but could also add to the image of legitimacy that the military was seeking to create around the 2010 elections. The proponents and opponents of engagement in the election process clearly weighed these arguments in different ways.

While the 'election boycott frame' might to some extent have resonated with local audiences who had little confidence in the election process, it went against the view held by other domestic and foreign actors that the 2010 elections should be seen as a step towards democracy, despite their obvious shortcomings. The announcement of the 2010 elections divided both political opposition parties and CSOs, as there was no unified strategy to participate in or boycott the elections. A split even occurred within the main opposition party NLD, as some members who chose to participate without Aung San Suu Kyi registered as a new party, the National Democratic Force (NDF). Within the various ethnic nationalities, there was also disagreement over whether the elections should be seen as an opportunity or as a trick by the military. The Mon political parties and CSOs, for example, were divided on their views towards the elections, which the Mon in exile wanted to boycott, but many in Myanmar did not, as they wanted the Mon voices to be heard in parliament.[8] Political actors among the Rakhine and the Shan were similarly divided, with some running in the elections and others deciding to boycott (TNI, 2015).

In a publication based on interviews with civil society members in Myanmar, the Centre for Peace and Conflict Studies (2010) identified six primary (although not necessarily mutually exclusive) perspectives on the 2010 elections, ranging from the 'do not participate' perspective (that is, the election boycott campaign) to the view that the election is 'an opportunity' for change to happen, although 'it will take time'. Respondents participating in a community development training in 2010 were equally divided in their views. Some were very pragmatic, saying that "we don't like this election, but we don't have a choice. We only have two options: ban or vote."[9] Some found the election boycott campaign better than doing nothing, while others preferred to view the elections, however flawed, as a building block: "I just want to give only an idea. We have to build our house, how it is useful for us. And later we can change and find some furniture or material step by step to put in the house, you know."[10]

In general, young respondents originating from inside the country showed a large amount of pragmatism, as well as hope that the elections would bring about change. Even though they disagreed with the way the elections were being conducted, they were willing to see them as a first step in building the 'democracy house'. This corresponds to some observers' assertion that the 2010 elections were 'the only game in town' (Irrawaddy, 2010). A respondent from Kachin State argued that he rejected the election boycott "because if we do not give our vote to the opposition party, who will win? The USDP and government will win. So if they win what will become of our country? So many bad things. So, as a Myanmar citizen, I will vote for the opposite party."[11] Another Kachin respondent was hopeful that "if we vote, maybe the Kachin representative can enter the lower government parliament."[12] It seemed that people from ethnic nationality backgrounds in particular saw the elections as an opportunity to gain political influence for their own groups, although these hopes did not materialize in all regions, such as Kachin State, where fighting soon erupted (TNI, 2013).

## Lobbying abroad for the election boycott campaign

As noted, one of the goals of the election boycott campaign was to convince the international community that any outcome of the elections should not be recognized as legitimate. Many foreign governments had been cautious but hopeful about the military's new step in the 'Roadmap', which would at least alter the status quo. The democracy movement therefore had to direct a significant proportion of its efforts towards an international audience. They undertook what Bob (2005: 24) refers to as 'targeted lobbying', including attending international conferences and making lobbying trips and 'solidarity tours' abroad, in order to conduct networking and gain international visibility. They often made use of 'norm entrepreneurs' (Carpenter, 2007: 104): international celebrities who could support their cause and ensure public attention for the human rights abuses committed in Myanmar. These included Nobel Peace Prize winner Jody Williams and the band U2, whose song 'Walk on' is inspired by Aung San Suu Kyi.

A number of young democracy activists based in Thailand had been given the opportunity to gain experience as interns with organizations in Europe or in Asia. Participants described how they had conducted two main activities during their internships: learning about democratic procedures in other countries (several of which had held elections at the time of their visit), and lobbying diplomats to support the calls for an election boycott. As the participants had noticed during their trips, these goals sometimes seemed to contradict each other. Moreover, some of them had had the opportunity to discuss their viewpoints with civil society representatives from inside the country who were also on an advocacy tour, which gave them exposure to proponents of the elections-as-opportunity counterframe. Some of the politicians they were lobbying complained that they were confused by the different views regarding the elections from various Myanmar groups. An advocacy consultant who had been brought in to train the democracy activists upon their return to Thailand emphasized that the participants had to send a clear and single message in their lobbying activities that the elections should be boycotted. For this purpose, however, the participants needed to determine the goals of the campaign and identify their potential allies and adversaries.

The efforts made by democracy activists to persuade the international community to reject the elections by framing them as undemocratic were hampered by the fact that the goals of the lobbying activities were not always clear to the individual activists themselves: did they want to inform people they could vote as they wished, or did they want to convince people to abstain from voting? A representative of the democracy movement explained that the goal was twofold:

> When we are doing voter education, for us it's a very basic sort of thing that people need to know. Because there is no such thing provided by the authorities in the country. So our people should be entitled to know what is it that they are facing, they are dealing with, what kind of rights do they have. But then the boycott campaign, it's a position taken by us, as an organization. That actually we send this message to the general public, informing them: look, because of these reasons, we as these organizations are boycotting this … But we never call on the people not to vote … Because we believe that people have the right to choose whatever they want.[13]

As this quote demonstrates, the campaigners wanted to both inform the public of their civil rights and lobby for their own position towards the elections. They hoped that this awareness raising would lead to a decision for people to boycott the elections. The question however is to what extent their audience can be expected to distinguish between 'neutral' information and specific advice on how to act, if these are coming from the same source at the same time. Moreover, this activist viewed a decision to vote primarily as an indication that people felt they had no choice, rather than a sign that people may have strategically chosen to participate in the election process; she said that "We don't deny the reality, if people are left with no chance but to vote." Apart from the unclear message and the prominent counterframe, the election boycott campaign suffered from another shortcoming in that those opposing the elections could not offer a concrete alternative, except holding on to previous demands such as inclusive dialogue (see also Win Tin, 2010). Although it might well be argued that it is not civil society's task to provide alternatives to a problematic election campaign orchestrated by a non-democratic government, in terms of advocacy the lack of alternatives could be considered a weak point.

Moreover, the election boycott campaigners were considered by some international audiences to be holding the losing hand. During the public event in 2010, a Western audience member asked the campaigners: "The elections are a fact. Your recommendations we already do. How will your movement deal with the actual new government?"[14] This comment was indicative of a growing international impatience with the failure of the democracy movement to provide effective political opposition to ongoing military rule, let alone an alternative. The panel members did not respond directly to the question, but reiterated their views, arguing that the small number of opposition members who might be elected would not have a chance to bring about change, and that the real power lay with the youth groups and the NLD, which were continuously scrutinized by the government. Another democracy activist added that "we should not be fighting for one seat, we should be fighting for peace and democracy in Burma". These answers avoided the question of how participation in or boycott of the elections could contribute to such goals.

## Adversarial framing

The proponents of participation in the 2010 elections provided a much clearer action perspective and became more of a threat to the democracy activists as they gained international support. The democracy movement therefore had to frame them publicly as adversaries. As a Western advocacy consultant explained to members of the democracy movement in Thailand in 2010: "We need more people from within the movement to speak out. Those apologists from inside the country, who think the elections will provide space, they are more consistent and more powerful in their lobbying."[15] The election boycott campaigners, she argued, were in need of a similarly consistent narrative: "Oppose or support? You need to give a clear message. There is no clear message, because there are different private opinions." Other critics referred to those that ran in the elections, including members of the NDF and ethnic nationality parties, as 'domestic apologists' and 'election cheerleaders' (Min Zin, 2010b). The fact that not only former NLD members, but also various ethnic nationality parties chose to run in the 2010 elections was particularly problematic for the democracy activists advocating for an election boycott, as an outright rejection of their participation could lead to accusations of Burman domination (Metro, 2011: 5). During the election boycott event in 2010, the democracy representative referred to ethnic parties that contested the elections as misguided: "The USDP has 21 million members. So the ethnic leaders can never make it, but they have the right to dream."[16]

While for advocacy purposes the diversity of views among Myanmar activists was perceived as an obstacle, many of the young activists who had had the chance to discuss the campaign abroad saw the elections as a unique opportunity to discuss the issue and learn about different views. Meanwhile, members of the Third Force actively promoted the elections as an opportunity both inside and outside the country. Democracy activists accused them of having a pro-government bias and of supporting the elections for their own benefit (see Wai Moe, 2010b). Myanmar Egress was pointed to as the main civil society voice of the pro-election lobby. They were seen by democracy activists as having an unfair advantage to lobby for the elections, given their access to platforms that were unavailable to the NLD and to other, smaller local groups, because of the restrictions they faced inside the country. This view very much emphasized the struggle between the two camps inside the country but overlooked the powerful voice of democracy activists in international lobbying platforms, which had actually been criticized by some actors inside the country.

When ethnic nationality parties eventually managed to secure seats after the elections, democracy representatives accused the military and election proponents such as Egress of having played 'the ethnic card' as a way to legitimize the election outcome. In this narrative, any win by ethnic nationality groups was seen as having been masterminded by the military, a view which denied the agency of, and domestic support for, ethnic parties that ran in the 2010 elections. Yet democracy activists rightly predicted an increase in armed conflict in the ethnic states after the elections. The example of the election boycott campaign confirms research findings that advocacy groups which appear to be united are better at gaining support than movements that give room to conflicting voices (Bob, 2005: 38). We will now turn to the question whether the election boycott campaign can be considered to have been successful, given that the elections eventually took place and resulted in a new, quasi-civilian government.

## Evaluating campaign success

Social movements, particularly those campaigning for democratization and human rights, face the challenge of presenting their long-term, idealistic goals in the language of concrete, achievable demands. In this process, obtaining or maintaining international attention for one's cause may become a goal in itself, and activists tend to focus on victories achieved along the way (Bob, 2005). At the time of the election boycott campaign, activists had been trying for decades without much success to achieve their long-term goal of democratization in Myanmar. Petitions for the release of political prisoners continued to draw attention but had little demonstrable results, while more complex causes such as the initiation of a second Panglong conference were met with limited foreign interest. For the democracy movement, the announcement of the 2010 elections provided a new opportunity to phrase their long-term ideals in the form of concrete demands. It also complicated their message, as there were different views within civil society regarding the prospect of the elections resulting in positive change, and democracy activists accused the government of manipulating the international community in its favour with what were in essence unfair elections.

While the elections took place as planned, the process was perceived internationally as undemocratic (TNI, 2010). Therefore, both proponents and opponents of the elections to a certain extent saw their predictions confirmed. Yet despite initial criticism, the 2010 elections eventually set in motion a political liberalization process under the guidance of President Thein Sein. This raised the question of whether the democracy movement could actually claim that its election boycott campaign had been a success. As discussed earlier, those who had been cautiously optimistic were hopeful that the elections would be the start of positive change in Myanmar. One of them looked back on the elections in 2011:

> Before, we had no parliament, people never speak out about politics. At least during this election time, most of the people say a lot about politics. In the streets and the tea shops, everyone speaks up about politics ... Even though the election was not free and fair, we gained something.[17]

This reaction exemplifies the patient approach of many activists inside the country who hoped for social and political change but realized that it might not come overnight. The democracy activists who had campaigned against the elections saw the resulting political transition in a less positive light, as one of them commented in hindsight: "The political parties that joined in the elections, they supported the regime to stay longer. For a game you need two players, and the parties that participated in the elections provided the team to play in the government's game."

Yet other democracy activists saw the election boycott campaign as successful, regardless of the outcome. A representative of Generation Wave commented in 2014: "It was not successful for the country. But it was successful for our movement. We could do a lot. We could raise awareness and mobilize people." This analysis shows that the primary goal of the election boycott campaign was not to have a direct effect on election results, but to raise awareness about the problematic role of the military and maintain attention on the goals of the democracy movement. Viewed from this perspective, the campaigners could claim success even if the boycott they called for had hardly been achieved. Looking back on this in 2013, a Western journalist who spoke at a public event in Amsterdam commented somewhat cynically that "the elections were only useful for editors as a hook to talk about other issues"; perhaps the same could be said about the democracy activists who ran the election boycott campaign. Their civil society adversaries, on the other hand, had a much easier job: they argued for a wait and see approach and for the need to support the small changes that were taking place inside the country. As developments unfolded, they could claim success, despite the fact that the political liberalization process was largely top-down and the long-term outcome remained uncertain. Given the increased opportunities for opposition parties to campaign before the 2015 elections, and the electoral victory of the NLD in 2015 and 2020, election boycotts were hardly an issue after 2010. At the time of writing, however, when the military has tentatively announced forthcoming elections, calls to boycott are again increasing, albeit in a more covert form than in 2010 given the heightened restrictions in the country (International Crisis Group, 2023b).

## A strategic shift to international justice campaigns

Even before the 2010 elections had taken place, some activists decided to diversify their strategies by highlighting another international campaign. In 2009, democracy organizations started calling for a UN Commission of Inquiry into past serious crimes committed by the military, a request that would remain relevant regardless of the election results. In September 2010, an open letter by NLD co-founder Win Tin was published in the *New York Times*, in which he commented: 'I wish that our friends from Europe would abandon their dream of expecting something impossible from the election, and start taking seriously action against the regime with the aim of starting dialogue. They should begin by creating a U.N. commission of inquiry to investigate human rights violations in Burma' (Win Tin, 2010).

Like the election boycott campaign, the Commission of Inquiry campaign served to frame the existing situation in a new language in order to maintain attention for the various human rights abuses committed by the military government. The call for UN involvement was in fact not new. As early as 2005, a report commissioned by Václav Havel and Desmond Tutu had called for Security Council action on Burma, arguing that the situation posed a threat to peace and stability in the region (DLA Piper Rudnick Gray Cary, 2005). Although the Security Council had discussed the human rights situation in Myanmar several times since 2006, attempts to come to an official resolution were vetoed by China and Russia. On 27 May 2009, Paulo Sérgio Pinheiro, former UN Special Rapporteur on Human Rights in Myanmar, mentioned the possibility of a UN Commission of Inquiry in a column in the *New York Times* (Pinheiro, 2009). The issue was subsequently taken up by the US Campaign for Burma, by parliamentarians from several countries (notably Japan and the United States), and by Pinheiro's successor, Tomás Ojea Quintana, but without much result. Burma Partnership and other democracy organizations had called for a Commission of Inquiry for several years and after the elections made it a primary international campaign focus.[18] They frequently referred to the content of Myanmar's 2008 constitution as evidence of the military government's lack of goodwill, particularly article 445, which offers immunity from prosecution to former government and military personnel. The campaigners called for justice for the victims of crimes committed by the military, as well as for a global arms embargo.

One of the earliest advocacy opportunities after the elections was Myanmar's Universal Periodic Review at the UN Human Rights Council in March 2011, in which many international organizations submitted reports emphasizing the need for international justice. After the UN General Assembly had issued over 40 resolutions on Myanmar without effect, the campaigners saw the need to phrase their calls for justice in a new terminology, in order to maintain attention for their cause. Moreover, the campaign for a Commission of Inquiry provided activists with a concrete call for action. The activists kept track of the number of countries that publicly supported the call for a Commission of Inquiry as a benchmark for measuring success, even in the absence of tangible impact on the Myanmar government. Despite the dim prospects of holding the military to account, they argued that an official UN investigation would send a message to the military government that their actions did not go unnoticed, and that evidence would be collected for possible use in future criminal proceedings.

Yet the prospect of international justice mechanisms also worried some commentators, who were reluctant to disrupt the anticipated political developments in the country after the 2010 elections. The International Crisis Group (2011: 12), a think tank known for its sometimes controversial positions on peace and conflict in Myanmar and criticism of Western sanctions policies, warned that

> [a]t a time when the new government is moving ahead with its reform agenda, including on human rights, pursuing the establishment of a UN commission of inquiry is unlikely to achieve anything. At this time, the international community should focus its efforts on ways to support the process of reform and encourage engagement.

A research project conducted by the Centre for Peace and Conflict Studies sought out responses from people in Myanmar regarding international justice initiatives. They found support for a Commission of Inquiry to be conditional on whether local people's views and preferences would be taken into account (Centre for Peace and Conflict Studies, 2011). Some feared retaliation by power holders against local civil society actors, and worried that it would affect their ongoing work on peacebuilding or access to foreign aid. Others commented that the time and resources would be better spent on economic developments and local needs, such as food and education. This study was largely based on respondents in Yangon, however, whereas the primary victims of human rights violations were located in ethnic areas where conflict continued, and benefits from the political transition remained largely absent.

Western human rights organizations mostly supported democracy activists' call for a Commission of Inquiry, although both foreign and local representatives privately expressed little trust that this would prevent human rights violations from taking place. According to a democracy activist, the campaign was meant "just to threaten" the government with legal accountability measures in the future: "It will not happen as long as they [the military] are in this position. One day if they have no power, they can be arrested and they can be put on trial. That's why we should collect information."[19] He also expressed a more cynical motive for international actors to support the campaign: "[T]his is necessary to do, because otherwise the international community, international organizations they don't have any work. They need work right? To find facts … Actually international governments, practically they cannot do so much. They can just issue statements." Respondents in the Centre for Peace and Conflict Studies report were even more critical, stating that the international community was "just playing their international politics" and abusing the situation in Myanmar (Centre for Peace and Conflict Studies, 2011: 53). Likewise, one of my respondents commented that "some people say other dictatorships have been changed from outside, but the Myanmar government is not like other dictatorships".

Even if there was little trust in the potential for the international community to prevent human rights violations in Myanmar, many democracy activists continued their transnational lobby activities. The Commission of Inquiry campaign, although ostensibly intended to gather evidence of human rights violations and eventually initiate criminal prosecutions against military leaders, in fact served primarily to maintain international attention for the broader cause of the democracy movement. It also served as a counter-strategy to the international optimism that arose during the early stages of the post-election transition period in response to the government's promise of top-down change. In the course of this optimism, however, democracy activists found international support for their campaign waning. One activist commented in 2012 that they had made a strategic decision to stop mentioning the Commission of Inquiry, because diplomats seemed to have become "allergic" to it. Another activist confirmed that "nowadays European and American leaders are reluctant to talk about crimes against humanity, they don't want to support a Commission of Inquiry, so we will not raise it for the time being. They are reluctant to disturb the reforms."

Such considerations indicate the need to adapt to international advocacy priorities, as activists had to delay their calls for justice when local and international actors wanted to give the new quasi-civilian government a chance to improve its human rights record. As stated, in the early years of the transition there was praise for President Thein Sein's reforms, his liberalization of civil rights and his attempts to hold peace talks with ethnic nationalities. The calls for justice would re-appear in later years, predominantly in response to the crimes committed against the Rohingya in 2017. The example of the Commission of Inquiry campaign shows that calls for justice can be strategically delayed if international campaign strategies and political priorities so require. But while the campaigns were stalled, activists' overall goals remained the same. It is the international community that shifted focus more radically based on perceived local changes, as the next chapter will demonstrate.

7

# Foreign Aid and
# the (De)politicization of
# Civil Society Assistance

Our main challenge is funding. Because without money we cannot
work. Normally we cannot get money from the community, because
people are still poor.[1]

For all the political sensitivities and organizational rivalries discussed
earlier, civil society's room to manoeuvre in Myanmar, as in any country,
is conditional on having the funds available to carry out activities. This
chapter describes both the opportunities provided and the challenges posed
by foreign donor assistance to civil society. [2] Although civil society actors
in Myanmar have become skilled at organizing activities with relatively
low budgets, many organizations, especially those without a clear religious
affiliation, suffered from the pervasive poverty levels in the country and
turned to outside funders for assistance. This partial dependence on
foreign donors and the sudden rise in donor funding during the political
transition period posed a number of challenges not unlike those described
in development literature on other recipient countries. Senders of aid have
been accused of prioritizing their own political, economic and geo-strategic
interests over the interests of beneficiaries, of distributing aid insufficiently
and inconsistently, and of paying lip service to values such as development
and democracy while actually pursuing economic agendas. At the same
time, donors have sometimes provided vital financial and moral support
in environments where the country's own government and local actors
are incapable or unwilling to do so. The pervasive role of the military in
Myanmar posed a number of unique challenges to donors and recipient
organizations alike, resulting in particularly vehement debates around the
politicization of aid.

Although funding for civil society can come from a number of sources, government assistance and private donations from inside the country are often ruled out in contexts of pervasive poverty levels and repressed civic space. As wealth in those contexts is often acquired in close collaboration with political and business elites, the more affluent sections of society tend to be reluctant to support activities that might challenge the status quo (Parks, 2008). Moreover, in authoritarian countries many organizations try to stay under the radar, which complicates their ability to fundraise (Cleary, 1997; Wells-Dang, 2012). This has certainly been the case in Myanmar; as a respondent commented in 2015: "I think we should also do fundraising inside the country. But those who have the money are the cronies."

Despite the Buddhist tradition of donating to religious causes, the idea of donating for social and humanitarian causes is a relatively new development in Myanmar (Jaquet and Walton, 2013). Some Buddhist initiatives have followed the example of Christian organizations that are more used to generating funding for civil society activities. Buddhist, Christian, Islamic and other organizations increasingly relied on foreign funding from the 1990s onwards, when Myanmar opened up to outside influences and Western democracy promotion gained popularity. Yet Western sanctions and a lack of international exposure also limited their opportunities to obtain foreign funding. This chapter first discusses the expansion and contraction of foreign aid throughout the periods of military rule. Depending on the type of activities, a distinction can be made between humanitarian aid, development assistance and capacity building of civil society.[3] Some donors explicitly focus their support on one of these areas, while others engage in a combination, either because they feel that certain goals are connected (such as development assistance and capacity building), or because they want to conceal their support for democratization under the banner of more neutral activities. This conflation of goals, however, further politicized the debate on aid to Myanmar, as discussed later in the chapter.

## Expansion and contraction of foreign aid during military rule

Since Asian donor agencies tend to provide economic and infrastructural assistance, which is mostly bilateral, Myanmar civil society organizations (CSOs) often have to rely on Western donors for support.[4] As mentioned, the earliest ties between 'Western-style' CSOs and foreign supporters were with Christian missionaries who entered the country in the colonial era. Although foreign missionaries were technically no longer allowed residency after 1962, strong ties between missionaries and the Christian churches in

Myanmar remained, and Christian donor organizations still play a significant role in Western donor policies in Myanmar (Sakhong, 2007; Rieffel and Fox, 2013). After independence in 1948, when the global aid chain was developing on a large scale, the country's bilateral relations were characterized by Cold War and post-colonial connections. In the 1950s, Burma received technical support from the British and post-war reparations as compensation for the Japanese occupation (Steinberg, 2010: 36; 45; 124). The post-1962 Burma Socialist Programme Party government tried to remain neutral amid Cold War rivalries but eventually had to seek out foreign assistance due to economic decline (Steinberg, 2010: 67). Bilateral and multilateral development assistance did not really take off until the end of the 1970s and was distributed exclusively through government channels (Perry, 2007: 39; Banki, 2009: 54). Japan remained the primary donor for decades, accounting for over 70 per cent of the official development assistance (ODA) in 1987 (Banki, 2009: 53).

The punitive approach that many Western countries have taken towards the Myanmar government was initiated after the 1988 crackdown and the denial of power to the National League for Democracy (NLD) after the 1990 elections. These events instilled on Western donors the idea that bilateral assistance to Myanmar contributed to repression, and that the military government should be coerced into democratization. As previously mentioned, this view was actively promoted by Aung San Suu Kyi and various exile organizations that gained a strong voice in determining foreign (and especially Western) policies on Myanmar after 1990. They nearly unanimously called for divestment, including withholding development assistance, which they argued primarily benefitted the military government. Democracy activists urged Western supporters to direct their support to the population in exile (both refugees and political activists, including the National Coalition Government of the Union of Burma [NCGUB]), whom they argued were in the best position to represent the Myanmar people. The Western sanction policies were subject to severe criticism, including by a number of scholars who argued that they ignored the needs of the majority of the Myanmar population (Taylor, 2009; Pedersen, 2012).

The Free Burma Coalition in the United States was particularly successful in getting a number of 'Free Burma Acts' passed that limited the possibility of investment in the country (Zaw Oo, 2006; Dale, 2011). The European Union adopted a Common Position in 1996, which contained an arms embargo and diplomatic sanctions, and suspended all non-humanitarian aid beyond immediate poverty alleviation (Steinberg, 2010: 177). This position was revised in 2004 to allow not only humanitarian assistance, but also projects on human rights, democracy and capacity building for civil society, as long as it was not distributed to or through the government (International Crisis Group, 2006: 3). Occasionally attempts were made to engage the Myanmar government, such as the Australian government's human rights training project for civil servants that was initiated in 1999 despite objections by the NLD (Kinley and Wilson, 2007). The Depayin incident in 2003 and the removal from office of General Khin Nyunt in 2004 put a premature end to this project. In general, though, the NLD and other opposition groups were effective in fostering the view that Western assistance was better distributed outside than inside the country. This politicization of the aid debate had a profound impact on the activities of civil society actors working inside the country under military rule.

In contrast to these Western responses, Asian countries did not impose political or economic sanctions on Myanmar, nor were they particularly supportive of non-governmental activities. Japan temporarily halted assistance after 1988 but soon resumed ties with Myanmar, although it was surpassed by China which became the largest provider of ODA to Myanmar (Bjarnegård, 2020; Décobert and Wells, 2020). However, both Japanese and Chinese aid has been distributed primarily through (inter)governmental agencies, and China in particular employed a broad definition of development assistance by contributing to infrastructure projects such as building the new capital Naypyidaw (Rieffel and Fox, 2013). Japanese governmental and non-governmental donors have long been active in Myanmar, particularly in agricultural training and other activities that fall within the Japanese aid philosophy of 'making persons' (Watanabe, 2014), but were less likely to contribute to politically contentious activities.

After 1988, most Asian countries pursued a policy of 'constructive engagement' with Myanmar, including successful attempts to include the country in the Association of Southeast Asian Nations (ASEAN) from 1997 onwards (Buszynski, 1998). ASEAN's engagement policy gained more international recognition when it was able to play a vital brokering role in post-Nargis humanitarian assistance efforts (International Crisis Group, 2008; Human Rights Watch, 2010). Among the Asian countries, India was most openly critical after the 1988 uprising and provided assistance to democracy activists and refugees based within its borders. This policy was reversed in the course of the 1990s, when India's 'Look East' policy called for closer political and economic ties with its eastern neighbours (Egreteau, 2011). Thailand has long hosted a significant section of the Myanmar population in exile, both activists and migrant workers, but has at the same time pursued hostile laws and extortive practices towards them (Hargrave, 2014; Simpson, 2014). Although ties with Thai activists have increased, especially since the rise of social media, the Thai government refuses to take a public position on the role of the military in Myanmar, presumably since Thailand has itself been ruled by the military since it staged a coup in 2014. Respondents confirmed that, despite their attempts at global advocacy, they mostly found political and financial support for their activities among Western donors. Contrary to Asian governmental policies, some non-state initiatives explicitly aim to support Myanmar civil society, for example the Thai-based Spirit in Education Movement, which contributes to capacity building through a Buddhist framework that differs from 'mainstream' Western development. However, this organization too receives funding from Western donors.

Despite general Western reluctance to become involved in any activities taking place inside Myanmar, a number of developments from the 1990s onwards increased opportunities for local actors to obtain foreign financial support. As mentioned, the ceasefires reached in several ethnic areas in the 1990s expanded the opportunities for local organizations to set up activities in these regions. The post-1988 military government also showed interest in receiving international development assistance, as long as it was limited to central Myanmar and the ceasefire areas that were under its control. Moreover, it preferred multi- or bilateral assistance such as from UN agencies that could be spent on technical reconstruction, rather than help from international non-governmental organizations (INGOs) that brought their own agendas and were considered difficult to oversee (International Crisis Group, 2002). Some of the ethnic armed organizations (EAOs) that had entered into ceasefires also sought out international assistance in order to develop the infrastructure and economy in their region, and INGOs were able to enter Kachin, Mon and Kayah States after signing Memoranda of Understanding (MOUs) with the government (Purcell, 1999). In addition, the government sought out assistance to target the gravest humanitarian needs such as poverty and HIV/AIDS, which it increasingly acknowledged as serious. In 1994, the State Law and Order Restoration Council officially announced that it would accept international development assistance to some of its border areas, as long as it did not pose a threat to national security. Opportunities thus increased for local humanitarian and peacebuilding organizations active in the accessible areas of the country.

Various Western organizations experienced an increase in humanitarian access in the early 2000s as a result of personal relationships with General Khin Nyunt. Humanitarian aid in Myanmar reportedly doubled between 2001 and 2005, while also reaching more remote areas (International Crisis Group, 2006). As the head of Military Intelligence and later briefly Prime Minister, Khin Nyunt had facilitated the ceasefires with various ethnic groups as well as informal talks with Aung San Suu Kyi. He was also responsible for foreign affairs, and actively sought out international involvement in the country. International organizations such as the International Labour Organization (ILO), the United Nations High Commissioner for Refugees and the International Committee of the Red Cross (ICRC) worked with Khin Nyunt to establish projects to reduce forced labour, facilitate prison visits and increase protection for civilians in conflict areas (International Crisis Group, 2006). General Khin Nyunt's sudden removal from power in 2004 directly affected the ability of intergovernmental organizations and INGOs to work inside the country. International organizations experienced decreased access to high-level government officials, increased surveillance, difficulty in obtaining permission for field trips and more pressure to work with government-organized NGOs (GONGOs). The ICRC had previously withdrawn operations due to the obstruction of its prison visits by the military government in 1995 and only resumed operations in 1999. It was forced to close all field offices inside Myanmar in 2006 after tensions arose when the Union Solidarity and Development Association (the main GONGO under the State Peace and Development Council) attempted to first join, and then compete with the ICRC prison visits programme (International Crisis Group, 2006: 8). The ICRC was only able to expand its operations again during the political transition.

The increased pressure culminated in the release of 'Guidelines for UN agencies, international organizations and INGOs/NGOs' by the Myanmar government in February 2006, which imposed strict rules on registration, oversight and funding of activities, and limited freedom to travel (International Crisis Group, 2006: 9). As a result, local CSOs could only legally obtain foreign support from donors who had established an MOU with the government, which in turn came with its own restrictions and oversight mechanisms. Some donors chose to channel funding through large partner organizations that did have an official presence in the country, such as Save the Children, which oversaw several multi-donor funds, but this increased local activists' dependency on large INGOs, as discussed subsequently.

Outside the government's framework, much more was possible. North American and European donor organizations were able to support the more politically oriented organizations that operated without official registration. However, since aid distributed outside Myanmar faced less obstruction from both the Myanmar government and Western sanctions, many donors found it easier and more efficient to support organizations in exile than those based inside the country. The American National Endowment for Democracy, for example, in 1999 reportedly spent $1.6 million on Burmese media, research and labour organizations in exile, including those of ethnic nationalities. It also supported the Norwegian-based media organization Democratic Voice of Burma, the NCGUB, and the US-based Burma Fund (Steinberg, 2001: 277; see Duell, 2014 for an overview of the main donors to the democracy movement in exile). In short, under military rule, a large proportion of the Western funding allocated for civil society support was spent on organizations outside the country, while humanitarian organizations active inside the country were subjected to strong scrutiny from both the government and the democracy movement.

## Politicization of the aid debate

Distributors of development assistance, and especially humanitarian aid, often have an interest in presenting their activities as politically neutral. Organizations such as the ICRC and Médecins Sans Frontières (MSF) are only able to operate in conflict areas under the condition that they remain impartial in the conflict and assist all sides equally. In reality, though, development assistance can become highly politicized. Humanitarian agencies can rightly or wrongly be accused of unequal distribution of aid, and assistance in the fields of development and democratization is even more likely to be politically charged. Research on African case studies in particular has shown how development aid has a strong political impact on the receiving countries and often comes with political intentions from the senders (De Waal, 1997; Sogge, 2002). The aid debate in Myanmar has at times been simplified to the question of whether to deliver aid through the military government, with the risk of displaced funding and continuation of conflict and oppression, or withhold aid from the government, and totally neglect the population inside the country (Décobert, 2016). Both local and Western organizations with an interest in Myanmar have actively tried to bring forth their own viewpoints on this issue, while discrediting the views of those taking a different approach. Their analyses of the situation often resulted in public policy advice about the desired distribution (or non-distribution) of assistance to Myanmar organizations.

As early as 1993, the International Council of Voluntary Agencies called for active INGO involvement inside the country, a suggestion that was rejected by the exile community. A variety of solidarity and exile organizations, including the NCGUB and some of the ethnic nationality organizations, argued that aid should be directed towards the Thai–Burma border instead (Purcell, 1999: 77). While some community leaders reportedly thought that the presence of international organizations could prevent human rights abuses from taking place, INGO representatives remained relatively secretive about their operations inside the country, in order to prevent problems both with the Myanmar government and with democracy activists who might criticize their work (Pedersen, 2012). Aid organizations wishing to be involved in military-ruled Myanmar were therefore presented with a policy dilemma: they wanted to attend to the needs of the people while at the same time promoting democratization and respecting calls from democracy activists in exile to withdraw support and assistance from the country (International Crisis Group, 2002, 2006). International Crisis Group (2006: 11) criticized 'the use of foreign aid by political actors whose first priority is regime change' and argued that organizations working on the ground faced serious limitations as a result of the principled stance taken by the United States and other Western states in terms of preventing money from flowing to the government, even indirectly. Some similarly argued that donors should give local organizations more room to design their own strategies, including inviting local authorities to their meetings if this was deemed beneficial (Ware, 2012).

As the climate for international organizations worsened over the course of 2004, two large INGOs decided to withdraw from the country. The French section of MSF argued that the new regulations limited their ability to travel and work, especially in minority areas. The withdrawal decision of the UN Global Fund for AIDS, Tuberculosis and Malaria, however, was attributed both to deteriorating implementation circumstances and to severe pressure from US-based activists who urged Congress to demand additional safeguards as a condition for American contributions to the fund (International Crisis Group, 2006; Currie, 2012). The EU and Australia reacted to the Fund's withdrawal by setting up the alternative Three Diseases Fund in 2006, which was less dependent on US funding. However, the total budget for combating these diseases was significantly reduced, resulting in adverse effects on the Myanmar population, as well as damaged relationships with government officials and GONGOs such as the Myanmar Red Cross, who had tried their best to cooperate with the Fund (International Crisis Group, 2006, 2008). Paulo Sérgio Pinheiro, the UN Special Rapporteur on Human Rights in Myanmar at the time, warned that "it would be a terrible mistake to wait for political normalisation of Myanmar to help the population and to reinforce the strengths of the community" (in International Crisis Group, 2006: 16).

Democracy organizations were much more sceptical about the benefits of aid to Myanmar. The Alternative ASEAN Network (Burma) (ALTSEAN-Burma [2002]) was one of the most vocal proponents of divestment. It argued that those in favour of humanitarian assistance were being naive and depoliticizing aid by using terminology such as 'crisis', which absolved the Myanmar government from direct responsibility. It argued that the military benefitted financially from foreign assistance, that it withheld aid from ethnic nationalities in areas of ongoing conflict and that it inhibited transparency, accountability and adequate monitoring of humanitarian work. By not bearing witness, ALTSEAN-Burma (2002: 48) argued, 'international agencies are responsible for the suffering of the people through their complicity'. Aid agencies based in Yangon, moreover, were accused of deliberately avoiding contact with organizations providing aid in the border areas. This view was also shared by researchers who argued that INGOs ceased to be impartial and were making a political choice by signing MOUs with the government (Purcell, 1999; Malseed, 2009). Such views, which were publicly aired by democracy organizations in exile, made many Western donors reluctant to offer support to local civil society initiatives (Décobert, 2016).

The limited availability of first-hand information from the ground made donors highly dependent on the information provided by advocacy organizations such as ALTSEAN-Burma on the one hand and think tanks such as International Crisis Group on the other. Humanitarian actors based inside the country had to both guard their fragile access on the ground and defend themselves against being labelled as 'regime apologists', as the previously discussed example of the 'After the storm' report illustrated. They also faced actual restrictions, for example on extending their services to known NLD supporters, and reported adjusting their language and the content of the reports they submitted to authorities (Purcell, 1999; Ware, 2012). Those humanitarian actors who were too critical of human rights violations, such as the United Nations Development Programme representative Charles Petrie, were denied access to the country (Currie, 2012: 26).[5] A few international organizations were uniquely well placed to combine engagement with and public condemnation of the military government, such as the ILO. In 1997, it ordered a public investigation into accusations of forced labour in Myanmar, while it later managed to cooperate with the government to reduce the use of forced labour and child soldiers (Horsey, 2011). This process was far from seamless, however. In 2003, two people were sentenced to death for treason after contacting the ILO representative.[6] The removal of General Khin Nyunt and his team in 2004 deprived the ILO of its primary contact points within the government, but it was able to re-engage with the government in the course of the political transition period.

As described earlier, the debate on the desirability of donor assistance to Myanmar intensified after cyclone Nargis in May 2008. The cyclone caused unprecedented damage, exposing the military government's inability to respond effectively to a large-scale crisis and provide effective delivery of aid. Meanwhile, Western aid suppliers tried to keep their support out of the hands of the authorities (Human Rights Watch, 2010; Larkin, 2010). International critics capitalized on the chaotic aftermath of the cyclone to highlight the military's continuing failure and lack of care for the population, and to renew their calls for democratization. Yet the personal involvement of UN Secretary General Ban Ki-Moon and the coordinating role taken up by ASEAN also offered new prospects for effective foreign intervention in what regional countries had thus far considered largely internal affairs (International Crisis Group, 2008; Rieffel and Fox, 2013).

Despite the initial restrictions on foreign aid entering the country, cyclone Nargis and its aftermath placed Myanmar more saliently on the international aid map. ODA to Myanmar increased from less than $3 per person in 2006 to a still modest $11 per person in 2008, then fell to $7 in 2010.[7] The number of INGOs active inside the country and their level of local staff rose significantly, particularly in the delta area. Some of this humanitarian assistance later transformed into regular development assistance, leading to long-term relationships between Western donors and local activists. Metta Development Foundation, which had been active since 1998, saw its budget expanding from $2 million to $12 million as a result of cyclone Nargis. Other organizations also continued to benefit from renewed contact and a growing reputation with international donors. The occurrence of cyclone Nargis thus shifted the balance, with CSOs inside the country seeing the opportunities for foreign assistance increase, sometimes at the expense of border-based groups, as described subsequently.

Both overly positive and overly negative depictions of INGO activities in Myanmar under military rule should be viewed in light of this politicized aid debate. The debate around humanitarian and development assistance to Myanmar prompted those involved to present two competing frames of the aid situation: one in which the international community was, intentionally or unintentionally, complicit in the regime's strategy to commit human rights abuses and enrich itself at the expense of the Myanmar people, and another in which the international community had been misled by democracy activists into believing that humanitarian assistance in Myanmar was largely ill-spent. The lack of information coming from inside the country made it difficult for any party to assess these claims, let alone obtain the views of the intended beneficiaries. These positions therefore had a significant impact on the ability of local activists to establish contact with Western donors. These donors, in turn, also used their financial and political leverage to foster democratization from below.

## Western democracy promotion

In the 1990s and early 2000s, a significant proportion of Western donor assistance to civil society in Myanmar could be labelled as 'democracy promotion', which was distributed to non-state actors (Bjarnegård, 2020). While exiled activists and students abroad were explicitly exposed to human rights training and civic education, the support for activists inside the country initially took a more covert form, such as English language training. Among Western donors, the US government was most explicit in its emphasis on democratization. Although diplomatic relations between the US and Myanmar had been limited, with no US ambassador in Myanmar between 1990 and 2012, the American Embassy maintained a presence in Yangon, and its American Center provided local activists the space to discuss politically sensitive issues. The United States also provided local CSOs with small grants of around $10,000, with the goal of fostering an active civil society as a key component of democratization. Australia and the EU channelled most of their donor funding through INGOs and UN organizations. Australia's minimum grant amount at the time was $100,000, which ruled out funding to small organizations. Individual European countries such as Denmark, Norway and Switzerland spent some of their funding for human rights and democracy directly on local organizations, while a significant proportion of their budgets were distributed among activists and media organizations in exile. Eastern European donor organizations were also particularly active supporters of Burmese democracy activists, for example through the Czech Republic's 'Transition Promotion Program', as they hoped to transfer their past revolutionary experiences to other contexts.

The UK, traditionally one of the most engaged countries in Myanmar due to its colonial ties, spent its budget for strengthening civil society mainly through trainings at the British Council in Yangon, and through its various 'Millennium Centres' around the country. The British Council also hosted Pyoe Pin, a multi-donor support programme for civil society in Myanmar. The UK's decision in 2011 to substantially increase assistance made it the largest bilateral donor in Myanmar. In most UK projects, strengthening civil society was presented as a first step towards ultimate democratization on the central political level. The military government attempted to stop or delegitimize such attempts at democratization and frequently accused foreign donors of false motives.[8] Where it could not exert much direct influence, such as at the American Center, it reportedly sent informers. The dual funding of organizations inside the country and those in exile was particularly sensitive, as it could have negative repercussions for local activists and often had to be publicly concealed. Consequently, some donors decided to fund only registered organizations, while others disguised their funding relations, leading to a certain level of overlap between donors (Décobert and Wells, 2020). Donor representatives were not always internally in sync either. Those close to the field were often more flexible towards organizations than their colleagues in headquarters, and individual preferences for supporting more radical or more moderate civil society initiatives also differed among diplomats and donor staff.

## Changing donor priorities during the political transition

The political transition process had a profound impact on donor policies and practices, particularly after Aung San Suu Kyi gained a seat in parliament in 2012. Donor funding for Myanmar rose sharply after 2011, coinciding with a 'gold rush' for foreign business opportunities (Bächtold, 2015).[9] Over $9 billion was committed in ODA between 2012 and 2015 (Campbell, 2023: 15). However, Western donor funding was increasingly spent through the Myanmar government, which was seen as essential for the building of a strong democratic state (Bjarnegård, 2020; Décobert and Wells, 2020; McConnachie, 2022). The United States withdrew its veto for international financial institutions to operate in Myanmar, and both the Asian Development Bank and the World Bank re-started operations in Myanmar after having been absent for several decades (Décobert and Wells, 2020).[10] New bilateral donors such as United States Agency for International Development (USAID) entered the country, while Western governments re-assessed their sanctions policies. This created significant opportunities for civil society actors. While previously they competed for a limited amount of donor funding, a new situation emerged in which the demand for local partners almost outgrew the supply. Respondents reported an increased demand for information as a result of the many scoping missions of new donors seeking to enter Myanmar. Some observers even questioned whether the amount of foreign aid entering Myanmar in the early years of the transition might be 'too much too soon' (Rieffel and Fox, 2013).

While political activities that had previously been considered sensitive could be conducted more openly, Western donor assistance itself became increasingly depoliticized. This was particularly visible in the area of peacebuilding. Donors allocated large amounts of money to peace initiatives that were decidedly unequal in set-up, put EAOs in a disadvantageous position, and ignored diversity within civil society (Bächtold, 2015; Wells, 2020; Loong, 2021), despite warnings from other conflict environments that supporting an imbalanced peace process may actually do more harm than good (Anderson, 1999; Stokke et al, 2022). The Thein Sein government initiated the Myanmar Peace Center in November 2012, which received substantial support from the European Union and other international actors (Su Mon Thazin Aung, 2016). This initiative was led by former leaders of the Third Force who had recently returned from exile. Although it was meant to be a neutral institute, it was strongly criticized for being untransparent and too close to the government (Saw Yan Naing, 2016; Su Mon Thazin Aung, 2016). The Myanmar Peace Support Initiative, another project intended to facilitate dialogue between EAOs, political parties and civil society, ran from 2012 to 2014 with Norwegian donor support but did not achieve much result (Hindstrom, 2012; Roy et al, 2021). A number of CSOs, including two women's groups and two Karen organizations, publicly expressed disappointment about the Norwegian government's 'flawed, rushed, and untransparent peace fund consultations' in relation to this initiative.[11] Norway was particularly criticized, because its peacebuilding involvement coincided with significant business investment in the country by Norwegian companies Telenor and Statoil in the telecom and oil and gas sector (Mon Mon Myat, 2014).

The International Crisis Group, a long-term proponent of foreign engagement with the Myanmar government, became subject to public criticism in November 2012 when it announced that it would honour President Thein Sein with an award for his peace efforts in the country (Horton, 2013). The national census in 2014 was conducted in collaboration with the UN Population Fund, which could not prevent the removal of

Rohingya as ethnic category and other contentious provisions (TNI, 2014; Ferguson, 2015; Min Zin, 2015). The European Union was criticized for its crowd management training offered to the Myanmar Police Force in 2014, as the police subsequently inflicted violence on peaceful protesters in Letpadan. From 2016 onwards, a group of Western donors pooled over $100 million into a Joint Peace Fund, which distributes funding to CSOs that could demonstrate a contribution to the peace process (Wells, 2020).[12] As a result, many respondents had to rephrase their rights-based projects in the more 'neutral' language of peacebuilding.

The situation of Myanmar activist and refugee organizations abroad and their ability to secure funding also changed dramatically because of these donor shifts. Political and advocacy organizations who had managed to create a role for themselves inside the country were able to benefit from the increase in donor support, while those that remained outside the country saw their funding options reduced (Duell, 2014; Décobert, 2016; Olivius, 2019). Several of the Western (particularly Scandinavian) donors began to shift funding from exile organizations to organizations working from inside Myanmar, whose position around the 2010 elections they found more constructive. Refugees in Bangladesh, Thailand and Malaysia experienced significant pressure to return to Myanmar, regardless of whether their area of origin was in fact accessible and free of conflict (Hargrave, 2014; McConnachie, 2022).[13] This also jeopardized civil society activities that could not be done safely inside the country, such as the documentation of human rights violations in the ethnic areas, and some inter-ethnic women's rights initiatives conducted from the Thai–Myanmar border (Olivius, 2019; Matelski et al, 2022).

## Foreign aid reinforcing societal divisions

Especially in situations of conflict, foreign aid may create or reinforce divisions in society (Anderson, 1999; Banki, 2009). The distribution of resources such as foreign aid can make ethnic, religious and geographical divisions more prominent, as it becomes rewarding to distinguish between one's own group members and outsiders. As previously discussed, ethnicity is one of the main identity markers in Myanmar. Within ethnic groups, divisions also exist between persons of various religious backgrounds, class and urban or rural origin. A further division exists between groups that have reached ceasefires with the military and those that have not (South, 2008b; Banki, 2009). People in remote and/or conflict areas often complain that they are less well served by aid agencies that tend to operate from central locations. Within aid organizations and their implementing partners, ethnic and religious divisions can also play a role. The divisions within Myanmar society complicated the hiring practices of donor and intermediary organizations. For example, people often accused Christian organizations of hiring mostly Christian staff (CDA, 2009). Some argue that (I)NGOs should hire staff from within communities who understand the local culture and needs, while others argue that they should refrain from hiring local staff members because they would favour their own (sub)group (CDA, 2009: 37).

In Rakhine State, existing distrust between ethnic and religious minority groups was exacerbated by the presence of Western aid agencies. Already in 2009, it was noted that the Rohingya in northern Rakhine State were far more likely to receive assistance from the international community, while the (Buddhist) ethnic Rakhine people were more likely to receive assistance from the Myanmar government (CDA, 2009: 10). Rakhine people in turn felt disadvantaged by INGOs operating in the area, because they were hiring Bengali-speaking staff in order to be able to communicate with the Rohingya population (CDA, 2009: 29).

The question of aid delivery in Rakhine State became even more relevant after violence between Buddhists and Muslims erupted in 2012. As aid levels finally started to rise during the political transition, people in Myanmar, and in Rakhine State in particular, were frustrated that the majority seemed to go to the Rohingya (Walton and Hayward, 2014). Significant street protests took place in opposition to the Organisation of Islamic Cooperation (OIC), which wanted to open offices in Rakhine State, after which the Myanmar government blocked the organization's access to the country; the president argued that the OIC's presence was "not in accordance with the desire of people" (BBC, 2012). The Rakhine people's suspicion that aid agencies were favouring Rohingya resulted in direct accusations and even violence against Western aid workers, after which the Myanmar government forced MSF Holland to withdraw from Rakhine State; they were allowed to re-enter in the course of 2014. Other aid agencies temporarily withdrew their Western staff members from the area for security reasons.[14]

The sudden international attention on Myanmar during the transition, on the political and economic level but also in terms of aid, contributed to the 'competitive victimhood' that had emerged from decades of violent repression of various ethnic nationalities, including the Rakhine (MacLean, 2022). The calls for justice and secession of violence against Rohingya from 2012 onwards were often perceived in that same light, and particularly opposed by Buddhist nationalists. When UN Special Envoy Yanghee Lee spoke out in support of Rohingya citizenship, Wirathu publicly called her a 'bitch' and a 'whore', and the NLD government banned her from the country in 2017 (Min Zin, 2015; Brooten, 2020).

## International justice initiatives

After the mass violence against and expulsion of Rohingya in 2017, the international call for justice initiatives grew. In 2018, the UN Human

Rights Council established the Independent International Fact-Finding Mission for Myanmar (IIFFMM) consisting of a body of experts tasked with the investigation of crimes committed in Myanmar since 2011 in order to support future domestic or international prosecutions. In August 2018, it called for the International Criminal Court (ICC) to prosecute five military leaders, including commander-in-chief Min Aung Hlaing, who would later stage the 2021 military coup. While a UN referral was unlikely given the composition of the Security Council, the ICC Prosecutor decided to open its own investigation into crimes committed against Rohingya who had since entered the territory of Bangladesh which, contrary to Myanmar, is a state party to the ICC. Proceedings began in late 2019 and are ongoing at the time of writing. The NLD government initially refused entry to the country for IIFFMM members but later decided to cooperate with the UN to a certain extent. The IIFFMM's mandate ended in September 2019, after which it transferred its documentation to the Independent Investigative Mechanism for Myanmar. A third international justice attempt was initiated in 2019 by the Burmese Rohingya Organisation UK, which successfully appealed to Argentina to use the principle of universal jurisdiction against the Myanmar military. On 20 January 2023, the NGO Fortify Rights filed a criminal complaint against the Myanmar military in Germany under the same principle. While the activists involved claim that the various international justice initiatives are mutually exclusive because they each have a different mandate, some experts have warned against the risk of over-documentation, and call for better coordination (see Matelski et al, 2022). ICC Prosecutor Karim Khan suggested that the international justice sector might be in need of a coordinating body similar to the UN Office for the Coordination of Humanitarian Affairs.[15]

The NLD government became stuck between international pressure to be more cooperative and domestic pressure from the military and Buddhist nationalists who were against any acknowledgement of the rights of Rohingya (Pedersen, 2019).[16] It eventually decided to challenge the ICC's jurisdiction over the events in Rakhine State. Meanwhile, the Gambia brought a case before the International Court of Justice, accusing the Myanmar state of breaching the genocide convention. In December 2019, Aung San Suu Kyi came to The Hague to defend her government against these accusations, after which she lost what little remained of her international reputation as a human rights defender. Amnesty International, the European Union, the UK city of Oxford and the US Holocaust Museum all withdrew awards they had granted to Aung San Suu Kyi; her Nobel Peace Prize was not withdrawn because the organization stated it has no such provision. While the internal reasoning for Aung San Suu Kyi's appearance in The Hague (and thus, her defence of military crimes) remains unclear, the military was able to use her reputation to its advantage, as international indignation focused almost exclusively on Aung San Suu Kyi's role. Despite his close involvement in the violence against the Rohingya, it would take until the 2021 coup before the leading role of Min Aung Hlaing in mass human rights violations started to receive international attention.

## Inequalities in donor relationships

The preceding discussion demonstrates that Western donors have had a variety of influences on civil society in Myanmar. They have provided important facilitation and support but have also influenced local activities with strong financial encouragement first towards democratization, and later towards depoliticized and largely technical peacebuilding activities. As a result of shifting donor priorities and increasingly technical reporting requirements, moreover, CSOs that rely on foreign funding have to spend a lot of their time meeting donor needs, often at the expense of their effectiveness in the field (see Hulme and Edwards, 1997; Parks, 2008; Ear, 2012). In the context of peacebuilding, it has been argued that accountability has shifted almost exclusively towards tax payers in donor countries, rather than to the communities that the aid is intended to help (Bächtold, 2021).

A further aspect of donor dependency pertains to the role of partnerships. Formal donor organizations such as UN agencies prefer to work with larger NGOs, as opposed to smaller community-based organizations with informal structures that might have a stronger link to local communities. Research on countries such as Cambodia and Vietnam has shown that Western donors tend to prioritize recipient organizations that resemble their own (Carothers and Ottaway, 2000; Salemink, 2006). Members of such organizations speak the same language (both literally speaking English, and knowing the right terminology), make use of familiar administrative processes, and report in a way that donors understand and approve of, in contrast to 'informal associations, social movements, and other kinds of networks, [that] are not set up to be administratively responsive to donor needs' (Carothers and Ottaway, 2000: 13).

The 'governmentality' of professionalized donors and (I)NGOs is often apparent in subtle indicators such as language use and project design (Li, 2007). Englund (2006: 33) noted how in Malawi, highly educated human rights activists uncritically accepted English as the lingua franca and showed contempt for others with different or lower literacy skills, despite their stated intentions to empower poor communities. Similar tendencies can be seen in Myanmar with many international staff's inability to speak Burmese, or local staff's insistence on using Burmese among ethnic nationalities who do not speak Burmese (either as their first language, or not at all). Even among civil society actors who do speak English, the use of technical terminology can create a subtle distance between local and 'professionalized' actors.

Such practices contribute to the impression noted by some anthropologists that development projects are hardly assessed based on their results on the ground but rather on their adherence to 'frameworks, tools and formulae' in order to ensure that the project is assessed as successful (Mosse, 2005; Crewe and Axelby, 2013). As a result, community development trainings such as the one I observed in Thailand focus a lot of their content on teaching the use and understanding of professional development terminology and technicalities in order to write successful funding proposals and project reports. Respondents conveyed how they sometimes lost funding because donors were unsatisfied with the professional level of their reporting or refused funding to organizations that did not have their own bank account. Such preconditions ruled out many experienced organizations that were successful in reaching local communities but did not meet the formal donor requirements due to government repression and/or lack of time and resources to live up to these demands.

In other cases, donor representatives, especially those close to the field, reportedly showed understanding of local conditions. These donors did not request receipts for small local expenses such as public transportation (which are obviously cheaper than flying or hiring a driver, but less easy to account for on paper), or even understood that a certain amount of bribery could be unavoidable to ensure effective implementation without obstruction by local officials. One respondent explained how they circumvented the requirement of registration with the government: "Some donors request registration. So most of the organizations in Burma, we have no registration. We explain that issue to them. My current donor partner, they never requested me to register … Most of the organizations they understand the situation in Burma."[17] Likewise, politically 'sensitive' organizations such as those working with political prisoners reported good and flexible working relationships with their donors, who understood that they often had to improvise or work secretly for security reasons.

An over-focus on reporting requirements may actually result in an ironic discrepancy between the evaluation of practices by donors and INGOs on the one hand and recipients of funding on the other. As Crewe and Axelby (2013: 186) note: 'There is a paradox between the low level of trust placed in professionals that has led to the perceived need for auditing and the high level of trust that attaches to auditors and evaluators.' Local organizations are viewed with suspicion and are judged by standards that do not apply to Western donor representatives and those evaluating projects on their behalf. Local organizations, moreover, are forced to partner with international agencies, even if they are used to handling large budgets, such as Metta Foundation. Its former director complained in 2015 about the distrust of local organizations: "The reality is, without the local NGOs, no international NGOs can implement projects on the ground." She pointed out double standards, whereby local NGO staff are continuously sent to trainings in financial management, despite their demonstrated ability to handle large projects: "And for us it's a very time-consuming process. But for that they don't pay. They don't even count the locals' time you know." She also complained that local organizations were forced to partner with INGOs that served as funding intermediaries:

> The problem with EU funding is ... they want to fund local NGOs, but then they don't provide seed funding. If you want to apply for funds, another institution has to put 10 per cent, for example. So where do you think local NGOs will get the 10 per cent? So that's the space for the INGO ... You can do this, but don't say it is civil society strengthening ... All EU funding went to international NGOs, and then [it must] trickle down to the local NGO. Don't call it our partner and then let us compete.[18]

A local NGO director quoted in a Paung Ku report made a similar comment regarding the unrealistic requirements the European Commission put on beneficiaries of its 'good governance programme' which aimed to reach grassroots organizations but realistically required at least $10,000 to prepare a funding proposal: "The EC think they are watering the plants, but the plants are somewhere else" (Paung Ku, 2011: 7). In response to these practices, some of the largest organizations tried to reduce their dependency on international NGOs by forming a bloc against them, but many of the smaller organizations were not in a strong enough position to bargain about the share taken by intermediary organizations.

UN agencies and large international NGOs have a financial monopoly position in Myanmar, as donors often choose to channel funding through these agencies, rather than directly to local actors. In one example, local non-state education providers were invited to a meeting in Yangon, where the United Nations Children's Fund (UNICEF) announced that it had $60 million to spend on education and wanted to extend its partnership with non-state actors. The non-state education providers (both Myanmar and foreigners), who were used to working with small budgets for many years, were initially very pleased and eager to share their thoughts on how the budget could be spent to make education accessible to more children throughout the country. However, they were disappointed and even became somewhat emotional when UNICEF mentioned that it could only work with one or two centralized INGOs as local partners, in order to shorten communication channels and minimize overhead costs. The atmosphere of working towards a shared communal goal was quickly lost when participants in the meeting realized that precisely their ability to make the most out of small budgets made them ineligible for donor support.[19]

The high overhead costs of UN agencies were particularly painful for local civil society actors. In May 2014, UNICEF in Myanmar became subject of a public scandal, when it transpired that the organization rented office space from a former military general for $87,000 per month. After this first news story, media reported that the World Health Organization, another UN agency, spent $79,000 per month on office space, which amounts to 10 per cent of its total annual budget for Myanmar (Kyaw Hsu Mon and Lewis, 2004). A contributor to an online platform on civil society in Myanmar commented in 2013 that the director of USAID spent $17,000 per month on rent alone, almost double the amount of the United States' full 'small grants' budget available to local organizations.[20] These scandals continued to emerge in the aftermath of the 2021 coup, as described in the next chapter.

# 8

# Interrupted Transition and Post-coup Resistance

After five years of contentious rule, Aung San Suu Kyi's National League for Democracy (NLD) party secured its largest victory to date in the elections of November 2020.[1] The military alleged voter fraud, despite widespread evidence to the contrary, and put pressure on the Union Election Commission (UEC) to hold off with the formation of a new government. When it became clear that the new parliament would convene as planned, Commander-in-Chief Min Aung Hlaing staged a coup on the morning of 1 February 2021. The military took control of parliament in Naypyidaw, imprisoned Aung San Suu Kyi, President Win Myint and other elected NLD leaders, and took over all powers under the name of the State Administration Council (SAC). The SAC appointed its own ministers as well as a new UEC, which subsequently confirmed mass voter fraud and cancelled the election results (Reny, 2022).

The 2021 military coup was a major setback in the transition process and a big surprise to the international community, which had largely underestimated the continued role of the military in Myanmar politics. The move was less surprising to local observers, as the military had been raising doubts about the election process and the role of the NLD-appointed UEC since mid-2020. In the months after the elections, at least 45 demonstrations were held protesting against presumed electoral fraud, mostly organized by the Union Solidarity and Development Party (USDP), which reportedly paid participants to demonstrate (Bynum, 2021). Although the 2008 constitution contains a provision for a military coup, the 2021 coup was widely considered to contravene that provision. Min Aung Hlaing would have been forced to retire as head of the military in June 2021 and had likely hoped to become president. The NLD's electoral victory deprived him of that opportunity and also posed a risk to the many military-controlled enterprises. The increasing number of international prosecutions of human rights violations involving the military probably also made its leadership less confident of a secure future (Jordt et al, 2021: 4).

The military initially seemed set on organizing elections mid-2023 in an effort to establish a legal basis for continued SAC rule. However, in early 2023 it extended the nationwide state of emergency without mentioning a new date for the election, which constitutionally should be held within six months after termination of a state of emergency (International Crisis Group, 2023b). As of mid-2023, further extensions have been announced. Meanwhile, the Myanmar population continues to challenge and resist the military coup in various ways. This chapter explores new repertoires of popular resistance as well as new forms of solidarity, but also new fault lines that emerged in the two years since the 2021 coup. It discusses how the military has been challenged on the local, national and international level, while various forces compete for legitimacy to represent the people of Myanmar and give shape to the country's future.

## Popular resistance and military repression since the 2021 coup

Almost immediately after the coup became known, protests were organized throughout the country. On 2 February 2021, a nationwide strike was launched by health care workers under the banner Civil Disobedience Movement (CDM). Civil servants refused to go to work, leading to disruptions in the health, education, transportation and banking systems. At one point, up to 50 per cent of civil servants (including nearly all railway workers) participated in the CDM, as did many employees of military-controlled enterprises (Jordt et al, 2021). That same week, protestors took to the streets in Mandalay and Yangon, and demonstrations in the ethnic states soon followed. Protests evolved under the banner of 'Spring Revolution' (later mostly called simply 'the revolution') in line with popular uprisings elsewhere, such as the earlier 'Arab Spring'. Notably, the street protests were organized by young people referred to as Generation Z, a group born between the mid-1990s and the early 2010s that comprise about a quarter of Myanmar's population (Jordt et al, 2021: 12). This was the first generation in Myanmar to grow up under a nascent (partial) democracy and with access to social media, while previous generations had known mostly military rule (Su Mon Thant, 2021).

A young medical doctor called Tay Zar San was one of the first to organize demonstrations in Mandalay on 4 February, after which several protestors were arrested (Walker, 2021). Two days later, the first protests emerged in Yangon, in which women played a prominent role. Factory workers organized themselves in an Anti-Junta Mass Movement Committee, while people throughout the country started banging pots and pans at 8 pm each night in resistance to the coup (Ko Maung, 2021). This ritual is a common form of protest with spiritual origins, which allows people who do not normally protest on the streets, including women, children and elderly, to join in (Phyu Phyu Oo, 2021). The first protests in Yangon were initially organized by labour unions and (often female) factory workers, but other young people soon joined in. Esther Ze Naw and Ei Thinzar Maung, both of ethnic nationality background, came to be perceived as two of the movement's leaders; later that year, they were named in *Time Magazine*'s list of 100 most influential persons of the year. This new generation of activists challenged existing power holders, not only from the side of the military but also within the political opposition, as detailed later in the chapter. They were supported by experienced activists from earlier generations who provided tactical information that, together with the use of social media, allowed them to mobilize effectively. Contrary to earlier demonstrations, Buddhist monks were not at the forefront of the anti-coup protests, although they participated in joint initiatives such as the General Strike Committee (Jordt et al, 2021; International Crisis Group, 2023a). The post-coup protests since 2021 have been described as more pluralistic, more inclusive and more secular than earlier protest movements (International Crisis Group, 2023a).

The protests continued peacefully for the first week, increasing in size to tens of thousands. The military repeatedly cut off the internet and mobile phone networks, as it had done in many of the ethnic states. On 8 February, it imposed a curfew and far-reaching restrictions on peaceful assembly, which in effect prohibited all public protest. When demonstrations continued, the military opened fire, leading to the first casualty on 9 February, when a young woman was shot in the head during a protest in Naypyidaw. On 22 February, millions of protestors united in the largest nationwide strike to date (Jangai Jap, 2021; Su Mon Thant, 2021). By March 2021, the military regularly resorted to violent repression, resulting in hundreds of casualties every month, sometimes even within a single day. One well-known victim of military violence was a 19-year-old student nicknamed Angel, who was shot in the head during a protest in Mandalay on 3 March. She was depicted shortly before her death in a T-shirt that stated 'everything will be ok', an image which inspired many artists and activists on social media. On 14 March, between 65-84 protestors in the Yangon township of Hlaing Thar Yar were killed (Campbell, 2023; Mon Mon Myat, 2023). On Armed Forces Day, 27 March, over 150 protestors were killed after the military had warned on its TV channel that anti-coup demonstrators could be 'in danger of getting shot to the head and back' (Human Rights Watch, 2022).

More than 1,000 protestors and bystanders had been killed by the end of 2021, and between 3,000 to over 6,000 by mid-2023, including significant numbers of women and children.[2] The military arrested approximately 20,000 political prisoners in the two years after the coup, including civil society leaders, dissident celebrities, CDM participants or supporters, and others who shared or possessed anti-coup messages on mobile devices. Because the street protests were largely leaderless, almost any citizen could be deemed suspicious. Detainees were taken for interrogation in military centres, where they were frequently subjected to torture and sexual abuse; several died in custody, while others were scarred for life. On 25 July 2022, the military broke its de facto moratorium on the death penalty by hanging four political activists, including Ko Jimmy of the 88 Generation Students, and Phyo Zayar Thaw, a famous rapper who, as discussed earlier, became MP in the first NLD government. As in many other cases, their bodies were not returned to the families. Several other activists were sentenced to death and remain at risk of unannounced executions, while some death sentences were commuted to life sentences in 2023. Activists hid in safe houses organized by the resistance movement in order to avoid arrest, while others fled the country. The military stepped up its blacklisting of dissidents. Suspected activists were shown on national television with names and pictures, while others were arrested at the airport before they could leave the country.

The military also intensified its repression on civil society organizations (CSOs) and the media. In response to the CDM, it declared labour organizations illegal. Existing laws that had been used to repress civil society, such as the Telecommunications Law, the Official Secrets Act and the Unlawful Associations Act, were combined with new amendments to the Penal Code that criminalized criticism of the military and incitement. A new Cyber Security Law was drafted to repress online activities, such as the use of virtual private networks (APHR, 2022). Over 100 local journalists were arrested in the years after the coup, as well as a Japanese and an American journalist who were initially sentenced to ten and eleven years in prison; both have since been released and deported. The threat to local and international journalists made it increasingly complex to cover the situation on the ground, and most international journalists left within the first years after the coup. The military also made use of strategic internet shutdowns to restrict communication between protestors, and to cover up its own human rights violations. It reintroduced the requirement to report overnight stays, searched houses without warrants and prohibited landlords from renting out to dissidents (Su Mon Thant, 2021). In response to frequent nightly raids, citizens established neighbourhood watches to warn against approaching soldiers in the absence of reliable internet access (Jordt et al, 2021).

On 28 October 2022, a new Registration Law for (International) Non-governmental Organizations ([I]NGOs) was announced, imposing mandatory registration and high criminal penalties for those associated with unregistered organizations. Critics warned that it would severely restrict civic space, as well as access to international donor funding and humanitarian aid. As of 2023, some respondents continue to work under the radar or with the various resistance movements operating from exile. Significantly, though, many of the civil society intellectuals who had continued living and working in the country during the transition started to leave in the course of 2022, either to secure a better future for their children or because they were on the military's wanted list, or both. As before, this contributed to a significant brain drain, though some of them were able to secure research positions on Myanmar with universities and other institutes abroad.

In order to fund military operations, extortion became increasingly common (Jordt et al, 2021). Soldiers were seen demanding money from people at cash machines in order to fund their operations and even stealing donations from the holy Shwedagon Pagoda. They frequently requested money from family members to release the bodies of people killed during protests or interrogations. Local officials started charging money to community-based organizations for authorization to hold meetings and demanded percentages of supplies that organizations wanted to distribute to communities. Given the restrictions imposed on media and formal organizations, reporting was increasingly done by citizen journalists, who in turn were obstructed, targeted and arrested. Medical staff were also criminalized and arrested for trying to provide assistance to victims of military violence. During the COVID-19 pandemic, soldiers issued fake calls for assistance, then arrested medics who responded to these calls. In June 2021, the former head of the COVID-19 vaccination programme was arrested and accused of treason for attempting to keep an international donation to the vaccination programme out of the hands of the military and for cooperating with the opposition forces (Maung Shwe Wah, 2021). In this case and several others, family members were intimidated or arrested in order to obstruct the work of dissidents: the head of the vaccination programme, for example, was detained along with her husband, her young son and their dog. The military continued its periodic issuing of mass prison amnesties.[3] In November 2022, it also released three prominent foreigners, including Australian academic and former NLD advisor Sean Turnell. As stated earlier, prison amnesties serve as much to reinforce military power as to placate the public (Cheesman, 2015). Moreover, most of those released were not considered political prisoners. In the first post-coup prison release in February 2021, over 20,000 criminals were freed to make room for anti-coup protestors. Some of those released were subsequently paid to carry out attacks in areas known to be opposition strongholds (Jordt et al, 2021).

Both Myanmar society as a whole and the opposition movement in particular have suffered economically since the military coup. While the economic situation had improved remarkably during the political transition, there was a significant downfall as a combined result of the global COVID-19 pandemic and the military coup. Respondents in 2021 often referred to the compounded effects of 'COVID-19, coup and conflict'. Tourism and trade relations were discontinued, while many informal workers lost their income as the country came to a standstill during the pandemic, which was also badly mishandled by the military. Over 1.6 million people had lost their jobs by the end of 2021, and 13 million people experienced food insecurity in 2022 (International Labour Organization numbers cited in APHR, 2022 and Campbell, 2023). The large-scale CDM further shut down public services, such as education and health centres. The Myanmar *kyat* lost 60 per cent of its value in 2021, and funders such as the Asian Development Bank and the World Bank withheld payment for development projects (Reny, 2022). Inflation hit the poorer sections of society particularly hard. As the CDM continued, protestors also faced trouble ensuring continued security and financial assistance for their activities, especially as support to the CDM was criminalized by the military (Su Mon Thant, 2021).

## Escalation of armed conflict and resistance

After the large-scale military violence against protestors and in some of the ethnic states in late March 2021, peaceful protests were increasingly supplemented with violent resistance tactics. SAC members were attacked, bombs were strategically detonated in Yangon and other main cities, and some newly appointed local officials were killed for their presumed ties with the military (Reny, 2022). In response to military violence, protestors started using improvised weapons to resist attacks and protect themselves and each other. People's Defence Forces (PDFs) were formed on the local level armed with hunting rifles, grenades, landmines and other hand-made weapons to attack the military when it entered specific townships (Reny, 2022). Armed resistance spread around the country but was most prevalent in the central Myanmar regions Sagaing and Magway, which had previously been known as bases for military support and recruitment (Ye Myo Hein, 2022).

Among ethnic armed organizations (EAOs), the Karen National Liberation Army (KNLA), the Kachin Independence Army (KIA), the Restoration Council of Shan State, the Chin National Front and the Karenni Army openly opposed the military coup. EAOs in Kachin, Karen and Kayah States attacked military outposts in their area, to which the military responded with bombing (Reny, 2022). Armed conflict soon resumed in these areas, resulting in hundreds of thousands of internally displaced people (IDP). Several EAOs, notably the Karen National Union (KNU), started offering protection and military training to protestors who had fled to areas under their control (Loong, 2021). The KNU's armed wing, the KNLA, attacked a military outpost on 27 March 2021 after refusing to participate in Armed Forces Day (Ye Myo Hein, 2022). In response, the military launched several airstrikes on KNU territory. Similar dynamics occurred with the KIA in Kachin State and with other EAOs.

Fighting continued throughout 2021–23. The military frequently torched and bombed villages they suspected of harbouring resistance fighters, whom they referred to as 'terrorists'. In October 2021, the military burnt down almost 200 houses and two churches during attacks in Chin State. On 24 December 2021, 35 people, including a child and two aid workers, were killed by a drone attack on their cars in Kayah State. On 23 October 2022, the military launched air strikes on a cultural festival organized by the Kachin Independence Organization and the KIA. Around 80 people were killed, including prominent Kachin artists, while survivors were denied access to medical services. Military violence increasingly expanded to areas in central Myanmar, where resistance had been growing (Ye Myo Hein, 2022). The first attacks in Sagaing Region were carried out in March 2021, and violent repression of resistance continued in the following years. In September 2022, the military carried out an air strike on a school which they accused of harbouring resistance fighters – 11 school children died in the attack, and dozens more were injured. The largest attack since the coup at the time of writing occurred on 11 April 2023, when the military carried out a series of airstrikes in Kanbalu Township in Sagaing. This attack resulted in at least 170 deaths, although it took days for the actual numbers to reach international media.

In response to these large-scale air attacks, activists stepped up international campaigns for a ban on the international supply of aviation fuel. Military tactics are partly weather-dependent, with a decrease in airstrikes reported during the rainy season (Ye Myo Hein, 2022). In a webinar directed at the international community, an activist commented that "winter is holiday season for you, but airstrike season for us", as it allows better access for fighter jets in the ethnic areas.[4] The role of the PDFs in trying to counter these attacks will be covered later in the chapter. First, I explore the new forms of protest and solidarity that occurred in the wake of the coup and the responses on the political level.

## New forms of protest and solidarity

In their protests, Generation Z activists made use of social media, international connections and English slogans. They challenged existing power relations and gender norms through playful protest methods such as street performances, collective car break-downs, sit-ins and placards with jokes (Jordt et al, 2021). In the months after the coup, traditionally marginalized groups such as the LGBTIQ+ community were remarkably visible in these protests, and soldiers were openly challenged in their masculinities and traditional beliefs. Women hung their traditional clothes (*htamein*) in public areas so that soldiers had to cross underneath to enter a neighbourhood; walking underneath a line of women's clothing is traditionally thought to diminish *hpoun*, a male-specific type of honour or glory (Egreteau, 2022;

Ferguson, 2023).[5] As the military response became more violent, protests-without-people, 'silent strikes' and flash mobs became increasingly common in order to evade arrest (Bynum, 2021). These practices emerged throughout the country and were shared on social media, particularly Facebook. The military, which had come under scrutiny for its role in spreading hate speech against Rohingya via Facebook, started using TikTok to issue threats to anti-coup protestors (Jordt et al, 2021: 26).

The anti-coup protests were marked by unprecedented links between urban and rural, remote and central areas. In many ethnic states, activists mixed modern forms of protest with traditional symbols (Jordt et al, 2021; Egreteau, 2022). The nationwide banging of pots and pans in resistance to military rule, for example, emerged from the spiritual tradition used to cast off evil spirits. Inter-ethnic solidarity also increased in the aftermath of the coup (Thawnghmung and Khun Noah, 2021; Vrieze, 2023). During the political transition period, Burman activists and politicians had occasionally shown interest in and solidarity with the plight of ethnic nationalities in Myanmar, for example around the campaign against the Myitsone Dam in Kachin State. The small group of activists that showed solidarity with the Rohingya, however, were subjected to threats and slander. As violence spread to central parts of the country, protestors realized how the military had treated ethnic nationalities in conflict areas for decades. Many Burman protestors publicly declared their solidarity with ethnic nationalities or apologized for not speaking out earlier in support of minorities. In March 2021, student unions were among the first to issue a formal apology to the Rohingya and other ethnic nationalities for their lack of solidarity in the face of human rights violations by the military (Jordt et al, 2021: 20). One month later, Susanna Hla Hla Soe, an NLD parliamentarian of Karen ethnicity, apologized to the ethnic nationalities on behalf of the NLD government (Loong, 2021). In June 2021, protestors posted pictures of themselves dressed in black as part of an online campaign called #Black4Rohingya, while a smaller group protested in downtown Yangon in solidarity with the Rohingya. The fourth anniversary of the mass violence against the Rohingya in August 2021 was the first to be publicly commemorated. Public statements were issued by several CSOs, such as the Women's League of Burma (2021).

Young activists borrowed tactics, slogans and revolutionary songs from earlier generations of student activists (Jordt et al, 2021). They established international connections through the Milk Tea Alliance, an Asian solidarity movement started in Hong Kong to resist China's repressive influence in the region, which has spread to Thailand and other countries (as in Myanmar, but unlike in China, tea in these countries is usually mixed with milk). The three-finger salute originating from the film series the Hunger Games became a symbol of resistance in both Thailand and Myanmar. Protestors also used more serious tactics, such as naming and shaming of military personnel, members of the police and prison wards, as well as 'social punishment' of their family members and calling for a boycott of military-owned businesses, including Myanmar Beer and the phone company MyTel (Jangai Jap, 2021; Irrawaddy, 2022; Ferguson, 2023; International Crisis Group, 2023b). In some cases, naming and shaming extended to citizens not associated with the military, such as civil servants who, often for financial reasons, chose not to participate in the CDM. Protestors and resistance fighters actively encouraged military soldiers and police officers to defect from their positions, using tactics of de-brainwashing and counter-psychological warfare, particularly via social media. Since the start of the coup, thousands of defections have been reported, although mostly on an individual basis and with various motives ranging from ideology to frustration and self-interest (Kyed and Lynn, 2021). Other soldiers maintained their position but privately support the opposition. Activists proudly refer to them as 'watermelons': soldiers (dressed in green) who sympathize with the NLD party, which uses red as its party colour (Ye Myo Hein, 2022).

## Political opposition to military rule

While protests appeared spontaneously on the streets, NLD law makers who evaded arrest also took action. Within a week after the coup, the Committee Representing Pyidaungsu Hluttaw (CRPH, or committee representing Union Parliament) was founded to act on behalf of the ousted MPs. It declared the military coup unconstitutional and presented itself as the genuine government of Myanmar. The CRPH, which appointed an interim government, initially consisted mostly of Burman politicians, but had begun negotiations with ethnic political leaders by early March (Loong, 2021: 18). It met with CSOs, politicians and rebel leaders of various ethnicities in an effort to start a pan-ethnic alliance (Vrieze, 2023). Together, they formed the National Unity Consultative Council (NUCC), an entity that was consciously designed as leaderless (Moe Thuzar, 2022). By the end of March, the NUCC agreed on the outlines of a Federal Democracy Charter containing provisions for a new constitution, a political roadmap and a political body that could replace the military; it also abolished the 2008 constitution (Moe Thuzar, 2022). Meanwhile, the CRPH floated suggestions for a federal army, which some EAOs had called for in previous years (Ye Myo Hein, 2022).

On 16 April 2021, a National Unity Government (NUG) was founded by the CRPH, consisting of a combination of elected parliamentarians and prominent civil society leaders. The NUG, a shadow government in exile similar to the National Coalition Government of the Union of Burma in earlier decades, consists of 26 cabinet members, including 30 per cent women and 50 per cent non-Burmans (Moe Thuzar, 2022). It is formally headed by President Win Myint and State Counsellor Daw Aung San Suu Kyi, although they remain imprisoned at the time of writing. Former civil society activist and NLD parliamentarian Susanna Hla Hla Soe was appointed Minister of Women, Youth and Children Affairs, while former student activist Ei Thinzar Maung became deputy minister. Aung Myo Min, former director of the Human Rights Education Institute of Burma/Equality Myanmar, was appointed Minister for Human Rights.[6] The NUG works with the NLD's representative to the UN, and has appointed new representatives in various countries and regions, as detailed subsequently.

The military first banned the CRPH and 'affiliated committees' under the Unlawful Associations Act and later declared both the CRPH and the NUG terrorist groups under the Counter-Terrorism Law. Since then, political opposition members have operated from remote locations, often EAO-controlled areas, while more than 100 others remain detained. Aung San Suu Kyi has been held practically incommunicado but appeared in military court periodically, where she was given multiple prison sentences. After calling for an election boycott, the NLD was dissolved by the military in March 2023. On the international level, both the NUG and the CDM have been nominated for the Nobel Peace Prize. The NUG, which gets most of its income from fundraising by activists and the diaspora, has been able to fund a small percentage of the CDM participants. According to the NUG Minister of Defence (quoted in Ye Myo Hein, 2022) the NUG had raised over $55 million dollars by November 2022, which it spent mostly to support armed resistance forces.[7] It has also established a mobile payment system called NUGPay to distribute donations to local activists and uses lotteries, taxes and shares in property as sources of fundraising (International Crisis Group, 2022).

## Armed opposition after the 2021 coup

As military violence increased in the months after the coup, the CRPH declared that civilians had the right to armed resistance. In response, many protestors started organizing themselves. On 5 May 2021, the NUG announced the creation of People's Defence Forces (PDFs), in order to organize the mostly young protestors who had turned to armed resistance in the face of military brutality. On 7 September, it announced a People's Defensive War. This inspired further attacks against the military throughout the country and an unprecedented number of guerrilla attacks in urban areas such as Yangon, Mandalay and Naypyidaw (Ye Myo Hein, 2022). The PDFs reportedly comprise three types of resistance groups: the larger PDFs which are recognized by the NUG and EAOs, Local Defence Forces (LDFs), which operate on the local level and are partly linked to the NUG, and People's

Defence Teams (PaKhaPha), which are characterized as localized guerrilla units formed by the NUG (Ye Myo Hein, 2022). The total number of PDF and LDF troops as of 2023 was estimated at 95,000 (of which 65,000 under NUG command) and 30,000 respectively (Connelly & Loong 2023). While PDFs are active in 250 out of 330 Myanmar townships, resistance is strongest in the central Sagaing and Magway regions.

Although some PDFs maintain links with the NUG, their forms, visions and functions often differ. PDF operations are hampered by weak centralized command and ineffective management of the already limited available resources (Ye Myo Hein, 2022). They lack armaments comparable to those of the Myanmar military, which receives a steady flow of heavy weaponry from international partners such as China, India and Russia. Yet the PDFs have a strong advantage in terms of troop morale as well as public support when compared to the military, which has seen a loss in both morale and manpower (Ye Myo Hein, 2022). PDFs and other guerrilla groups have stepped up their fight against the military, carrying out bomb attacks around military bases and offices, as well as assassinations of people suspected (rightly or wrongly) of being associated with the military (Bynum, 2021; Reny, 2022; Ye Myo Hein, 2022). The implications of these attacks, which often occurred in the centres of large cities, will be discussed later in the chapter. While the PDFs and the EAOs together claim control over a significant section of the country's territory, such claims are difficult to verify and remain contested between activists and observers.

The military retaliated against the armed resistance by seizing the houses and properties of suspected resistance fighters and detaining their family members. It also formed its own urban militias and death squads (Bynum, 2021; Ye Myo Hein, 2022). While initially deploying mostly released criminals, the military increasingly mobilized militia groups to attack members and supporters of the NLD, the NUG and the PDFs and their families. In April 2022, it announced the formation of the Thway Thout Ah-Pwe (Blood-sworn group) militia, which tortured and killed dozens of NLD members in its first weeks of existence and shared pictures of the victims on social media (Maung, 2022). One significant militia is the Pyu Saw Htee, which consists of former members of the nationalist Buddhist organization MaBaTha (Min Zaw Oo and Tønnesson, 2023; Thiha & Nilsen 2023). The monk Wirathu, who had played a large role in distributing hate speech about Muslims in earlier years, publicly pledged support for the SAC, while responses by other monks have been mixed and largely low profile (Thu Thu Aung and McPherson, 2022; International Crisis Group, 2023a). Analysts warn that the country is becoming 'locked in a cycle of violence' and is at risk of territorial fragmentation, as various parties continue to fight each other with no overarching coordinating or intervening actor in sight (Ye Myo Hein, 2022). The coup and the post-coup resistance movements have created a legal vacuum in which security is either absent or in the hands of the military and other armed forces. Consequently, individual security and adherence to human rights remain at the discretion of power holders, either from the side of the military or from the various opposition forces.

## Contested representation within the opposition

Generation Z openly resisted the NLD's party politics, which had revolved largely around party loyalty and had disappointed many young people and ethnic nationalities (Jordt et al, 2021). The situation after the coup opened up the space for new activists to come forward. The quickly growing, visible influence of this new youth movement also prompted adaptations among politicians of older generations. The CRPH and NUG took steps to increase cooperation with ethnic nationality organizations. On 17 March 2021, they decriminalized all EAOs and instead declared the Myanmar military to be terrorist, given that it was responsible for most of the indiscriminate violence throughout the country (Loong, 2021; David et al, 2022). Next, the CRPH recognized the NLD's past failure to stand up for the rights of minorities: first through the previously mentioned statement by Susanna Hla Hla Soe, and later by issuing a formal policy paper which promised justice and citizenship to Rohingya in the future (David et al, 2022: 103). The NUG also appointed an advisor to deal with the question of Rohingya citizenship, as well as accountability for the crimes committed against them (APHR, 2022; Moe Thuzar, 2022). In July 2023, it appointed Aung Kyaw Moe as its first Rohingya representative in the position of deputy Human Rights Minister.[8]

Despite these efforts, the NUG and CRPH have come under criticism for their lack of inclusiveness of both ethnic nationalities and young people. Although it appointed former youth activist Ei Thinzar Maung as deputy minister, NUG membership exists predominantly of people over 35 years old (Su Mon Thant, 2021). Concerns were also raised about NUG members, including Aung San Suu Kyi and two ministers, who were known defenders of the military violence against the Rohingya in 2017. In online events and other media outlets, Rohingya representatives and their advocates complained that the Rohingya are increasingly forgotten in reporting on post-coup developments, from the release of political prisoners which tends to exclude imprisoned Rohingya, to the continued marginalization of Rohingya refugees and IDPs in Bangladesh and Rakhine State. The appointment of Aung Kyaw Moe mid-2023 may be viewed as a response to this critique. Other ethnic nationality representatives within the NUG include the acting President Duwa Lashi La, who is Kachin; Prime Minister Mahn Win Khaing Than, who is Karen; and several appointed Ministers. Yet critics contend that the NUG prioritizes unity over genuine concern for diverse interests (Myo Min, 2022; see also Walton, 2015a on the 'disciplining discourse of unity in Burmese politics').

Different motives can be identified among youth activists as well. Su Mon Thant (2021) distinguishes between democrats, federalists and intersectionalists. The democrats' aspirations are closest to the 2020 electoral victory of the NLD – they therefore aim for maximum local, regional and international recognition of the NUG. Federalists do not wish to return to the outcome of the 2020 elections but seek the creation of a new federal political system to replace the one that existed prior to the coup. This group, which hails mostly from ethnic nationality communities, does not necessarily trust or support the CRPH and the NUG, given the Burman reluctance to support federalism in the past. Intersectionalists aspire both a federal system and a regime that supports universal human rights, including gender equality and rights for sexual and religious minorities. The three groups share the aspiration of ending military rule but otherwise differ in their envisioned future for the country.[9] This makes coordination or centralized decision making among opposition members more complex.

Ethnic nationalities have also been divided in their response to the coup and the resistance that emerged in its wake (Ye Myo Hein, 2022). EAOs in Chin, Kachin, Karen and Kayah States have been strongest in their resistance to the coup. These groups are known for their close connections to broad civilian constituencies (Vrieze, 2023: 11). The KNU protected both Karen protesters and other fleeing activists, including participants in the CDM and members of the NLD, in the areas under its control. Other Nationwide Ceasefire Agreement signatories which had already been more divided in their approach towards the military such as the Mon, the Pa-O and some Shan groups stayed mostly quiet, presumably as a survival strategy (Vrieze, 2023). A number of armed groups in Rakhine and Shan States, including the United Wa State Army, refrained from supporting the resistance altogether, and some initiated peace talks with the military (APHR, 2022). Among ethnic nationality politicians, a small group openly supported the resistance; as a result, they had to leave their parties to avoid retaliation by the military (Vrieze, 2023: 18). Ethnic human rights organizations such as the Karen Human Rights Group were more independent in their reporting on human rights violations from various sides than the EAOs with which they are affiliated (Loong, 2021; Matelski et al, 2022).

Debates about responses to the coup differ not only between EAOs, but also within them. High-level KNU members have publicly disagreed on the desired response but nevertheless managed to act in a coherent manner (Ye Myo Hein, 2022). In Mon State too, debates over the preferred strategy continued. The Mon Unity Party has cooperated with the military, while other Mon leaders, including within the party itself, strongly disagreed (Min

Naing Soon, 2021). Lastly, significant gaps exist between ordinary citizens and elites among the ethnic communities (Jangai Jap, 2021). Ever since the peace process, political and business elites among the EAOs, just like their Burman counterparts, have been able to benefit from their position, including access to resources and political and economic interactions with the Myanmar military (Loong, 2021). Thus, the process of 'ceasefire capitalism' identified in earlier decades continues in Myanmar (Woods, 2011, 2017). Jangai Jap (2021) rightly draws attention to the intersection of ethnicity and class when she argues that '[p]olitical behaviors of an ethnic minority person are not determined by their minority experiences only but rather by [a] myriad of identities they hold'. A study conducted in 2021 on the position of ethnic minority women in CSOs shows that gender, age or generation and education level can be added to this list of intersecting identities (Matelski and Nang Muay Noan, 2022).

## Contested international legitimacy

At the time of writing, the NUG and affiliated bodies are struggling for legitimacy on various levels. They need to demonstrate to young people that they do not aim to return to the situation under previous governments, where their voices were not heard. They must convince the ethnic nationalities that they take their voices and demands seriously, even in case of future NLD rule, while maintaining support from those who voted for the NLD in the 2015 and 2020 elections. Many stakeholders wonder what the future of the democracy movement will look like, and whether the political opposition will succeed in being more inclusive of youth, ethnic and other minorities than in the past.

The opposition is also fighting for legitimacy on the international level, from online webinars to the UN General Assembly. After the coup, Myanmar's ambassador to the UN, Kyaw Moe Tun, pledged support to the opposition and aligned himself with the NUG (Moe Thuzar, 2022). The military sought to replace him but as of mid-2023 had been unsuccessful in doing so. The UN Credentials Committee postponed the decision on the representation of Myanmar within the General Assembly, and activists started a campaign for the UN to accept an NUG representative instead. As a consequence of the stalemate in UN representation, however, individual states have been left to decide how to deal with the SAC and the NUG, both of which claim to represent the Myanmar people (APHR, 2022). As the situation remained unclear to the international community, some states and UN bodies started communicating with the military about ongoing matters, while many Western parliamentarians pledged public support for the NUG. In October 2021, the French Senate (but not the government) publicly recognized the NUG and CRPH as legitimate representatives of

Myanmar. The European Parliament did the same, and in December 2022 invited NUG Minister Aung Myo Min for formal meetings. In November 2022, the NUG was allowed to open a diplomatic representative office in Washington, DC, and in December, the US House of Representatives passed a National Defense Authorization Act which pledges the provision of non-military assistance to both EAOs and PDFs in Myanmar.

Other international actors, particularly UN agencies, were less forthcoming in meeting the wishes of the opposition. Local CSOs were particularly appalled that UN agencies such as the Office for the Coordination of Humanitarian Affairs, the United Nations Children's Fund, the Food and Agriculture Organization and the International Organization for Migration decided to present credentials to the SAC in order to be allowed to continue operations (APHR, 2022). In September 2022, over 600 CSOs wrote a letter to the UN Secretary-General to oppose UN entities that 'legitimize' the military by entering into letters of agreements and Memoranda of Understanding (MOUs).[10] The CSOs feared that perceived public recognition for the military would be used to strengthen its legitimacy in the country. When UN Special Envoy Noeleen Heyzer visited Myanmar in August 2022 she was unable to meet with any political opposition forces or civil society members, and her visit was presented in state propaganda as a sign of UN acceptance (APHR, 2022); in 2023 she resigned from her position. A visit of former UN Secretary-General Ban Ki-Moon in April 2023 on behalf of The Elders (an independent group of global leaders founded by Nelson Mandela) generated a similar result, as he was photographed extensively with military leadership while the military continued its airstrikes on civilian targets in the ethnic states. Contestations also played out around the international courts where cases have been brought against the Myanmar state or individual military representatives. The NUG has stated its support for the International Criminal Court (ICC) and its intention to accept its jurisdiction over Myanmar. In contrast, the military continued sending its own representatives to International Court of Justice (ICJ) hearings, who were accepted as state representatives despite some military leaders being on the international sanctions list.

## International responses and the search for global recognition

The anti-coup protests were initially reported extensively in international media, largely due to the images emerging from citizen journalists and local activists. As violence continued and internet access diminished, however, Myanmar largely disappeared from the international news. The Taliban reclaimed large parts of Afghanistan in August 2021, and Russia invaded Ukraine in February 2022, two significant developments that for months made international headlines. At a film festival organized by Amnesty International in The Hague in April 2022, extra screenings were added of the documentary on Russian opposition leader Alexei Navalny, whereas the screenings of *Myanmar Diaries*, a documentary on the aftermath of the 2021 military coup, drew a very small audience. Solidarity protests in Amsterdam showed a similar pattern. Meanwhile, protestors in Myanmar also started carrying banners expressing solidarity with Ukraine and other repressive situations throughout the world. By mid-2022, the human rights situations in Qatar (where the football World Cup was held) and in Iran (where protests emerged in September) received extensive news coverage, and women worldwide cut their hair to show their support of (female) protestors in Iran.

Myanmar, meanwhile, had lost its 'human rights icon' Aung San Suu Kyi since the violence against the Rohingya, as well as the initial international interest sparked by the popular protests in 2021. The military succeeded in banning the majority of independent foreign journalists and frustrating the work of local journalists who remained in the country, although citizen journalists continued to share reports of local developments. I was contacted repeatedly by Dutch media who wanted to report on Myanmar; in a series on forgotten conflicts, and in response to the air strike of 11 April 2023, for example. Yet none of these enquiries after 2021 resulted in news items, as I was informed that access to information had proven difficult and the airstrike had quickly been "overtaken by other news". Western media largely used the detention of their own citizens as a hook, such as Australian academic Sean Turnell who was released after almost two years in prison, and former UK ambassador Vicky Bowman, head of the Myanmar Centre for Responsible Business, who was detained for a number of months in 2022 with her Myanmar husband. UN Special Rapporteur on Myanmar Tom Andrews and former rapporteur Yanghee Lee continued to raise the situation in international platforms but came to the conclusion that the world had failed Myanmar (Lee, 2022). Yanghee Lee co-founded the Special Advisory Council for Myanmar (with a somewhat unfortunate similar acronym to the post-coup military), a solidarity and advocacy group consisting of 'international experts working to support the peoples of Myanmar in their fight for human rights, peace, democracy, justice and accountability'.[11]

While activists in Myanmar had initially called for the Responsibility to Protect (R2P) to be invoked in response to military violence, they soon came to the realization that no international actors would come to their aid. They urged individual countries to join the Gambia in its case at the ICJ, or to start their own universal jurisdiction as Argentina had done earlier. In webinars, activists expressed their deep disappointment with the international community as well as with former aid and business partners who they felt had abandoned them. Protest banners were often written in English to be shared with an international audience via (social) media. Initially, they referred mainly to the desire for democracy and the wish to have their votes respected. Later, they started appealing to the international community by requesting an intervention, or at least material support for their struggle. After nearly a year of international inaction, the messages became more cynical regarding international involvement. When the UN Secretary General issued a statement condemning the execution of four activists in July 2022, a Kachin activist wrote on Twitter: 'We stand in solidarity with the UN for feeling sorry for us. Take your time, we still have millions of people still alive.'[12]

Although sanctions were imposed on the military, they were limited in scope. The European Union and individual European governments re-instated a number of sanctions that had been in place before the political transition, and trade and travel restrictions were imposed on military leaders of the SAC and their businesses. Embargoes imposed on the UN level remained non-binding. In June 2021 the General Assembly adopted a resolution calling on all member states to prevent the flow of arms into Myanmar, but Security Council members China and Russia abstained from voting and continued their trade relations with the military, including large-scale supply of weapons. In September 2022, a report commissioned by the UN Human Rights Council (2022) was released which called for more state efforts to cut the military's access to arms and revenue. However, all these measures lack enforcement mechanisms, and the international community had its hands full with Russia's warfare against Ukraine. After the coup, a number of prominent international companies such as the beer manufacturer Kirin and the French TotalEnergies left Myanmar, though some argued this happened rather late, given the history of human rights violations especially around energy projects. Unfortunately, many of the departing companies failed to take responsibility for the people they left behind. Most garment workers lost their jobs, and the Norwegian company Telenor sold its telecom services, including sensitive information on activists, to a Lebanese investor which transferred part of its oversight to a Myanmar company with strong ties to the military. The United States took the lead in continuing to impose new sanctions on Myanmar throughout 2021-23.

As previously stated, people in Myanmar have long had higher expectations of international actors and partners than of the military. As academic Mary Callahan (quoted in Nhu Truong, 2022) stated after the coup, 'people in Myanmar fear being forgotten or ignored by the world even more than they fear a bullet'. Neighbouring states, however, have not been able to help either, as Bangladesh and Thailand periodically attempt to push back refugees, and the Association of Southeast Asian Nations (ASEAN) fails to take a decisive stance against the Myanmar military, despite the efforts of Indonesian and Malaysian representatives. ASEAN initially insisted on a five-point consensus;

when the military did not meet any of the demands, its representatives were barred from attending subsequent ASEAN meetings. However, economic and political relations with individual ASEAN members continue, and some voted against an arms embargo on Myanmar in the UN General Assembly.

As in previous eras, such as in the aftermath of cyclone Nargis in 2008 and the Rakhine conflict in 2014, aid in Myanmar has again become compromised and politicized. As of late 2022, an estimated 15 million people inside the country, including over 1 million IDPs, were in need of humanitarian assistance (APHR, 2022), and the number is expected to exceed 17 million by 2023. Yet the military closed off areas to aid organizations, demanded a percentage of their support and even carried out attacks against aid workers. Examples include the violent attacks in Kayah State in December 2021 and March 2022, which killed local staff members of Save the Children and of the local organization Free Burma Rangers. As access decreased and the risks increased for international aid workers, humanitarian assistance was mostly left to local actors close to the ground, including members of the CDM (Slim, 2022). In May 2023, a new cyclone named Mocha swept western Myanmar, and the military again restricted the work of humanitarian aid organizations (Schlein, 2023).

Donors to CSOs reacted to the military coup with a combination of cautious assistance and withdrawal. Apart from those that signed MOUs with ministries acting under control of the military, foreign donors according to respondents became more conservative in their activities and partnerships in Myanmar. Western donor assistance was spent mostly through pre-existing contacts and in areas with an established (I)NGO presence such as Rakhine State, rather than through new actors that had emerged in the post-coup period. As before the transition, donor representatives were reluctant to speak out publicly against the military for fear of losing access. Civil society representatives argued, however, that a neutral position in post-coup Myanmar could be equated to support for the military, as it controlled most formal platforms. They also warned against leaving the risks of local aid delivery mostly to local organizations and their staff, who already had lower budgets and more to lose. A civil society representative commented in a webinar in October 2022 that for local organizations, partnering with an international organization had become "almost a daydream".[13]

Donors faced practical difficulties getting their funding to local respondents, such as the high inflation in the country and the local banking crisis. The new registration law for (I)NGOs announced in October 2022 further complicated the relationship between foreign donors and local organizations. Some organizations decided to relocate to the Thai border, although critics argued that many of the populations with the highest needs, such as those in central Myanmar, would not be reached through that route. Others operated on a dual scheme, with low-profile operations inside the country and interaction with ethnic nationalities and international partners mostly outside the country. Some local organizations considered disbanding, in order to avoid making the choice between collaborating with military–run ministries or risking significant prison sentences.

Since the coup, CSOs inside and outside the country have organized regular online events to draw attention to the plight of the opposition movement. Framing of the situation in Myanmar centres on denial of legitimacy for the military, ranging from contestations over its territory, to consistent reference to the coup as attempted, failed, or unconstitutional. The elections initially announced for 2023 were referred to as 'sham' or unrealistic (given that millions of people are displaced, and the military controls only part of the country), and the military itself is called *sit-tat* rather than the more honorary *tatmadaw* used in previous years. Transnational activists have run a number of campaigns, ranging from recognition of the NUG before the UN and the ICC, to campaigns for sanctions on military companies (the so-called Blood Money campaign), and calls to ban aviation fuel to Myanmar (since only the military has airpower). Calls for an election boycott have also surfaced, although it has been difficult to campaign around this given the absence of an anticipated election date (International Crisis Group, 2023b). As in earlier years, activists have used these campaigns partly to keep international attention on the ongoing human rights violations in Myanmar amid new global crisis situations.

## Avoiding the blame game?

As the post-coup situation in Myanmar continues without a clear winner in sight, it becomes increasingly tempting for involved actors to point fingers. While the military remains the main culprit in everyone's view except its own, opinions on the desired role of the NUG and the PDFs vary widely. Observers accused the PDFs of contributing to instability by staging attacks in public areas which in some cases led to civilian casualties, with or without alleged connections to the military. Accidents with land mines and other explosive devices were increasingly common, and some PDFs publicly accepted responsibility for possible civilian deaths. Incidents include the killing of 21 local inhabitants by a PDF group in Sagaing Region in November 2021, including ten of its own members, after which the NUG announced an investigation (Radio Free Asia, 2022). In October 2022, eight people were killed and 18 others injured when a bomb exploded at the entrance of Insein prison in Yangon. Among the casualties were family members of (political) prisoners. Respondents in 2022 spoke of increased lawlessness, extortion practices and fear of 'so-called revolutionists' taking advantage of the situation to retaliate against personal enemies under the guise of resistance against military associates or informants. Such incidents increase the feelings of insecurity in Myanmar's central cities and bring the levels of fear closer to those experienced by ethnic nationalities in conflict areas. Critics argue that the PDFs need to be better trained and should establish codes of conduct similar to the more experienced EAOs in order to avoid casualties among bystanders.

Activists have countered criticism on the use of armed force by the PDFs, arguing that they merely respond to large-scale violence conducted by the military. Moreover, they point out that despite repeated requests, and in contrast to Ukraine, they have hardly received any international support, let alone weapons (Ye Myo Hein and Myers, 2022). Others show concern that the plight of the ethnic nationalities, including the Rohingya, will again become secondary to the focus on Burman protestors. Despite violence having spread to central Myanmar after the coup, populations in the ethnic border areas continue to suffer more and more intense consequences of armed conflict and repression of cultural and religious life (Loong, 2021). The CRPH, the NUCC, the NUG and the NLD certainly have a long process of introspection ahead of them in terms of interaction with various minorities and the future of their federalist aspirations, regardless of the role of the military. The abolition of the 2008 constitution continues to be a vital demand for most ethnic groups, as they fear that, in the words of a Kachin commander (quoted in Loong, 2021: 20), "whosoever in power, under this constitution they will become a dictator".

## Debating ways forward and the role of international observers

The severely restricted access to the country since the 2021 military coup and the many lives and livelihoods that are at stake have made it difficult to hold well-informed discussions about the current situation and the future of Myanmar. Nevertheless, the preceding COVID-19 crisis had helped transfer discussions partly to online platforms. This continued after the coup in the form of webinars and online conferences, which allowed people from inside Myanmar to participate. Emotions ran high during those discussions, especially in the first months after the coup, as participants from Myanmar conveyed their personal losses and the sacrifices they themselves and their family, friends and colleagues had to make in the post-coup situation, as well as their feelings of survivor's guilt. Faced with these emotions, foreign participants sometimes became very quiet as they felt powerless and unable to give adequate assistance or reassurance to their Myanmar contacts. Some local activists criticized foreign 'self-proclaimed experts' analysing post-coup scenarios, a hypothetical undertaking that was far removed from the needs and experiences of people who suffer violence, repression and poverty on a daily basis. They also expressed disappointment with their Western contacts who had entered the country during the transition in search of opportunities but had become quiet in the years since the COVID-19 pandemic and the coup, or had simply shifted attention to other contexts. Two young academics, Chu May Paing and Than Toe Aung (2021), have been sharing their critique of Westerners with long-term engagement in Myanmar, stating that 'just because they have spent all their lives living in Burma, researching Burma, learning the language(s), loving the food, and taking Burmese names, it does not mean they share our pain'. The overarching sentiment is that local voices continue to be underrepresented in international platforms, whether on the policy level or in academia (see Metro, 2023).[14] Equal criticism has been raised of Burmese 'political intellectuals' who have often been trained abroad and now advocate neutrality and dialogue with the military (Banyar Aung, 2022).

Observers with long-term experience in Myanmar, however, also faced challenges discussing their concerns about the post-coup situation. Based on their understanding of the country, some had strong doubts about the opposition's claims regarding the amount of territory under its control, or the assertion that the revolution was bound to succeed. Their counter-arguments related to the material strength of the military compared to armed opposition groups, the limited capacity and coordination efforts of the resistance forces, and the general security situation, which could potentially result in protracted civil war rather than a peaceful federal democracy. Some even called for dialogue with the military to be resumed, though in a tactical manner that would not convey additional legitimacy towards the SAC. However nuanced, such views went against the preferences of more activist-oriented scholars, who viewed this as a zero-sum game in which one simply had to side with either the military, as represented by the SAC, or the people, as represented by the NUG and various opposition forces.

With its pervasive violence and restrictive laws on civic space and association, the military has again succeeded in narrowing the space for open dialogue and fostering the construction of adversaries and framing disputes as discussed in earlier chapters. However, the developments within civil society during the earlier years of transition and the increased internet access and use of social media means that at least more voices than before can be heard in international platforms. Even activists on the run can often still participate from their safe houses, despite occasional connection issues. Their calls for solidarity are clearly conveyed to those willing to listen, as they continue expressing their views on the desired future of Myanmar and their hope not to be forgotten by the international community.

# Conclusion

This book has explored the forms and functions of organized civil society as it developed before, during and after Myanmar's political transition period between 2011 and 2020. Starting from the pre-2010 era, when the country was relatively isolated and civil society presumed largely absent, I traced back the origins of some of the organizations and movements that became visible to outside observers in the early years of political transition. I showed that both welfare organizations and democracy activists that gained prominence in the 1990s have partial roots in forces that emerged around independence from British colonialism. The military's top-down 'Roadmap to Democracy' from 2003 onwards generated opportunities for some civil society actors to engage more openly in political debates, especially around the three national elections that were held between 2010 and 2020. As this book testifies, some people in Myanmar experienced increased room to manoeuvre, while others, particularly in the ethnic areas, saw their opportunities decreasing. The military coup of February 2021 brought an end to this decade of political transition, and the resistance in response to renewed violent repression led to the emergence of a number of younger and more progressive groups that sought out new alliances both within and beyond Myanmar.

When discussing the forms and functions of civil society, this book has focused on two types of contestation. The first, which dominates the country's modern history, is contested political power and resistance against the military, both in central Myanmar and in the ethnic border regions. The impact of over five decades of military rule on the country and its (civil) society cannot be overstated. The formally military-ruled era from 1962 until 2010 and the power struggle between the military, the people and their elected representatives which has intensified since 2021 have been characterized by widespread repression, violence and destruction of the economy and social services. A series of repressive laws, some of which stemmed from colonial times, criminalized most forms of civic association from the 1960s onwards, while organizations that continued to operate often worked under the radar and were subject to intrusive surveillance. The arbitrary application of rules and the absence of an independent judiciary made people in Myanmar subject to the whims of the military, leading to widespread fear, distrust and self-censorship. Significant popular uprisings in 1988, 1996 and 2007 and the presence of armed resistance movements in the ethnic regions resulted in further repression and an increase in the number of refugees and political prisoners.

The political transition process from 2010, which was initiated from above but eagerly seized upon by civil society, brought various actors the opportunity to step up their social and political activities and allowed some dissidents to return from exile. The enthusiasm around these changes in central Myanmar and internationally was not shared by those in the border areas who continued to be marginalized, particularly as some of the previous ceasefires in the ethnic states broke down. While Aung San Suu Kyi and her National League for Democracy (NLD) party managed to return to politics in 2012 and won the 2015 elections, violence broke out which targeted mostly Muslim minorities. The Rohingya particularly fell victim to renewed military violence in the early years of NLD rule, and Aung San Suu Kyi lost her reputation as a human rights icon in the eyes of Western audiences while trying to defend the military. This period after 2015 also saw a further decrease in opportunities for civil society to engage with political actors and contribute to policy making. Meanwhile dissidents, particularly those opposing large-scale development projects and land confiscation, were again pushed to the margins. The international community maintained a largely one-sided focus first on the political liberalization process and then on the plight of the Rohingya, and ignored the pleas of civil society actors who warned against uncritical engagement with the Myanmar government. New forms of resistance against the military since 2021 resulted in a brief period of international attention, particularly when masses of people took to the streets. Attention faded as soon as these public manifestations were suppressed, however, underscoring the argument in this book that international attention focuses too narrowly on formal political processes and displays of public dissent and overlooks more covert manifestations of civil society that may nevertheless contribute to social and political change.

The second type of contestation, perhaps less unique to Myanmar, concerns the question of who constitutes civil society in the eyes of both local and transnational actors. In the absence of responsive and accountable state entities, Western democracy and human rights promotion is often aimed at civil society organizations (CSOs) viewed as representative of the broader population. What emerges from my research, however, is an ambiguous picture of CSOs' ability to represent a population as vast and diverse as that of Myanmar. Despite a plethora of organizations active inside and outside the country, several sections of the population continued to feel underrepresented by prominent civil society spokespersons, who are often middle-aged Burman males with an urban background and relatively high education levels. This was the case for ethnic, religious, gender and sexual minorities but also for youth, and for those with intersecting minority identities such as young women in ethnic communities or organizations (Matelski and Nang Muay Noan, 2022). The transnational reach of the democracy movement provided some minorities the opportunity to emancipate their struggle by linking up with international movements around women's rights, indigenous peoples or the environment. Simultaneously, a new generation of civil society actors was able to increase its status by making use of opportunities for education and training provided by foreign supporters, especially when interest in local activism increased after the post-Nargis relief efforts in 2008.

Another development that underscores the importance of keeping an open eye towards manifestations of civil society concerns the rise in nationalist Buddhist movements during the political transition period. Although their goals diverged significantly from progressive civil society actors, MaBaTha (Organization for the Protection of Race and Religion) and related organizations undeniably had significant support among the Buddhist majority in Myanmar, to the surprise of some Western observers (Arnold and Turner, 2019). Their strong influence on political and policy processes in the country, such as the Race and Religion Laws passed in 2015 but also the close affiliation between some Buddhist and military leaders up to the present day, demonstrates the various forms that organized (un)civil society may take, but also the potential intertwining of state and non-state actors, including in the business sector. These and more benign forms of Buddhist organizations were not the focus of this book, and their identities and activities have been covered extensively elsewhere (Kyaw Yin Hlaing, 2008; Schober, 2011; Walton and Hayward, 2014; Walton, 2015b, 2016). Their significant influence in Myanmar and other majority Buddhist countries such as Sri Lanka should be taken into account, however, even if they do not meet Western expectations of civil society or do not adhere to Western conceptualizations of human rights.

This book shows that the preferred sequence and prioritization of social and political change differs widely among various actors who operate under the banner of Myanmar civil society. While the popular uprisings demonstrated the potential for large-scale dissent in the face of economic hardship and injustice, up to 2021 they were largely initiated by urban-based (former) students. These protestors may have voiced the concerns of many but often struggled to align their high-level political demands with the day-to-day needs of more marginalized sections of the population, for whom the practical outcomes of political changes had more immediate relevance. The post-coup protestors since 2021 faced different circumstances and had better access to social media, which allowed them to bring multiple voices and visions to the fore. Yet new democracy activists have similarly struggled to present a viable alternative to the military, as decades of divisions and distrust cannot be easily undone.

Related to this contestation over identity and representation is the professionalization of civil society as a result of transnational interactions. Several conjunctures in the country's recent history contributed to the institutionalization of civil society and its relationships with foreign supporters. The rising international interest in democracy assistance through civil society in the 1990s, for example, coincided with an increase in international non-governmental organization (INGO) activities in Myanmar as a result of the country opening up to the outside world, and the realization of ceasefires between the military and several ethnic armed organizations (EAOs). The imposition of sanctions by several Western countries, however, which were actively pursued by democracy activists and the political opposition led by Aung San Suu Kyi, limited the overall levels of development assistance to organizations inside the country, while government restrictions on politically motivated activities constrained external efforts aimed at democracy promotion. Up to the late 2000s, therefore, a large proportion of financial and political assistance for Myanmar was distributed to activists and refugees in exile.

The occurrence of cyclone Nargis in 2008 and the elections organized in 2010 marked the start of a redirection of Western support to less antagonistic civil society actors, who made use of new opportunities to contribute to gradual social and political change. In this context, civil society actors selectively framed their message in order to keep the situation in Myanmar on the international agenda. These framing efforts concerned the questions of who could legitimately represent the wishes of the people of Myanmar, how the political changes that were occurring should be evaluated, and what responses were desired from the international community. In the course of the political transition, donors shifted funds and attention towards governmental initiatives such as institution building and a resumption of the contentious peace process, while organizations with a more critical stance, as well as populations in the border areas, lost some of their support. These developments were partly reversed after the 2021 military coup, as local organizations again had to go under the radar or operate from exile in order to survive. Some organizations felt abandoned as donors imposed unrealistic expectations on them after the coup, forced them to cooperate with the military, or simply dismantled their operations in the country. While the overall impression of Western donors among respondents in this study has been positive compared to the military, this does not absolve them from taking the responsibility that comes with being a powerful political and economic actor in the country. This chapter therefore presents not only theoretical insights, but also a number of recommendations for donors.

# Identifying civil society in repressive environments

This book focuses on the early years of the political transition period and ends just over two years after the military coup of February 2021. By exploring the forms and functions of civil society in Myanmar and in exile over time, it seeks to make a number of contributions to the debate about independent civil society in repressive environments which may be of use to academics, donors and policy makers working in similar contexts. First, I refute the claim made by some researchers and activists that no independent civil society existed in Myanmar during military rule. Such misguided assumptions resulted from narrow Western expectations that civil society can and should speak out publicly against oppression, but also from local organizations' attempts to stay under the radar of the government, and from the prominent position of politicized (and often exiled) activists in international debates.

In reality, social welfare and cultural organizations have existed parallel to an activist democracy movement that sought to bring down the military government, but their informal structures and focus on the local level made them less visible to outside observers. I describe the ways such actors manoeuvred between the restrictions and opportunities provided by various actors during the political transition such as the Myanmar government, democracy activists and foreign donors. Local organizations inside the country strategically adapted their activities and affiliations to the unpredictable circumstances on the ground, including the sudden onset of political change and the corresponding increase in international attention. Although overall these organizations were hindered rather than helped by the authorities, some nevertheless managed to establish productive working relationships on various levels, while maintaining some operational independence. This was not the case for organizations that adopted a more openly confrontational stance towards the government, which mostly encountered repression. These findings indicate the importance of researching civil society based on actual daily experiences rather than relying on formal registration numbers or other public indicators.

In academic literature on civil society in repressive circumstances, two contrary approaches can be identified. One measures civil society vibrancy by the occurrence of (successful) popular uprisings, while the other presumes civil society under repressive rule to advance primarily through co-optation by, or close interaction with the authorities. As I demonstrate, each approach has its shortcomings in describing the functioning of civil society in contemporary Myanmar. Popular uprisings, at least until the 2021 coup, have arguably been regarded too much as an end goal, rather than a means to achieve long-term social and political change. Many Burmese CSOs and political opposition groups spent more time identifying problems and culprits than envisioning a future for the country. In contrast, research that focuses on common forms of association in repressive environments finds that authorities may be influenced more successfully through cooperation and strategic clientelism than through outright opposition. In authoritarian Myanmar too, many CSOs conduct part or all of their activities outside the view of the state, report on their activities selectively or in disguised terminology, and seek to placate the relevant authorities by granting them symbolic roles, tokens of appreciation or actual assistance. Academic approaches focused on such collaborations, however, tend to ignore the more activist section of society that is frequently presumed to be non-existent, but in fact has been forcibly restricted to a position in exile or in hiding, and may be visible mostly in online activism. Since the 2021 coup, as in earlier decades, many Myanmar dissidents have again had to flee or ended up in prison.

More importantly, perhaps, academic approaches focused on collaborative relations over-emphasize the 'mutual need' and underestimate the 'mutual suspicion' that Spires (2011) identifies as constituting a relationship of 'contingent symbiosis' between civil society and the government. While respondents during the political transition could and did achieve significant concessions by strategically liaising with authorities on various levels, the foundations of such cooperation remained unstable, with activities being approved one day and prohibited the next. Abrupt leadership changes, moreover, such as General Khin Nyunt's removal from power in 2004, the political power shifts between 2011 and 2020 and the military coup of 2021 significantly impacted personal relationships that had been carefully built up over time. The ability for civil society actors to have a durable influence within a repressive environment should therefore be neither underestimated nor overestimated but assessed within the particular local and temporal context.

Overall, it has been the Myanmar government, and by extension mostly the military, that has influenced civil society's room to manoeuvre. Since 2010, successive governments have organized elections, decided the fates of political prisoners, adapted the rules for political participation, introduced regulations pertaining to freedom of speech and association, and initiated peace talks with EAOs. Concessions granted were often arbitrary and conditional rather than secured by law and could be revoked at any time, while existing laws were applied selectively. Organizations and activists that operated in a ceasefire zone one moment could be thrown back to armed conflict the next, and political activists in central Myanmar faced similarly unpredictable circumstances, particularly after the 2021 military coup.

A balanced picture of civil society under repressive rule must take into account the aspiration of short- and long-term goals, of revolutionary and pragmatic pathways to change, and of more and less visible actors. A selective focus on either of these is likely to play into the agendas of repressive states or of certain foreign or local actors that seek to benefit from developments in the political or economic sphere. In conclusion, I endorse calls from researchers on civil society operating in other restrictive environments such as China and Vietnam to look beyond public manifestations of associational life such as formal registration or popular uprisings (Howell, 2007; Hsu, 2010; Spires, 2011; Wells-Dang, 2012; Salmenkari, 2013) but reject conceptualizations of civil society in which there is no room for critical voices, or in which politically motivated action is perceived as entirely externally inspired. By showing both manifestations of civil society in Myanmar, this book aims to diminish the 'theoretical poverty' that Salmenkari (2013) identified in relation to Chinese civil society, but which arguably applies to the Southeast Asian region as a whole (see Weiss and Hansson, 2023). This is especially relevant as many countries in the region have experienced democratic backsliding in recent years (Spires and Ogawa, 2022).

## Policy recommendations for donors

Donors wishing to support civil society actors striving towards democracy or development will have to accept that their local partners have various identities, goals and strategies and should rely on thorough context analysis for a detailed understanding of local power relations. While many donors prefer to work with 'moderate' sections of civil society whose views on political change are expressed in terms that are compatible with Western priorities, it must be kept in mind that civil society's ability to express and act on its political views is partly conditional on the room granted by the government (and sometimes donors) to operate. Moderate actors often have more room to manoeuvre than actors with dissenting political or economic views, who nevertheless raise important points in relation to human rights promotion and protection. Moreover, a one-sided focus on partial improvements during political transition risks overlooking populations who may in fact be worse off, such as ethnic minorities but also many of the women, youth and working classes underrepresented in formal civil society or operating in areas and sectors at risk of exploitation by local and international elites. Throughout Myanmar's political transition period, both the military and the former NLD government attempted to exclude or silence more critical sections of civil society, which emphasizes the need for external facilitation of dissent. It also shows the importance of looking beyond the occurrence of elections to assess the full extent of democratic progress in the country, as well as potential risk factors. The occurrence of the 2021 military coup has made this painfully clear.

In the course of the political transition period, donors were quick to reward Myanmar's liberalization by redirecting attention and resources from civil society to state actors. This shift had some questionable consequences, such as the training of future human rights abusers or the depoliticization of the peace process. After the 2021 coup, large donors again prioritized INGO partners and in some cases gave credentials to the military in order to be allowed to operate and distribute aid throughout the country. Given the controversial donor spending in previous decades, civil society actors have understandably been very critical of such interactions. Donors who feel they need to establish relations with illegitimate governments in order to secure humanitarian access should be very careful about the way these interactions are depicted and interpreted by various stakeholders, in order not to appear as pawns of repressive power holders.

In a society as deeply divided and traumatized as Myanmar, the importance of building trust cannot be overestimated. Trusted local contacts should be cherished and not bypassed if situations deteriorate. Donors and intermediaries that simply enter a community, distribute products and then leave encourage local actors to focus on short-term benefits rather than lasting change. In formulating reporting requirements for local recipients, moreover, restrictions on travel, communication, registration and administration must be taken into account. Donor commitment to sectors that will help the population in a durable manner, such as education, environmental sustainability and responsible investment, is essential for the realization of inclusive growth. Such investments are perhaps difficult, but not impossible in circumstances of renewed repression, and local actors are best placed to indicate the possibilities and limitations when interacting with donors. Local agencies such as the Pandita Development Institute (2022) have been providing concrete suggestions on how donors can best work with local advocacy organizations in Myanmar.

Donors that choose to offer capacity building trainings should avoid duplicating programmes with the most popular and easy to reach representatives of civil society. Local organizations that to Westerners appear unorganized and incoherent may actually know more about dynamics on the ground than 'donor darlings' claiming to speak for the population as a whole. A trickle-down effect of capacity building beyond the elite level should not automatically be assumed but actively fostered by distributing resources equally among various sections of the population. Capacity building should be aimed at the development of long-term, locally relevant capacities rather than socializing trainees into Western donor priorities and practices. Western donors and INGOs should value experienced domestic actors with knowledge of the local context at least as much as external consultants that are brought in to provide technical expertise, by granting them responsibility for financial and strategic decision making. Consultation with civil society, whether by donors, governments or companies, should be treated as more than a box-ticking exercise. For each decision taken in consultation with civil society, donors should indicate who has been consulted, what their position is and whom they claim to represent.

Donor practices, moreover, should be consistent with broader political and economic foreign policies. Investment in short-term, incidental projects while simultaneously maintaining unsustainable business practices has the effect of giving with one hand and taking with the other. The same goes for donors who individually fund local civil society actors, but through UN or other international organizations partner with military entities that directly obstruct the goals of these actors. The situation in Myanmar further shows the importance of donor strategies going beyond the country-wide level, as the political progress made in some areas of the country did not expand to several of the ethnic states, and moreover has been nullified by the 2021 military coup.

## The future of civil society in Myanmar

At the time of writing, Myanmar has passed its second year since the military coup. The situation on the ground has deteriorated in so many respects that it is difficult to predict the future of civil society, let alone anticipate developments in the short run. Yet this book has testified to the resilient spirit of the Myanmar people and the country's many manifestations of civil society. Myanmar's postcolonial history has been characterized by at least as many popular uprisings as military coups, and the most recent opposition movement has shown remarkable new manifestations that could point towards more equality and inclusivity. Foreign actors, whether donors, human rights activists or academics, should continue to amplify and support these various voices coming from Myanmar, including those from the now once again growing diaspora and refugee communities. International attention is inherently fragmented and partial, but pragmatic preferences for a single narrative in transnational advocacy should not go at the expense of the diversity of claims and narratives coming from Myanmar society.

It is important to look beyond international headlines and support local activists, especially when international attention risks drifting elsewhere. As this book has shown, much-needed work goes on in various capacities on the ground to contain the malicious role of the military and secure a better future for the people of Myanmar. One important development is the growing presence of Myanmar voices in international research and policy circles (see Chu May Paing and Than Toe Aung, 2021; Metro, 2023). This could be further fostered by offering more support for people from Myanmar to access education, jobs and consultancy opportunities inside and outside the country. A dual focus on local opportunities and involvement of refugee and exile communities will remain needed until dissidents and minorities risk less repression. Regardless of their identity, geographical location and experiences with repression and resistance, a multitude of civil society actors will continue to strive towards social and political change in Myanmar.

# Notes

## Introduction

[1] Since 1982, the state officially recognizes 135 ethnic groups (*taingyintha*) and eight 'national races' (Bamar, Chin, Kachin, Kayah, Kayin, Mon, Rakhine and Shan), with the Bamar (or Burman in English) majority comprising about 60 to 70 per cent of the population. These categories were also used in the contentious 2014 national census, where people were prohibited from self-identifying as Rohingya (Ferguson, 2015; Kyaw Zeyar Win, 2018). According to figures released after the 2014 census, an estimated 88 per cent of the Myanmar population is Buddhist, with Christians and Muslims comprising about 6 per cent and 4 per cent, 0.8 per cent animist and 0.5 per cent Hindu (Thawnghmung and Robinson, 2017).

[2] The term ethnic armed organizations (EAOs) is commonly used to refer to ethnic armed groups in Myanmar, though some of them prefer the terms 'ethnic resistance' or 'ethnic revolutionary' organizations to emphasize their goal of resisting or overthrowing the Myanmar military (see Thiha 2023 on this terminology).

[3] As detailed subsequently, some data are included from later visits between 2017 and 2019 and from online interactions, particularly since the COVID-19 pandemic of 2020.

[4] The role of 'government-organized NGOs', or GONGOs, will be discussed in Chapter 3.

[5] Among my respondents who had been political prisoners in the past, some continued to openly resist the military, while others chose more covert ways to operate after their release.

[6] As explained in Chapter 1, the British colonial administration and later military governments encouraged people to artificially identify with a single ethnic group.

[7] Notable exceptions at the time included a number of in-depth studies on ethnic nationalities in the border areas (Smith, 1991; South, 2004, 2008ab; Gravers, 2007; Walton, 2008; Kramer, 2011) and on the Buddhist *sangha*, or community of monks and nuns (Schober, 2011; Walton, 2012a, 2015b, 2016), as well as several seminal books discussing life in authoritarian Myanmar more generally (Lintner, 1990; Fink, 2009). However, studies on local experiences in and with civil society were relatively scarce, with the exception of a few individual studies (Kyaw Yin Hlaing, 2004, 2007abc, 2008; Lorch, 2007, 2008; Malseed, 2009) and publications on related issues such as the rule of law (Cheesman, 2015 and earlier articles) and the role of the media (Brooten, 2004, 2006).

## Chapter 1

[1] Karen, Kachin, Chin and other groups (including Anglo-Burmese) made up the majority (Charney, 2009: 54; Steinberg, 2010: 29).

[2] Also spelled as 'Saya San'. *Saya* (*sayama* for women) means teacher in Burmese.

[3] The term 'nationalism' is commonly used not only to refer to the Burman majority, but also to describe ethnic minority groups' prioritization of, and pride in, their own ethnic group. See, for example, South (2003).

4    The Mon and Arakanese were excluded from the meeting, because they were considered to fall under Ministerial Burma which was under direct British control (Walton, 2008: 902). Karen observers also attended but did not participate in the meeting (TNI, 2017).

5    Sao Shwe Thaike, a prominent Shan leader, became the first president. The role of president rotated among the ethnic nationalities in order to 'placate' them (Steinberg, 2010: 57).

6    In 1989, the CPB split into four armed organizations: Burma National United Party and Army (which later became the United Wa State Army [UWSA]), the Myanmar National Democratic Alliance Army, the National Democratic Alliance Army in East Shan State, and the New Democratic Army(-Kachin) (Lintner, 2019).

7    The Myanmar army generally refers to itself as *Tatmadaw*, or 'Royal Armed Forces', while critics refer to it as 'the regime' or 'the junta'. Since the 2021 military coup, critics have argued that the term *tatmadaw* should no longer be used, due to its controversial honorary and imperialist connotations (Ye Myo Hein, 2022). The term *sit-tat*, simply meaning armed forces, is becoming increasingly common.

8    Also referred to as 'Bogyoke Government', after General (*bogyoke*) Ne Win.

9    Interestingly, Burma also delivered the third Secretary General of the UN, U Thant, during this period.

10   In the 2008 constitution, the term 'divisions' has been replaced by 'regions'.

11   In an apparent public relations exercise, the SLORC changed its name to SPDC in November 1997.

12   While unacceptable to the NLD, this was not in fact a surprise to most observers, who had noted that the army had already backtracked before the elections by proclaiming that a new constitution was to be drafted before power could be transferred (Tonkin, 2007).

13   The country would be without a constitution until 2008.

14   The controversy surrounding her Nobel Peace Prize and her response to the Rohingya crisis will be covered later in the book.

15   Some authors have objected to the internationally used term 'Saffron Revolution' (Fink, 2009: 102; Holliday, 2011: 25; Aung-Thwin, 2013). One reason is the fact that the monks mostly wore maroon, not saffron robes. More importantly, however, it has been questioned whether it is appropriate to refer to monastic activities with Western terms such as 'revolution', which might misportray the original intentions of the monks.

16   By 2008, Myanmar had the largest number of political prisoners thus far, estimated somewhere between 1,700 (Taylor, 2009: 424) and 2,200 (Holliday, 2011: 64). The definition (and therefore calculation) of 'political prisoners' remains contested, especially given the generally malfunctioning legal system (see Assistance Association for Political Prisoners (Burma) [AAPP(B)], 2011 and Cheesman, 2015). Since the 2021 military coup, the number of political prisoners (of which the AAPP keeps an online record) far exceeds this previous peak.

17   In 2022, it was estimated that 5 per cent of political prisoners arrested after the 2021 coup have been permanently disabled due to torture (Irrawaddy, 2022).

18   The most prominent opposition parties were the National Democratic Force, consisting of former NLD-members who disagreed with the election boycott, and a number of ethnic minority parties, of which the Shan Nationalities Democratic Party (SNDP) was the largest.

19   The second largest parties were the NUP and the SNDP with 5 per cent each, and the Rakhine Nationalities Development Party (which later transformed into the Arakan National Party) with 3 per cent of the votes (TNI, 2010).

20   Several international garment companies such as H&M and Adidas started operating in Myanmar during these years, and the first KFC opened in 2015 (Campbell, 2023: 12). International development banks also entered, as discussed in Chapter 7.

21 Estimates of the total number of EAOs range somewhere between 20 and 40. The largest one is the UWSA with around 30,000 soldiers.
22 When the constitution was 'approved' in 2008, it did not result in further disarmament (Steinberg, 2010: 44).
23 Other signatories were smaller parties or splinter factions plus the All Burma Students' Democratic Front (introduced in the next chapter), a group of Burman student activists with its own armed wing. For an overview, see Stokke et al (2022).

## Chapter 2
1 See Kanbawza Win in Kyaw Yin Hlaing (2007b: 38): '[I]f we put two Myanmar in a cell they will form three political parties.'
2 Apart from prominent Buddhist nationalist groups, students were also active in the anti-colonial movement. In the 1920s and 1930s, university students actively opposed British rule, particularly in Rangoon (Charney, 2009: 34).
3 The government-organized peasants' organization and workers' organization claimed nearly 8 million and over 5 million members, respectively, out of a population of about 25–30 million (Taylor, 2009: 326, 360).
4 Several elected representatives of the NLD and ethnic nationalities parties also fled the country and formed the National Coalition Government of the Union of Burma.
5 Min Ko Naing (meaning 'conqueror of king[s]'), whose real name is Paw Oo Tun, has remained one of the best known Burmese dissidents since the 1980s.
6 'Liberated Area' refers to certain ethnic areas in Myanmar that were under de facto insurgent control when these movements were started. Although some of the organizations mentioned were initially based in these areas, eventually they acted predominantly from abroad.
7 These groups mostly resided in neighbouring countries such as Thailand; a list of solidarity groups established in Western countries is provided in Chapter 3.
8 Another influential media outlet, Myanmar Now, was founded in 2015. For more insights on the role of independent media in contemporary Myanmar, see the work of Lisa Brooten (2004, 2006) and especially the edited volume by Brooten et al (2019).
9 The relationship between EAOs and their affiliated CSOs differs widely between groups. Some EAOs are professionally run military forces with high levels of legitimacy among local constituencies, whereas others operate more like private business ventures with limited grassroots support (Thawnghmung and Saw Eh Htoo, 2022; Vrieze, 2023).
10 For a detailed discussion of the evolution of these laws and civil society advocacy, see Doi Ra and Khu Khu Ju (2021).
11 The number 969 stands for 'the nine qualities of Buddha, the six qualities of Buddha's teaching, and the nine qualities of monastic community' (Min Zin, 2015: 382).
12 Section 66 of the Telecommunications Law criminalizes defamation and is often used against those who publicly criticize the government or the military, for example through social media. In 2019, for example, the law was used against the founder of the Human Rights Human Dignity Festival for criticizing the strong constitutional role of the military on Facebook. His request for bail was denied despite his need for urgent medical treatment. He was eventually released in February 2020.
13 Interestingly, after the 2010 elections, five Rohingyas had served as national and regional representatives of the military-backed USDP (Simpson and Farrelly, 2020: 487).
14 The ICJ case is ongoing at the time of writing, and the label genocide remains contested, due to its legal implications. However, reports on violence against the Rohingya consistently find strong indications of genocidal intent (see, for example, Fortify Rights, 2015). See Matelski et al (2022) for a discussion on the documentation of human rights

violations by non-state actors inside and outside Myanmar which feeds into this and other legal cases.

## Chapter 3

1. A smaller number of civil society actors (often educated abroad) self-identifies as agnostic or atheist.

2. Information in this section stems from interviews with the co-founders conducted in Thailand in January 2010, February 2011 and July 2011, and from public documents.

3. Cardinal Bo was later criticized for posing with the leader of the 2021 military coup, Min Aung Hlaing, in his capacity as Archbishop of Yangon at a Christmas event. At many other points, however, he has been openly critical of the post-2021 military leadership.

4. Smaller minority groups within ethnic areas, such as the Danu or the Pa-O in Shan State, were in some cases allowed to have self-administered zones but were less able to benefit from the post-ceasefire development opportunities for civil society than some of the ceasefire groups.

5. Under President Thein Sein, the NCA was signed by eight non-state armed groups, including the KNU. Two more groups signed later under NLD rule. Despite the increasingly acknowledged demands for a federal system, ethnicity-based territories seem unlikely to be established, as it would weaken the position of minorities-within-minority areas, such as the Pa-O in Shan State or the Rohingya in Rakhine State (Thawnghmung and Saw Eh Htoo, 2022).

6. Bertrand et al (2022) similarly describe how the state and the military made use of the peace process between 2011 and 2021 to strengthen their position and 'neutralize' ethnic nationality groups.

7. Information in this section stems from interviews with one of its members conducted in Thailand in 2010 and in Yangon in 2014, and observations in public events.

8. Phyo Zayar Thaw was hanged after receiving the death penalty in July 2022, along with Ko Jimmy, a prominent member of the 88 generation, and two lesser-known activists, all convicted under the anti-terrorism law for their resistance to the military coup. It was the first time in over 30 years that the government formally carried out death sentences.

9. Research in other (former) authoritarian contexts such as Indonesia and China points towards a similar increase in political and social space for civil society actors in the aftermath of natural disaster (Antlöv et al, 2006; Teets, 2009).

10. This section is based on an article published in the *Journal of Burma Studies* (Matelski and Nang Muay Noan, 2022).

11. In Myanmar, the category 'youth' is rather loosely applied to persons up to the age of about 35. Many of the political youth organizations, for example, consist of members in their 30s.

12. Woman from Mon state, 27 years old. Interviewed in Chiang Mai, November 2010 (ethnicity and geographical origin are identical unless otherwise stated). Thin Lei Win (2019) makes a similar argument with regard to the media.

13. Interview conducted in Mae Sot, June 2011.

14. Burma Center Netherlands (BCN), the organization where I volunteered between 2004 and 2006, was founded in 1993 in collaboration with the Amsterdam-based Transnational Institute (TNI), and initially advocated for economic sanctions. In 2015, BCN moved most of its activities to Myanmar. The centre was formally discontinued in November 2018, while TNI has continued its programme on Myanmar.

15. This section is based on an interview conducted in Mae Sot, June 2011; see also earlier section under 'Generation and gender'.

16. Also spelled Hlaingthaya. While poverty is higher in the rural areas, inequality is higher within the urban areas of Myanmar (Warr, 2020).

17  Woman from Mon state, 27 years old. Interviewed in Chiang Mai, November 2010.
18  Man from Kachin state, 27 years old. Interviewed in Chiang Mai, October 2010.
19  Muslim man from Yangon, 36 years old. Interviewed in Yangon, March 2011.
20  Observation during a public civil society meeting in Yangon, 2014.
21  Burman male representative of a Yangon-based organization. Interviewed in March 2014.
22  The CBI emerged out of a training programme for Burmese staff set up by INGOs in the early 1990s to increase the competency of local NGOs and has been operating under the name CBI since 2001. The organization started offering trainings for local organizations in 2005 and consultancies in 2006. In 2010, it was transformed into a local NGO.
23  The Local Resource Centre was set up by the Australian Burnet Institute and other INGOs in 2008 to coordinate local and international relief efforts after Nargis. After 2010, it shifted focus to the 'holistic development' of local NGOs.
24  Paung Ku (meaning 'bridge' or 'arch') was set up in 2007 by an INGO consortium led by Save the Children. Its goals are to build capacity of and encourage networking among local CSOs, improve practice within the international development community and enhance advocacy towards policy actors.
25  Pyoe Pin (meaning 'green shoots') was a project of the British Department for International Development with additional Danish and Swedish funding started in 2007. It aimed to promote strategic partnership among governmental and non-governmental actors in order to bring about social and economic development.
26  Information based on an interview with one of the founders in Chiang Mai, November 2010.
27  This section is based on informal discussions with several respondents, including former trainees of Myanmar Egress, and a visit to the Egress office in Yangon in 2010. Some of the information was confirmed in later writings, including by co-founder Kyaw Yin Hlaing (2014). The organization's founder, Nay Win Maung, died unexpectedly from a heart attack on 1 January 2012. For a detailed account of the activities of Myanmar Egress, see Lidauer (2012), Lall (2016), Mullen (2016), and Mon Mon Myat (2023).

## Chapter 4

1  Woman from Mon state, 27 years old. Interviewed in Chiang Mai, November 2010.
2  Tactics mentioned by several respondents from CSOs interviewed between 2010 and 2014.
3  Burman man from Yangon, 27 years old. Interviewed in Chiang Mai, October 2010.
4  Man from Dawei, 28 years old. Interviewed in Chiang Mai, October 2010.
5  Muslim man from Yangon, 30 years old. Interviewed in Chiang Mai, October 2010.
6  Man from Karen state, 29 years old. Interviewed in Chiang Mai, October 2010.
7  Muslim man from Yangon, 33 years old. Interviewed in Yangon, February 2011.
8  Man from Karen State, 29 years old. Interviewed in Chiang Mai, October 2010.
9  Rakhine man from Yangon, 22 years old. Interviewed in Chiang Mai, November 2010.
10  Woman from Mon State, 27 years old. Interviewed in Chiang Mai, November 2010.
11  Man from Kachin State, 35 years old. Interviewed in Chiang Mai, October 2010.
12  Muslim man from Yangon, 36 years old. Interviewed in Yangon, March 2011. This was a particularly outspoken respondent, who is indeed unafraid to criticize anything. He was among the first to speak out in defence of the Rohingya, and openly criticized the military, the elected government and the opposition before and after the 2021 military coup. Most of these outspoken respondents, who were determined to stay in the country, sadly had to flee in the course of 2022 as violence against dissidents intensified.
13  Man from Kachin State, 27 years old. Interviewed October 2010 in Chiang Mai.
14  Conversation between two respondents, November 2010 in Chiang Mai.
15  Muslim man from Yangon, 30 years old. Interviewed in Chiang Mai, October 2010.
16  Interview with one of the members in Yangon, March 2014.

17  See The Best Friend (2012) 'We need more tourists like Garrett', [online] 26 October, Available from: http://thebestfriendint.blogspot.com/2012/10/we-need-more-touri sts-like-garrett.html [Accessed 18 May 2023].

18  Email discussion with Burman respondent, January 2014.

## Chapter 5

1  Retrieved from BCN's website in 2015.

2  Personal conversation, 2010.

3  Unsigned letter dated 29 September 2010, retrieved from EBO's website in 2015.

4  EBO letter dated 20 October 2010, retrieved from EBO's website in 2015.

5  Muslim man from Yangon, 33 years old. Interviewed in Yangon, February 2011.

6  The Unlawful Association Act of 1908 provides for prison sentences for formal or informal association with unlawful organizations and is frequently used to sentence dissidents.

## Chapter 6

1  See Burma Partnership/Ten Alliances (2010) 'Burma's Ten Alliances call for "People's Elections" on 27 May', [online] 12 May, Available from:https://burmapartnership.net/2010/05/burmas-ten-alliances-call-for-peoples-elections-on-27-may/ / [Accessed 18 May 2023].

2  *Matha ko hpauda yaik teh*, according to this respondent, is a common saying in Mandalay, meaning 'to beautify a corpse'.

3  See Burma Partnership/Ten Alliances (2010), 'Burma's Movement for Democracy and Ethnic Rights Launches Global Campaign Against 2010 Elections', [online] 19 March, Available from: https://burmapartnership.net/2010/03/burmas-movement-for-democr acy-and-ethnic-rights-launches-global-campaign-on-2010-elections/ [Accessed 18 May 2023].

4  See Note 1.

5  One of them referred to themselves as 'We, the united voice of people, communities, and organizations from Burma and around the globe.' See Burma Campaign UK/ALTSEAN-Burma et al. (2009), 'Calling for Genuine Political Reconciliation Before Elections in Burma', [online] 10 December 2009, Available at: http://burmacampaign.org.uk/collect ive-statement-on-2010-elections [Accessed 18 May 2023].

6  'Examining the wider reality of Burma's elections: perspectives from stakeholders on the ground', 2 November 2010, Foreign Correspondents' Club of Thailand, Bangkok. A representative of the Karen Women's Action Group was among the other speakers.

7  A 17-minute documentary with this title produced by Burma Partnership can be viewed at http://www.youtube.com/watch?v=agq2_kI0HqE [Accessed 18 May 2023].

8  As conveyed by a woman from Mon State, 27 years old. Interviewed in Chiang Mai, November 2010.

9  Rakhine man from Yangon, 22 years old. Interviewed in Chiang Mai, November 2010.

10  Woman from Shan State, 31 years old. Interviewed in Chiang Mai, October 2010.

11  Man from Kachin State, 27 years old. Interviewed in Chiang Mai, October 2010.

12  Man from Kachin State, 35 years old. Interviewed in Chiang Mai, October 2010.

13  Interview conducted in Thailand in 2011.

14  See Note 6.

15  In this quote, border based groups are equated to the democracy movement. This shows that the boundaries of the movement were rather fluid. Most (but not all) of the participants in this training indeed came from an ethnic nationality organization on the Thai border.

16  See Note 6.

[17] Muslim man from Yangon, 33 years old. Interviewed in Yangon, February 2011.

[18] In a concept paper, the objectives of the campaign were phrased as follows: (1) for more governments to support a Commission of Inquiry; (2) for those governments that already expressed support to take concrete steps to bring about the establishment of a Commission of Inquiry; (3) for a UN resolution to include language establishing a Commission of Inquiry; (4) for governments that will not support a Commission of Inquiry to refrain from obstructing its establishment; (5) to promote greater understanding and/or support among civil society, the public and non-state armed groups for a Commission of Inquiry; and (6) for media to amplify the call for the establishment of a Commission of Inquiry.

[19] Interview conducted in Thailand, July 2011.

## Chapter 7

[1] Burman man from Yangon, 27 years old. Interviewed in Chiang Mai, October 2010.

[2] Part of this chapter was previously published in Kosem, S. (2016) *Border twists and Burma trajectories: perceptions, reforms, and adaptations*, Chiang Mai: Chiang Mai University, Center for ASEAN Studies. Reproduced here with the permission of the copyright holder.

[3] See Purcell's (1999: 70–6) discussion of David Korten on four 'generations' of NGO strategies described earlier.

[4] Japan, which is one of the largest providers of development assistance to Myanmar, may be considered either Western, Eastern or Asian, depending on one's definition. As detailed in this chapter, its assistance has been distributed primarily through (inter)governmental agencies. However, see Watanabe (2014) for a notable exception.

[5] In 2012, Petrie returned to the country at the invitation of the Myanmar government to lead the Myanmar Peace Support Initiative, described later in the chapter.

[6] The sentences were later converted to prison terms, and the men were released as part of an amnesty in 2005.

[7] According to figures cited by International Crisis Group (ICG, 2008), the average assistance to comparatively poor countries in 2006 was $58 per person, and even other countries with repressive governments received between $21 (Zimbabwe) and $63 (Laos) per person.

[8] As evidenced by the title of a press conference by General Khin Nyunt in 1997: 'Some Western powers have been aiding and abetting terrorism committed by certain organizations operating under the guise of democracy and human rights by giving them assistance in both cash and kind' (quoted in Callahan, 2010: 64).

[9] In line with many other Western countries, the Netherlands opened a business mission in 2013 and a full embassy in Yangon in 2016.

[10] In 2012, the World Bank foresaw a 'triple transition' in Myanmar: from military rule to democracy, from conflict to peace, and from a centrally managed to a market economy (in McConnachie, 2022).

[11] They issued an open letter to the Norwegian ambassador expressing disappointment with the lack of adequate civil society consultation. See Eurasia Review (2012), 'Burma: Open Letter to Norway Ambassador Nordgaard on MPSI Consultation', [online] 30 August, Available from: https://www.eurasiareview.com/30082012-burma-open-letter-to-norway-ambassador-nordgaard-on-mpsi-consultation [Accessed 18 May 2023].

[12] The Joint Peace Fund still exists at the time of writing but has sized down. The initiative started with 11 donors and the current website mentions eight (Canada, the European Union and six European countries); see https://www.jointpeacefund.org [Accessed 18 May 2023].

[13] In April 2020, UNHCR estimated the official number of refugees and asylum seekers from Myanmar at 859,000 in Bangladesh, 178,990 in Malaysia and 93,227 in Thailand

(McConnachie, 2022: 664). These numbers are likely an underestimate of the total number of refugees and have gone up significantly since the 2021 military coup.

[14] These events, perhaps not entirely coincidently, took place around the very sensitive 2014 census process which was expected to influence the official population numbers in Rakhine State (Ferguson, 2015).

[15] Personal observation at ICC meeting in The Hague, December 2022.

[16] These various perspectives were reflected in the naming and framing of the situation, which was referred to alternately as Rakhine problem, Rohingya question (or, in nationalist terms, Bengali question), Rohingya crisis, or genocide.

[17] Muslim man from Yangon, 33 years old. Interviewed in Yangon, February 2011.

[18] Interviewed in The Hague, February 2015.

[19] Personal observation, reported in Matelski (2015, 2016).

[20] The page of the Paung Ku Platform has since changed to https://www.pkforum.org [Accessed 18 May 2023].

## Chapter 8

[1] The NLD won 83 per cent of the seats in parliament, whereas the military's USDP won only 7 per cent.

[2] Daily briefings on casualties and arrests since the coup can be found on www.aappb.org [accessed 18 May 2023]. The Assistance Association for Political Prisoners (Burma), which has emerged as the main source of numbers on post-coup violence, estimates the actual number of deaths to be twice as high as reported, since they only count those cases they can fully identify and corroborate (APHR, 2022). Min Zaw Oo and Tønnesson (2023) put the number of post-coup civilian casualties by mid-2023 at over 6,000.

[3] Amnesties to date were issued in February, April and October 2021, in November 2022, and in April and May 2023. A number of released political prisoners were instantly re-arrested.

[4] Webinar 'The Myanmar crisis: is there light at the end of the tunnel?' organized by Forum-Asia, Progressive Voice and ALTSEAN-Burma, 3 November 2022. The number of airstrikes by the military in the first two years since the 2021 coup is estimated to be over 1,400, according to Mizzima (2023).

[5] See also other articles in volume 27(1) of the *Journal of Burma Studies* issued in 2023, which is dedicated to the gender dynamics in anti-coup resistance and in Myanmar society more generally.

[6] A full list of ministers appointed by the NUG is available at https://www.nugmyanmar. org/en/ [Accessed 18 May 2023].

[7] One of the largest international fundraising initiatives is Mutual Aid Myanmar (www. mutualaidmyanmar.org), an initiative by Tun Myint, a US-based academic from Myanmar, together with the American academic James Scott and the Thai academic Chayan Vaddhanaphuti. As of mid-2023, they report having sent $833,000 to over 16,000 CDM participants in Myanmar.

[8] One month earlier, his brother had been killed after his affiliation as advisor to the NUG became known.

[9] Secession is another aspiration among some of the ethnic nationalities, though it has not received much attention in post-coup reporting.

[10] See 638 Civil Society Organizations (2022) 'Letter to the UN Secretary General: Regarding UN Agencies, Funds, Programmes and Other Entities Engagement with the Military Junta', Progressive Voice, [online] 23 September, Available from: https://progressivevoice myanmar.org/2022/09/23/un-agencies-funds-programmes-and-other-entities-engagem ent-with-the-military-junta/ [Accessed 18 May 2023].

[11] See https://specialadvisorycouncil.org/ [Accessed 18 May 2023].

[12] See Twitter message by 'FreeKachin', 26 July 2022. Available from: https://twitter.com/FreeKachin/status/1551750179811987458 [Accessed 18 May 2023].

[13] Online report launch "Seeking Effective Assistance for a Future: Reflections of Local Advocacy Organisations in Myanmar", Pandita Development Institute, 26 October 2022.

[14] A side campaign has been started on social media against the existence of 'manels': (near) all-male panels of experts, whether Burmese or foreign, that continue to dominate discussions on Myanmar.

# References

Action Aid, ADRA, Burnet Institute, Care, CESVI, Danish Church Aid et al (2009) 'Joint response to "After the storm: voices from the delta"', Rangoon, 8 April, Available from: http://www.burmalibrary.org/docs07/Joint_INGO_Response_to_After_theStorm.pdf [Accessed 18 May 2023].

Akman, A. (2012) 'Beyond the objectivist conception of civil society: social actors, civility, and self-limitation', *Political Studies*, 60(2): 321–40.

Alagappa, M. (2004) 'Introduction', in M. Alagappa (ed) *Civil society and political space in Asia: expanding and contracting democratic space*, Stanford: Stanford University Press, pp 1–21.

ALTSEAN-Burma (2002) 'A peace of pie? Burma's humanitarian aid debate,' Bangkok: ALTSEAN-Burma, Available from: https://www.burmalibrary.org/en/a-peace-of-pie-burmas-humanitarian-aid-debate [Accessed 18 May 2023].

Amnesty International (2022) 'The social atrocity: META and the right to remedy for the Rohingya', London: Amnesty International.

Anderson, M.B. (1999) *Do no harm: how aid can support peace – or war*, Boulder, CO: Lynne Rienner Publishers.

Antlöv, H., Ibrahim, R. and Van Tuijl, P. (2006) 'NGO governance and accountability in Indonesia: challenges in a newly democratizing country', in L. Jordan and P. Van Tuijl (eds) *NGO accountability: politics, principles and innovations*, London: Earthscan Publications, pp 147–64.

APHR (2022) '"Time is not on our side": the failed international response to the Myanmar coup', ASEAN Parliamentarians for Human Rights.

Arnold, D. and Campbell, S. (2017) 'Labour regime transformation in Myanmar: constitutive processes of contestation', *Development and Change*, 48(4): 801–24.

Arnold, D. and Turner, A. (2019) 'Why are we surprised when Buddhists are violent?', *KNOW: A Journal on the Formation of Knowledge*, 3(1): 159–66.

Assistance Association for Political Prisoners – Burma (2011) 'AAPP calls to bridge the gap on political prisoner numbers', 8 November, Available from: https://democracyforburma.wordpress.com/2011/11/08/aapp-calls-to-bridge-the-gap-on-political-prisoner-numbers-eng/ [Accessed 18 May 2023].

Aung-Thwin, M. (2001) 'Parochial universalism, democracy jihad and the Orientalist image of Burma: the new evangelism', *Pacific Affairs*, 74(4): 483–505.

Aung-Thwin, M. (2011) *The return of the Galon King*, Singapore: NUS Press.

Aung-Thwin, M. (2013) 'Those men in saffron robes', *Journal of Burma Studies*, 17(2): 243–334.

Aung-Thwin, M. and Aung-Thwin, M. (2012) *A history of Myanmar since ancient times: traditions and transformations*, London: Reaktion Books.

Bächtold, S. (2015) 'The rise of an anti-politics machinery: peace, civil society and the focus on results in Myanmar', *Third World Quarterly*, 36(10): 1968–83.

Bächtold, S. (2017) 'An eclipse of Myanmar's civil society?', Heinrich Böll Stiftung, Available from: https://www.boell.de/en/2017/07/05/eclipse-myanmars-civil-society [Accessed 18 May 2023].

Bächtold, S. (2021) 'Donor love will tear us apart: how complexity and learning marginalize accountability in peacebuilding interventions', *International Political Sociology*, 15(4): 504–21.

Banki, S. (2009) 'Contested regimes, aid flows, and refugee flows: the case of Burma', *Journal of Current Southeast Asian Affairs*, 28(2): 47–73.

Banks, N., Hulme, D. and Edwards, M. (2015) 'NGOs, states and donors revisited: still too close for comfort?', *World Development*, 66: 707–18.

Banyar Aung (2022) 'Myanmar's "neutral" intellectuals are poison', Irrawaddy, 12 December, Available from: https://www.irrawaddy.com/opinion/guest-column/myanmars-neutral-intellectuals-are-poison.html [Accessed 18 May 2023].

Baud, M. and Rutten, R. (2004) *Popular intellectuals and social movements: framing protest in Asia, Africa, and Latin America*, Cambridge: Cambridge University Press.

BBC (2012) 'Burma blocks opening of office for Islamic body OIC', BBC, 15 October, Available from: https://www.bbc.com/news/world-asia-19949414 [Accessed 18 May 2023].

Beaulieu, E.A. (2006) 'Protesting the contest: election boycotts around the world, 1990–2002', Unpublished doctoral thesis, University of California, Available from: https://escholarship.org/uc/item/1h22t7g6#page-1 [Accessed 18 May 2023].

Benford, R.B. and Snow, D.A. (2000) 'Framing processes and social movements: an overview and assessment', *Annual Review of Sociology*, 26: 611–39.

Bertrand, J., Pelletier, A. and Thawnghmung, A.M. (2022) *Winning by process: the state and neutralization of ethnic minorities in Myanmar*, Ithaca/London: Cornell University Press.

Bjarnegård, E. (2020) 'Introduction: development challenges in Myanmar; political development and politics of development intertwined', *The European Journal of Development Research*, 32: 255–73.

Bob, C. (2005) *The marketing of rebellion: insurgents, media, and international activism*, Cambridge: Cambridge University Press.

Bob, C. (2011) 'Civil and uncivil society', in M. Edwards (ed) *The Oxford handbook of civil society* (online edn), Oxford: Oxford University Press.

Brees, I. (2009) 'Burmese refugee transnationalism: what is the effect?', *Journal of Current Southeast Asian Affairs*, 2: 23–46.

Brooten, L. (2004) 'Human rights discourse and the development of democracy in a multi-ethnic state', *Asian Journal of Communication*, 14(2): 174–91.

Brooten, L. (2006) 'Political violence and journalism in a multiethnic state: a case study of Burma (Myanmar)', *Journal of Communication Inquiry*, 30(4): 354–73.

Brooten, L. (2013) 'The problem with human rights discourse and freedom indices: the case of Burma/Myanmar media', *International Journal of Communication*, 7: 681–700.

Brooten, L. (2020) 'When media fuel the crisis: fighting hate speech and communal violence in Myanmar', in J. Matthews and E. Torsen (eds) *Media, journalism and disaster communities*, Basingstoke: Palgrave Macmillan, pp 215–30.

Brooten, L., McElhone, J. and Venkiteswaran, G. (2019) *Myanmar media in transition: legacies, challenges and change*, Singapore: ISEAS.

Burma Campaign UK (2005) 'EU Burma meeting a sham', 4 April, Available from: http://burmacampaign.org.uk/eu-burma-meeting-a-sham/ [Accessed 18 May 2023].

Burma Center Netherlands and Transnational Institute (1999) *Strengthening civil society in Burma: possibilities and dilemmas for international NGOs*, Chiang Mai: Silkworm Books.

Buszynski, L. (1998) 'Thailand and Myanmar: the perils of "constructive engagement"', *The Pacific Review*, 11(2): 290–305.

Bynum, E. (2021) 'Myanmar's Spring Revolution', Armed Conflict Location & Event Data Project (ACLED).

Callahan, M.P. (2003) *Making enemies: war and state building in Burma*, Ithaca/London: Cornell University Press.

Callahan, M.P. (2010) 'The endurance of military rule in Burma: not why, but why not?', in S.L. Levenstein (ed) *Finding dollars, sense, and legitimacy in Burma*, Washington, DC: Woodrow Wilson International Center for Scholars, pp 54–76.

Callahan, M.P. (2018) 'Myanmar in 2017: crises of ethnic pluralism set transition back', *Southeast Asian Affairs*: 243–64.

Campbell, S. (2023) 'Interrogating Myanmar's "transition" from a post-coup vantage point', *SOJOURN Journal of Social Issues in Southeast Asia*, 38(1): 1–27.

Campbell, S. and Prasse-Freeman, E. (2022) 'Revisiting the wages of Burman-ness: contradictions of privilege in Myanmar', *Journal of Contemporary Asia*, 52(2): 175–99.

Carothers, T. and Ottaway, M. (2000) 'The burgeoning world of civil society aid', in M. Ottaway and T. Carothers (eds) *Funding virtue: civil society aid and democracy promotion*, Washington, DC: Carnegie Endowment for International Peace, pp 3–17.

Carpenter, R.C. (2007) 'Setting the advocacy agenda: theorizing issue emergence and nonemergence in transnational advocacy networks', *International Studies Quarterly*, 51(1): 99–120.

CDA (2009) 'Listening project: field visit report Myanmar/Burma', August–December, CDA Collaborative Learning Projects/Shalom Foundation/Centre for Peace and Conflict Studies.

Centre for Peace and Conflict Studies (2009) 'Listening to voices from inside: Myanmar civil society's response to Cyclone Nargis', Phnom Penh: Centre for Peace and Conflict Studies.

Centre for Peace and Conflict Studies (2010) 'Listening to voices from inside: people's perspectives on Myanmar's 2010 election', Siem Reap: Centre for Peace and Conflict Studies.

Centre for Peace and Conflict Studies (2011) 'Myanmar voices on the Commission of Inquiry', Siem Reap: Centre for Peace and Conflict Studies.

Chambers, R. (1997) *Whose reality counts? Putting the last first*, London: ITDG Publishing.

Chambers, S. and Kymlicka, W. (2002) 'Introduction: alternative conceptions of civil society', in S. Chambers and W. Kymlicka (eds) *Alternative conceptions of civil society*, Princeton/Oxford: Princeton University Press, pp 1–10.

Chandhoke, N. (2007) 'Civil society', *Development in Practice*, 17(4–5): 607–14.

Charney, M.W. (2009) *A history of modern Burma*, Cambridge: Cambridge University Press.

Cheesman, N. (2003) 'School, state and Sangha in Burma', *Comparative Education*, 39: 45–63.

Cheesman, N. (2015) *Opposing the rule of law: how Myanmar's courts make law and order*, Cambridge: Cambridge University Press.

Cheesman, N. (2017) 'How in Myanmar "national races" came to surpass citizenship and exclude Rohingya', *Journal of Contemporary Asia*, 47(3): 461–83.

Cheesman, N. and Kyaw Min San (2013) 'Not just defending: advocating for law in Myanmar', *Wisconsin International Law Journal*, 31(3): 702–33.

Chu May Paing and Than Toe Aung (2021) 'Talking back to White "Burma experts"', *Agitate! Journal*, Available from: https://agitatejournal.org/talking-back-to-white-burma-experts-by-chu-may-paing-and-than-toe-aung/ [Accessed 18 May 2023].

Chua, L.J. and Gilbert, D. (2015) 'Sexual orientation and gender identity minorities in transition: LGBT rights and activism in Myanmar', *Human Rights Quarterly*, 37(1): 1–28.

Cleary, S. (1997) *The role of NGOs under authoritarian political systems*, London: Macmillan Press.

Cohen, J.L. and Arato, A. (1994) *Civil society and political theory*, Cambridge, MA: MIT Press.

Connelly, A. and Loong, S. (2023) 'Conflict in Myanmar and the international response', in The International Institute for Strategic Studies, *Asia-Pacific Regional Security Assessment 2023: Key developments and trends*, Routledge, pp 138–59.

Cowan, J.K., Dembour, M. and Wilson, R.A. (2001) *Culture and rights: anthropological perspectives*, Cambridge: Cambridge University Press.

Crewe, E. and Axelby, R. (2013) *Anthropology and development: culture, morality and politics in a globalised world*, Cambridge: Cambridge University Press.

Currie, K. (2012) 'Burma in the balance: the role of foreign assistance in supporting Burma's democratic transition', Arlington: The Project 2049 Institute.

Dale, J.G. (2011) *Free Burma: transnational legal action and corporate accountability*, Minneapolis/London: University of Minnesota Press.

David, R., Aung Kaung Myat and Holliday, I. (2022) 'Can regime change improve ethnic relations? Perception of ethnic minorities after the 2021 coup in Myanmar', *Japanese Journal of Political Science*, 23(2): 1–16.

De Waal, A. (1997) 'Democratizing the aid encounter in Africa', *International Affairs*, 73(4): 623–39.

De Waal, A. (2003) 'Human rights organizations and the political imagination: how the West and Africa have diverged', *Journal of Human Rights*, 2(4): 475–94.

Décobert, A. (2014) 'Sitting on the fence? Politics and ethics of research into cross-border aid on the Thailand–Myanmar/Burma border', *Journal of Burma Studies*, 18(1): 33–58.

Décobert, A. (2016) *The politics of aid to Burma: a humanitarian struggle on the Thai–Burmese border*, Oxon: Routledge.

Décobert, A. and Wells, T. (2020) 'Interpretive complexity and crisis: the history of international aid to Myanmar', *The European Journal of Development Research*, 32: 294–315.

Diamond, L. (1999) *Developing democracy: toward consolidation*, Baltimore/London: Johns Hopkins University Press.

Dittmer, L. (2008) 'Burma vs Myanmar: what's in a name?', *Asian Survey*, 48(6): 885–8.

DLA Piper Rudnick Gray Cary (2015) 'Threat to the peace: a call for the UN Security Council to act in Burma.' Report commissioned by Václav Havel and Desmond Tutu, Available from: https://burmacampaign.org.uk/media/threat-to-the-peace.pdf [Accessed 18 May 2023].

Doffegnies, A. and Wells, T. (2022) 'The vernacularisation of human rights discourse in Myanmar: rejection, hybridisation and strategic avoidance', *Journal of Contemporary Asia*, 52(2): 247–66.

Doi Ra and Khu Khu Ju (2021) 'Nothing about us, without us: reflections on the challenges of building Land in Our Hands, a national network in Myanmar/Burma', *The Journal of Peasant Studies*, 48(3): 497–516.

Donnelly, J. (1999) 'Human rights and Asian values: a defense of "Western" universalism', in O.R. Bauer and D.A. Bell (eds) *The East Asian challenge for human rights*, Cambridge: Cambridge University Press, pp 60–87.

Dorning, K. (2006) 'Creating an environment for participation: international NGOs and the growth of civil society in Burma/Myanmar', in T. Wilson (ed) *Myanmar's long road to national reconciliation*, Singapore/Canberra: Institute of Southeast Asian Studies/Asia Pacific Press, pp 188–217.

Dudley, S. (2003) '"External" aspects of self-determination movements in Burma', Oxford: QEH Working Paper Series, Available from: https://www.qeh.ox.ac.uk/publications/external-aspects-self-determination-movements-burma [Accessed 18 May 2023].

Duell, K. (2014) 'Sidelined or reinventing themselves? Exiled activists in Myanmar's political reforms', in N. Cheesman, N. Farrelly and T. Wilson (eds) *Debating democratization in Myanmar*, Singapore: ISEAS, pp 109–35.

Ear, P. (2012) *Aid dependence in Cambodia: how foreign assistance undermines democracy*, New York: Columbia University Press.

EAT/JHU CPHHR (2009a) 'After the storm: voices from the delta', Mae Sot/Baltimore: Emergency Assistance Team (Burma) and Johns Hopkins Bloomberg School of Public Health, Center for Public Health and Human Rights, Available from: https://reliefweb.int/report/myanmar/myanmar-after-storm-voices-delta [Accessed 18 May 2023].

EAT/JHU CPHHR (2009b) 'Statement of Emergency Assistance Team – Burma and the Johns Hopkins Center for Public Health and Human Rights regarding the report "After the storm: voices from the delta"', 20 April, Available from: https://www.burmalibrary.org/docs07/EAT-CPHHR_Response_to_Joint_INGO_Statement-ocr.pdf [Accessed 18 May 2023].

Edwards, M. (2009) *Civil society* (2nd edn), Cambridge: Polity Press.

Edwards, M. (2011) 'Introduction: civil society and the geometry of human relations', in M. Edwards (ed) *The Oxford handbook of civil society* (online edn), Oxford: Oxford University Press.

Egreteau, R. (2011) 'A passage to Burma? India, development, and democratization in Myanmar', *Contemporary Politics*, 17(4): 467–86.

Egreteau, R. (2012) 'Burma in diaspora: a preliminary research note on the politics of Burmese diasporic communities in Asia', *Journal of Current Southeast Asian Affairs*, 31(2): 115–47.

Egreteau, R. (2022) 'Blending old and new repertoires of contention in Myanmar's anti-coup protests', *Social Movement Studies*: 1–8.

Englund, H. (2006) *Prisoners of freedom: human rights and the African poor*, Berkeley: University of California Press.

Farrelly, N. (2018) 'The capital', in A. Simpson, N. Farrelly and I. Holliday (eds) *Routledge handbook of contemporary Myanmar*, Abingdon/ New York: Routledge, pp 55–63.

Ferguson, J.M. (2015) 'Who's counting? Ethnicity, belonging, and the national census in Burma/Myanmar', *Bijdragen tot de taal-, land- en volkenkunde*, 171(1): 1–28.

Ferguson, J.M. (2023) 'Editor's note: special issue; gender and social change in Myanmar', *Journal of Burma Studies*, 27(1): 1–27.

Fink, C. (2009) *Living silence in Burma: surviving under military rule* (2nd edn), London/Chiang Mai: Zed Books/Silkworm Books.

Fink, C. (2018) 'Dangerous speech, anti-Muslim violence, and Facebook in Myanmar', *Journal of International Affairs*, 71(1.5): 43–52.

Fink, C. and Simpson, A. (2018) 'Civil society', in A. Simpson, N. Farrelly and I. Holliday (eds) *Routledge handbook of contemporary Myanmar*, Abingdon/ New York: Routledge, pp 257–67.

Foley, M.W. and Edwards, B. (1996) 'The paradox of civil society', *Journal of Democracy*, 7(3): 38–52.

Forbes, E. (2019) 'Migration, informal settlement, and government response: the cases of four townships in Yangon, Myanmar', *Moussons: Recherche en Sciences Humaines sur l'Asie du Sud-Est*, 33: 95–117.

Ford, M., Gillan, M. and Htwe Htwe Thein (2015) 'From cronyism to oligarchy? Privatisation and business elites in Myanmar', *Journal of Contemporary Asia*, 46(1): 18–41.

Fortify Rights (2015) 'Persecution of Rohingya Muslims: is genocide occurring in Myanmar's Rakhine State? A legal analysis', Fortify Rights/ Allard K. Lowestein International Human Rights Clinic, Yale Law School.

Giddens, A. (1986) *The constitution of society: outline of the theory of structuration*, Cambridge: Polity Press.

Glasius, M. (2010) 'Uncivil society', in H.K. Anheier and M. Juergensmeyer (eds) *Encyclopedia of global studies*, Los Angeles/London/New Delhi/ Singapore: Sage Publications, pp 1583–88.

Glasius, M. (2012) 'Gramsci's trenches: civil society as "warfare"', *International Studies Review*, 14: 670–3.

Glasius, M., Lewis, D. and Seckinelgin, H. (2004) 'Exploring civil society internationally', in M. Glasius, D. Lewis and H. Seckinelgin (eds) *Exploring civil society: political and cultural contexts*, Oxon/New York: Routledge, pp 3–10.

Gravers, M. (2007) (ed) *Exploring ethnic diversity in Burma*, Copenhagen: Nordic Institute of Asian Studies.

Griffiths, M.P. (2019) *Community welfare organisations in rural Myanmar: precarity and parahita*, London: Routledge.

Hargrave, K. (2014) 'Repatriation through a trust-based lens: refugee–state trust relations on the Thai–Burma border and beyond', Refugee Studies Centre, University of Oxford, Working Paper Series no 104, Available from: http://www.rsc.ox.ac.uk/files/publications/working-paper-series/wp104-repatriation-through-a-trust-based-lens_2014.pdf/ [Accessed 18 May 2023].

Harriden, J. (2012) *The authority of influence: women and power in Burmese history*, Honolulu: University of Hawai'i Press.

Harvey, G.E. (1925) *History of Burma: from the earliest time to the end of the first war with British India*, Calcutta/New Delhi: Asian Educational Services.

Hedman, E.E. (2006) *In the name of civil society: from free election movements to people power in the Philippines*, Honolulu: University of Hawai'i Press.

Hedström, J. (2016) 'We did not realize about the gender issues. So, we thought it was a good idea', *International Feminist Journal of Politics*, 18(1): 61–79.

Heidel, B. (2006) *The growth of civil society in Myanmar*, Bangalore: Books for Change.

Henry, N. (2011) 'Civil society amid civil war: political violence and non-violence in the Burmese democracy movement', *Global Society*, 25(1): 97–111.

Hewison, K. and Prager Nyein, S. (2010) 'Civil society and political oppositions in Burma', in Li Chenyang and Wilhelm Hofmeister (eds) *Myanmar: prospect for change*, Singapore/Kunming: Select Publishing/Yunnan University, pp 13–24.

Hindstrom, H. (2012) 'Can Norway forge peace in Burma?', *Democratic Voice of Burma*, 19 July, Available from: https://english.dvb.no/can-norway-forge-peace-in-burma/ [Accessed 18 May 2023].

Holliday, I. (2011) *Burma redux: global justice and the quest for political reform in Myanmar*, Hong Kong/Chiang Mai: Hong Kong University Press/Silkworm Books.

Holliday, I. (2013) 'Myanmar in 2012: toward a normal state', *Asian Survey*, 53(1): 93–100.

Hopgood, S. (2013) *The endtimes of human rights*, Ithaca: Cornell University Press.

Horsey, R. (2011) *Ending forced labour in Myanmar: engaging a pariah regime*, Oxon/New York: Routledge.

Horton, G. (2013) 'Burma's shame: why the ICG's peace award for Thein Sein Is unconscionable', Irrawaddy, 29 April, Available from: https://www.irrawaddy.com/opinion/guest-column/burmas-shame-why-the-icgs-peace-award-for-thein-sein-is-unconscionable.html [Accessed 18 May 2023].

Houtman, G. (1999) *Mental culture in Burmese crisis politics*, Tokyo: ILCAA Institute for the Study of Languages and Cultures of Asia and Africa Monograph Series No 33, Tokyo University of Foreign Studies.

Howell, J. (2007) 'Civil society in China: chipping away at the edges', *Development (Supp. China)*, 50(3): 17–23.

Howell, J. and Pearce, J. (2002) *Civil society and development: a critical exploration*, Boulder, CO: Lynne Rienner Publishers.

Hsu, C. (2010) 'Beyond civil society: an organizational perspective on state–NGO relations in the People's Republic of China', *Journal of Civil Society*, 6(3): 259–77.

Hughes, C. (2009) *Dependent communities: aid and politics in Cambodia and East Timor*, Ithaca: Cornell Southeast Asia Program.

Hulme, D. and Edwards, M. (1997) *NGOs, states and donors: too close for comfort?*, Basingstoke/London: Macmillan Press.

Human Rights Watch (2009) 'The resistance of the monks: Buddhism and activism in Burma', New York: Human Rights Watch.

Human Rights Watch (2010) '"I want to help my own people": state control and civil society in Burma after Cyclone Nargis', New York: Human Rights Watch.

Human Rights Watch (2013) '"All you can do is pray": crimes against humanity and ethnic cleansing of Rohingya Muslims in Burma's Arakan State', New York: Human Rights Watch.

Human Rights Watch (2022) 'Myanmar: Armed Forces Day spotlights atrocities', New York: Human Rights Watch.

International Crisis Group (2002) 'Myanmar: the politics of humanitarian aid', Bangkok/Brussels: International Crisis Group.

International Crisis Group (2006) 'Myanmar: new threats to humanitarian aid', Yangon/Brussels: International Crisis Group.

International Crisis Group (2008) 'Burma/Myanmar after Nargis: time to normalise aid relations', Yangon/Brussels: International Crisis Group.

International Crisis Group (2011) 'Myanmar: major reform underway', Jakarta/Brussels: International Crisis Group.

International Crisis Group (2022) 'Crowdfunding a war: the money behind Myanmar's resistance', Yangon/Melbourne/Brussels: International Crisis Group.

International Crisis Group (2023a) 'A silent Sangha? Buddhist monks in post-coup Myanmar', Bangkok/Brussels: International Crisis Group.

International Crisis Group (2023b) 'A road to nowhere: the Myanmar regime's stage-managed elections', Bangkok/Brussels: International Crisis Group.

Irrawaddy (2010) 'Reasons to vote and not to vote', Irrawaddy, 2 November, Available from: https://www2.irrawaddy.com/opinion_story.php?art_id=19917 [Accessed 18 May 2023].

Irrawaddy (2022) 'Myanmar political prisoners issue list of torturers in junta's Insein prison', Irrawaddy, 17 October, Available from: https://www.irrawaddy.com/news/burma/myanmar-political-prisoners-issue-list-of-torturers-in-juntas-insein-jail.html [Accessed 18 May 2023].

Jangai Jap (2021) 'Protestors and bystanders: ethnic minorities in the pro-democracy revolution', Tea Circle, [online] 22 March, Available from: https://teacircleoxford.com/politics/protesters-and-bystanders-ethnic-minorities-in-the-pro-democracy-revolution/ [Accessed 18 May 2023].

Jaquet, C. and Walton, M.J. (2013) 'Buddhism and relief in Myanmar: reflections on relief as a practice of dāna', in H. Kawanami and G. Samuel (eds) Buddhism, international relief work, and civil society, New York: Palgrave Macmillan, pp 51–74.

Johnston, H. (2006) '"Let's get small": the dynamics of (small) contention in repressive states', Mobilization: An International Journal, 11(2): 195–212.

Jordt, I. (2007) Burma's mass lay meditation movement: Buddhism and the cultural construction of power, Athens: Ohio University Press.

Jordt, I., Tharaphi Than and Sue Ye Lin (2021) 'How Generation Z galvanised a revolutionary movement against Myanmar's 2021 military coup', Trends in Southeast Asia 7, Singapore: ISEAS.

Kagwanja, P. (2005) 'Zimbabwe's March 2005 elections: dangers and opportunities', African Security Review, 14(3): 5–18.

Karen Human Rights Group (2008) 'Village agency: rural rights and resistance in a militarized Karen State', Karen Human Rights Group.

Keck, M. and Sikkink, K. (1998) Activists beyond borders: advocacy networks in international politics, Ithaca: Cornell University Press.

Kiik, L. (2020) 'Confluences amid conflict: how resisting China's Myitsone Dam project linked Kachin and Bamar nationalisms in war-torn Burma', Journal of Burma Studies, 24(2): 229–73.

Kinley, D. and Wilson, T. (2007) 'Engaging a pariah: human rights training in Burma/Myanmar', Human Rights Quarterly, 29: 368–402.

Kirchherr, J. (2018) 'Strategies of successful anti-dam movements: evidence from Myanmar and Thailand', Society & Natural Resources, 31(2): 166–82.

Ko Htwe (2010) 'Election boycott campaign heats up', Irrawaddy, 17 August, Available from: https://www2.irrawaddy.com/article.php?art_id=19236 [Accessed 18 May 2023].

Ko Maung (2021) 'Myanmar's Spring Revolution: a history from below', Open Democracy, 15 December, Available from: https://www.open democracy.net/en/beyond-trafficking-and-slavery/myanmars-spring-rev olution-a-history-from-below/ [Accessed 18 May 2023].

Kramer, T. (2011) 'Civil society gaining ground: opportunities for change and development in Burma', Amsterdam: Transnational Institute/Burma Center Netherlands.

Kramer, T. (2015) 'Ethnic conflict and lands rights in Myanmar', *Social Research: An International Quarterly*, 82(2): 355–74.

Kramer, T. (2021) '"Neither war nor peace": failed ceasefires and dispossession in Myanmar's ethnic borderlands', *The Journal of Peasant Studies*, 48(3): 476–96.

Kyaw Hsu Mon and Lewis, S. (2014) 'Rangoon rental costs in the spotlight after UNICEF outcry', Irrawaddy, 30 May, Available from: https://www.irrawaddy.com/news/burma/rangoon-rental-costs-spotlight-unicef-out cry.html [Accessed 18 May 2023].

Kyaw Yin Hlaing (2004) 'Burma: civil society skirting regime rules', in M. Alagappa (ed) *Civil society and political change in Asia: expanding and contracting democratic space*, Stanford: Stanford University Press, pp 389–418.

Kyaw Yin Hlaing (2007a) 'Associational life in Myanmar: past and present', in N. Ganesan and Kyaw Yin Hlaing (eds) *Myanmar: state, society and ethnicity*, Singapore/Hiroshima: Institute of Southeast Asian Studies/Hiroshima Peace Institute, pp 143–71.

Kyaw Yin Hlaing (2007b) 'The state of the pro-democracy movement in authoritarian Burma', Washington, DC: East–West Center Washington Working Papers.

Kyaw Yin Hlaing (2007c) 'The politics of state–society relations in Burma', *South East Asia Research*, 15(2): 213–54.

Kyaw Yin Hlaing (2008) 'Challenging the authoritarian state: Buddhist monks and peaceful protests in Burma', *The Fletcher Forum of World Affairs*, 32(1): 125–44.

Kyaw Yin Hlaing (2014) 'Political impasse in Myanmar', in Kyaw Yin Hlaing (ed) *Prisms on the golden pagoda: perspectives on national reconciliation in Myanmar*, Singapore: NUS Press, pp 17–67.

Kyaw Zeyar Win (2018) 'Securitization of the Rohingya in Myanmar', in J. Chambers, G. McCarthy, N. Farrelly and Chit Win (eds) *Myanmar transformed? People, places and politics*, Singapore: ISEAS, pp 251–76.

Kyed, H.M. (2019) 'Informal settlements and migrant challenges in Yangon', *Moussons: Recherche en ciences Humaines sur l'Asie du Sud-Est*, 33: 65–94.

Kyed, H.M. and Lynn, A. (2021) 'Soldier defections in Myanmar: motivations and obstacles following the 2021 military coup', Copenhagen: Danish Institute for International Studies.

Lakshmibai, G. (2010) 'A wave of dissent-activists start campaign opposing elections', Democratic Voice of Burma, 13 August, Available from: https://engl ish.dvb.no/a-wave-of-dissent-activists-start-campaign-opposing-elections/ [Accessed 18 May 2023].

Lall, M. (2016) *Understanding reform in Myanmar: people and society in the wake of military rule*, London: Hurst.

Lall, M. and South, A. (2014) 'Comparing models of non-state ethnic education in Myanmar: the Mon and Karen national education regimes', *Journal of Contemporary Asia*, 44(2): 298–321.

Larkin, E. (2010) *Everything is broken: life inside Burma*, London: Granta Books.

Laungaramsri, P. (2006) 'Imagining nation: women's rights and the transnational movement of Shan women in Thailand and Burma', *Focaal – European Journal of Anthropology*, 47: 48–61.

Lee, J.C.H., Huat, W.C., Wong, M. and Guan, Y.S. (2010) 'Elections, repertoires of contention and habitus in four civil society engagements in Malaysia's 2008 general elections', *Social Movement Studies*, 9(3): 293–309.

Lee, Y. (2022) 'The United Nations is failing the people of Myanmar', Washington Post, 2 November, Available from: https://www.washington post.com/opinions/2022/11/02/un-failing-myanmar-burma-people-revolution/ [Accessed 18 May 2023].

Levitt, P. and Merry, S. (2009) 'Vernacularization on the ground: local uses of global women's rights in Peru, China, India and the United States', *Global Networks*, 9(4): 441–61.

Lewis, D. (2001) 'Civil society in non-Western contexts: reflections on the "usefulness" of a concept', London: London School of Economics, Civil Society Working Paper 13. Available from: http://eprints.lse.ac.uk/29052/1/CSWP13_web.pdf [Accessed 18 May 2023].

Lewis, D. (2004) 'On the difficulty of studying "civil society": reflections on NGOs, state and democracy in Bangladesh', *Contributions to Indian Sociology*, 38(3): 299–322.

Li, T.M. (2007) *The will to improve: governmentality, development, and the practices of politics*, Durham/London: Duke University Press.

Lidauer, M. (2012) 'Democratic dawn? Civil society and elections in Myanmar', *Journal of Current Southeast Asian Affairs*, 31(2): 87–114.

Liddell, Z. (2001) 'International policies towards Burma: Western governments, NGOs and multilateral institutions', in International Institute for Democracy and Electoral Assistance (ed) *Challenges to democratization in Burma: perspectives on multilateral and bilateral responses*, Stockholm: IDEA, pp 131–82.

Lieberman, V.B. (1984) *Burmese administrative cycles: anarchy and conquest, c.1580–1760*, Princeton: Princeton University Press.

Liljeblad, J. (2016) 'The 2014 Enabling Law of the Myanmar National Human Rights Commission and the UN Paris Principles: a critical evaluation', *Journal of East Asia and International Law*, 9: 427–47.

Liljeblad, J. (2017) 'The efficacy of human rights institutions seen in context: lessons from the Myanmar Human Rights Commission', *Yale Human Rights and Development Journal*, 19: 70–86.

Lintner, B. (1990) *Outrage: Burma's struggle for democracy*, Bangkok: White Lotus.

Lintner, B. (2019) 'Peaceworks: the United Wa State Army and Burma's peace process', Washington, DC: United States Institute of Peace.

Loong, S. (2021) 'Centre–periphery relations in Myanmar: leverage and solidarity after the 1 February coup', Singapore: ISEAS.

Lorch, J. (2007) 'Myanmar's civil society – a patch for the national education system? The emergence of civil society in areas of state weakness', *Südostasien aktuell – Journal of Current Southeast Asian Affairs*, 3: 54–88.

Lorch, J. (2008) 'Stopgap or change agent? The role of Burma's civil society after the crackdown', *Internationales Asienforum*, 39: 21–54.

MacLean, K. (2022) *Crimes in archival form: human rights, fact production, and Myanmar*, Berkeley: University of California Press.

Malseed, K. (2009) 'Networks of noncompliance: grassroots resistance and sovereignty in militarised Burma', *The Journal of Peasant Studies*, 36(2): 365–91.

Matelski, M. (2014) 'On sensitivity and secrecy: how foreign researchers and their local contacts in Myanmar deal with risk under authoritarian rule', *Journal of Burma Studies*, 18(1): 59–82.

Matelski, M. (2015) 'Fulfilling the right to education? Responsibilities of state and non-state actors in Myanmar's education system', in K. Mills and D.J. Karp (eds) *Human rights protection in global politics: responsibilities of states and non-state actors*, Basingstoke/New York: Palgrave Macmillan, pp 201–20.

Matelski, M. (2016) 'Civil society, foreign aid, and donor dependency in transitional Myanmar', in S. Kosem (ed) *Border twists and Burma trajectories: perceptions, reforms, and adaptations*, Chiang Mai: Center for ASEAN Studies, Chiang Mai University, pp 93–126.

Matelski, M., Dijkstra, R. and McGonigle Ley, B. (2022) 'Multi-layered civil society documentation of human rights violations in Myanmar: the potential for accountability and truth-telling', *Journal of Human Rights Practice*, 14(3): 794–818.

Matelski, M. and Nang Muay Noan (2022) 'Grassroots roles and leadership aspirations: the experiences of young ethnic women in Myanmar civil society organizations', *Journal of Burma Studies*, 26(1): 95–131.

Maung, M. (2022) 'In post-coup Myanmar: "death squads" and extrajudicial killings', *The Diplomat*, 3 November, Available from: https://thediplomat.com/2022/11/in-post-coup-myanmar-death-squads-and-extrajudicial-killings/ [Accessed 18 May 2023].

Maung Maung (1980) *From Sangha to laity: nationalist movements of Burma, 1920–1940*, New Delhi: Manohar.

Maung Shwe Wah (2021) 'Health official who kept Covid-19 vaccine funds from junta hit with corruption charge', Myanmar Now, 2 December, Available from: https://myanmar-now.org/en/news/health-official-who-kept-covid-19-vaccine-funds-from-junta-hit-with-corruption-charge/ [Accessed 18 May 2023].

May, R.A. and Milton, A.K. (eds) (2005) *(Un)civil societies: human rights and democratic transitions in Eastern Europe and Latin America*, Lanham: Lexington Books.

McAdam, D., McCarthy, J.D. and Zald, M.N. (1996) 'Introduction: opportunities, mobilizing structures, and framing processes – toward a synthetic, comparative perspective on social movements', in D. McAdam, J.D. McCarthy and M.N. Zald (eds) *Comparative perspectives on social movements: political opportunities, mobilizing structures, and cultural framings*, Cambridge: Cambridge University Press, pp 1–22.

McCarthy, G. (2019) 'Class dismissed? Explaining the absence of economic injustice in the NLD's governing agenda', *Journal of Current Southeast Asian Affairs*, 38(3): 358–80.

McCarthy, G. and Farrelly, N. (2020) 'Peri-conflict peace: brokerage, development and illiberal ceasefires in Myanmar's borderlands', *Conflict, Security & Development*, 20(1): 141–64.

McConnachie, K. (2022) 'Refugee policy as border governance: refugee return, peacebuilding, and Myanmar's politics of transition', *Modern Asian Studies*, 56(2): 661–90.

Mercer, C. (2002) 'NGOs, civil society and democratization: a critical review of the literature', *Progress in Development Studies*, 2(1): 5–22.

Merry, S.E. (2006) *Human rights and gender violence: translating international law into local justice*, Chicago/London: University of Chicago Press.

Metro, R. (2011) 'The divided discipline of Burma/Myanmar studies: writing a dissertation during the 2010 election', Southeast Asia Program Bulletin (Cornell University), Available from: https://www.academia.edu/22104025/The_divided_discipline_of_Burma_Myanmar_studies_Writing_a_dissertation_during_the_2010_election [Accessed 18 May 2023].

Metro, R. (2023) 'How can scholars from formerly colonizing countries assist in decolonizing Burma Studies?', *Journal of Burma Studies*, 27(1): 171–86.

Michio, T. (2007) 'Who are the Shan? An ethnological perspective', in M. Gravers (ed) *Exploring ethnic diversity in Burma*, Copenhagen: Nordic Institute of Asian Studies (NIAS), pp 178–99.

Min Naing Soon (2021) 'The current crisis in Myanmar: the different political position of the Mon people', Transnational Institute, 2 November, Available from: https://www.tni.org/en/article/the-current-crisis-in-myanmar-the-different-political-position-of-the-mon-people [Accessed 18 May 2023].

Min Zaw Oo and Tønnesson, S. (2023) 'Counting Myanmar's dead: reported civilian casualties since the 2021 military coup', PRIO paper 2023. Peace Research Institute Oslo (PRIO). Available from: https://reliefweb.int/report/myanmar/counting-myanmars-dead-reported-civilian-casualties-2021-military-coup [Accessed 18 May 2023].

Min Zin (2010a) 'Opposition movements in Burma: the question of relevancy', in S.L. Levenstein (ed) *Finding dollars, sense, and legitimacy in Burma*, Washington, DC: Woodrow Wilson International Center for Scholars, pp 77–94.

Min Zin (2010b) 'Burma's road to 3G democracy', Irrawaddy, 14 July, Available from: https://www2.irrawaddy.com/opinion_story.php?art_id=18965 [Accessed 18 May 2023].

Min Zin (2015) 'Anti-Muslim violence in Burma: why now?', *Social Research*, 82(2): 375–97.

Mizzima (2023) 'Myanmar Junta's Airstrikes Linked to 'Four-Cuts' Strategy', [online] 28 May, Available from: https://mizzima.com/article/myanmar-juntas-airstrikes-linked-four-cuts-strategy [Accessed 28 May 2023].

Moe Thuzar (2013) 'Myanmar's 2014 ASEAN chairmanship: a litmus test of progress?', Washington, DC: National Bureau of Asian Research.

Moe Thuzar and Htet Myet Min Tun (2022) 'Myanmar's National Unity Government: a radical arrangement to counteract the coup', Singapore: ISEAS.

Mon Mon Myat (2014) 'Norway's changing role in Burma: driven by peace or business?', Irrawaddy, 5 December, Available from: https://www.irrawaddy.com/opinion/guest-column/norways-changing-role-burma-drive-peace-business.html [Accessed 18 May 2023].

Mon Mon Myat (2023) 'Failure of Third Force's role in unlinking Myanmar political changes with Aung San Suu Kyi', in M. Takeda and C. Yamahata (eds), *Myanmar's changing political landscape*, Springer, pp 151–183.

Mosse, D. (2005) *Cultivating development: an ethnography of aid policy and practice*, London: Pluto Press.

Mullen, M. (2016) *Pathways that changed Myanmar*, London: Bloomsbury Publishing.

Mutua, M. (2001) 'Savages, victims and saviors: the metaphor of human rights', *Harvard International Law Journal*, 42(1): 201–45.

Myo Min (2022) 'Common enemy: a hollow slogan for solidarity in Myanmar', New Mandala, 7 November, Available from: https://www.new mandala.org/common-enemy-a-hollow-slogan-for-solidarity-in-myanmar/ [Accessed 18 May 2023].

Nhu Truong (2022) 'People's power and resistance in Southeast Asia in comparison: a roundtable', New Mandala, 1 June, Available from: https://www.newmandala.org/peoples-power-and-resistance-in-southeast-asia-in-comparison-a-roundtable/ [Accessed 18 May 2023].

Nyein Nyein (2015) 'ABSDF report finds torture, leaves questions in killing of its own', Irrawaddy, 16 March, Available from: https://www.irrawaddy.com/news/burma/absdf-report-finds-torture-leaves-questions-in-killing-of-its-own.html [Accessed 18 May 2023].

Öjendal, J. (2014) 'In search of a civil society: re-negotiating state–society relations in Cambodia', in G. Waibel, J. Ehlert and H.N. Feuer (eds) Southeast Asia and the civil society gaze: scoping a contested concept in Cambodia and Vietnam, Oxon/New York: Routledge, pp 21–38.

Oliver, P.E. and Johnston, H. (2000) 'What a good idea! Ideologies and frames in social movement research', Mobilization: An International Quarterly, 5(1): 37–54.

Olivius, E. (2019) 'Time to go home? The conflictual politics of diaspora return in the Burmese women's movement', Asian Ethnicity, 20(2): 148–67.

Pandita Development Institute (2022) 'Seeking effective assistance for a future: reflections of local advocacy organisations in Myanmar', Myanmar: Pandita Development Institute, Available from: https://www.pandita.org/blog/20221031 [Accessed 18 May 2023].

Parks, T. (2008) 'The rise and fall of donor funding for advocacy NGOs: understanding the impact', Development in Practice, 18(2): 213–22.

Paung Ku (2011) 'The European Commission "Good Governance" programme: is it strengthening civil society?', Yangon: Paung Ku.

Pedersen, M.B. (2007) Promoting human rights in Burma: a critique of Western sanctions policy, Lanham: Rowman & Littlefield Publishers.

Pedersen, M.B. (2012) 'Rethinking international assistance to Myanmar in a time of transition', in N. Cheesman, M. Skidmore and T. Wilson (eds) Myanmar's transition: openings, obstacles, and opportunities, Singapore: ISEAS, pp 271–86.

Pedersen, M.B. (2014) 'Myanmar's democratic opening: the process and prospect of reform', in N. Cheesman, N. Farrelly and T. Wilson (eds) Debating democratization in Myanmar, Singapore: ISEAS, pp 19–40.

Pedersen, M.B. (2019) 'Myanmar in 2018', Southeast Asian Affairs: 225–42.

Pepper, M. (2018) 'Ethnic minority women, diversity, and informal participation in peacebuilding in Myanmar', Journal of Peacebuilding & Development, 13(2): 61–75.

Perry, P.J. (2007) *Myanmar (Burma) since 1962: the failure of development*, Aldershot/Burlington: Ashgate.

Petry, C. and South, A. (2013) 'Mapping of Myanmar peacebuilding civil society', European External Action Service for the European Commission: Civil Society Dialogue Network, Available from: http://www.ashleysouth. co.uk/files/EPLO_CSDN_Myanmar_MappingMyanmarPeacebuilding CivilSociety_CPetrieASouth.pdf [Accessed 18 May 2023].

Phyu Phyu Oo (2021) 'The importance of Myanmar's pots and pans protests', The Lowy Institute, [online] 11 February, Available from: https://www. lowyinstitute.org/the-interpreter/importance-myanmar-s-pots-pans-protests [Accessed 18 May 2023].

Pinheiro, P.S. (2009) 'End Burma's system of impunity', The New York Times, 27 May, Available from: http://www.nytimes.com/2009/05/28/ opinion/28iht-edpineiro.html?_r=0 [Accessed 18 May 2023].

Prasse-Freeman, E. (2012) 'Power, civil society, and an inchoate politics of the daily in Burma/Myanmar', *The Journal of Asian Studies*, 71(2): 371–97.

Prasse-Freeman, E. and Phyo Win Latt (2018) 'Class and inequality', in A. Simpson, N. Farrelly and I. Holliday (eds) *Routledge handbook of contemporary Myanmar*, Abingdon: Routledge, pp 404–16.

Purcell, M. (1999) '"Axe-handles or willing minions?" International NGOs in Burma', in Burma Center Netherlands and Transnational Institute (eds) *Strengthening civil society in Burma: possibilities and dilemmas for international NGOs*, Chiang Mai: Silkworm Books, 69–102.

Radio Free Asia (2022) 'Local PDF Leader Confirms Killing of 10 in Myanmar's Sagaing Region', [online] 19 March, Available from: https:// www.voanews.com/a/local-pdf-leader-confirms-killing-of-10-in-myan mar-s-sagaing-region/6492224.html [Accessed 18 May 2023].

Renshaw, C. (2019) 'Myanmar's transition without justice', *Journal of Current Southeast Asian Affairs*, 38(3): 381–403.

Reny, M. (2022) 'Myanmar in 2021: the military is back in power', *Asian Survey*, 62(1): 137–44.

Rieffel, L. and Fox, J.W. (2013) 'Too much too soon? The dilemma of foreign aid to Myanmar/Burma', Arlington, VA: Nathan Associates.

Roy, C., Ware, A. and Laoutides, C. (2021) 'The political economy of Norwegian peacemaking in Myanmar's peace process', *Third World Quarterly*, 42(9): 2172–88.

Sadan, M. (2013) *Being and becoming Kachin: histories beyond the state in the borderworlds of Burma*, Oxford: Oxford University Press.

Sakhong, L.H. (2007) 'Christianity and Chin identity', in M. Gravers (ed) *Exploring ethnic diversity in Burma*, Copenhagen: Nordic Institute of Asian Studies (NIAS), pp 200–26.

Salem-Gervais, N. and Metro, R. (2012) 'A textbook case of nation-building: the evolution of history curricula in Myanmar', *Journal of Burma Studies*, 16(1): 27–78.

Salemink, O. (2006) 'Translating, interpreting, and practicing civil society in Vietnam: a tale of calculated misunderstandings', in D. Lewis and D. Mosse (eds) *Development brokers and translators: the ethnography of aid and agencies*, Bloomfield: Kumarian Press, pp 101–26.

Salmenkari, T.M. (2013) 'Theoretical poverty in the research of Chinese civil society', *Modern Asian Studies*, 47(2): 682–711.

Saw Yan Naing (2016) 'Where has Burma's peace money gone?', Irrawaddy, 1 April, Available from: https://www.irrawaddy.com/news/burma/where-has-burmas-peace-money-gone.html [Accessed 18 May 2023].

Schlein, L. (2023) 'Restrictions in Myanmar impede efforts to help victims of Cyclone Mocha', *VOA News*, 16 May, Available from: https://www.voanews.com/a/restrictions-in-myanmar-impede-efforts-to-help-victims-of-cyclone-mocha-/7096003.html [Accessed 18 May 2023].

Schober, J. (2011) *Modern Buddhist conjunctures in Myanmar: cultural narratives, colonial legacies, and civil society*, Honolulu: University of Hawai'i Press.

Scott, J.C. (1985) *Weapons of the weak: everyday forms of peasant resistance*, New Haven/London: Yale University Press.

Sekine, Y. (2023) 'Agrarian struggles in the era of climate change, populism and authoritarianism in Myanmar', Unpublished PhD thesis, International Institute of Social Studies, Erasmus University Rotterdam.

Selth, A. (1998) 'Burma's intelligence apparatus', *Intelligence and National Security*, 13(4): 33–70.

Selth, A. (2013) 'Burma's security forces: performing, reforming or transforming?', Griffith Asia Institute, Regional Outlook Paper 45, Available from: https://www.files.ethz.ch/isn/173085/Regional-Outlook-Paper-45-Selth.pdf [Accessed 2023].

Selth, A. (2015) 'Burma's Tatmadaw: a force to be reckoned with', in A. Selth (ed) *Interpreting Myanmar: a decade of analysis*, Acton: ANU Press, 2020, pp 373–77.

Sen, A. (1997) 'Human rights and Asian values', 16th Morgenthau Memorial Lecture on Ethics and Foreign Policy, New York: Carnegie Council on Ethics and International Affairs.

Shwe Shwe Sein Latt, Kim N. B. Ninh, Mi Ki Kyaw Mint and S. Lee (2017) 'Women's Political Participation in Myanmar. Experiences of women parliamentarians 2011–2016', The Asia Foundation and Phan Tee Eain.

Sikkink, K. (2011) *The justice cascade: how human rights prosecutions are changing world politics*, New York: W. W. Norton & Company.

Simpson, A. (2014) *Energy, governance and security in Thailand and Myanmar (Burma)*, Farnham, Surrey: Ashgate.

Simpson, A. and Farrelly, N. (2020) 'The Rohingya crisis and questions of accountability', *Australian Journal of International Affairs*, 74(5): 486–94.

Skidmore, M. (2004) *Karaoke fascism: Burma and the politics of fear*, Philadelphia: University of Pennsylvania Press.

Slim, H. (2022) 'Humanitarian resistance: its ethical and operational importance', London: Humanitarian Practice Network.

Smith, M. (1991) *Burma: insurgency and the politics of ethnicity*, London: Zed Books.

Smith, M. (1999) 'Ethnic conflict and the challenge of civil society in Burma', in Burma Center Netherlands and Transnational Institute (eds) *Strengthening civil society in Burma: possibilities and dilemmas for international NGOs*, Chiang Mai: Silkworm Books, pp 15–53.

Snow, D.A. and Benford, R.D. (1988) 'Ideology, frame resonance, and participant mobilization', *International Social Movement Research*, 1: 197–218.

Snow, D.A. and Benford, R.D. (1992) 'Master frames and cycles of protest', in A.D. Morris and C. McClurg Mueller (eds) *Frontiers in social movement theory*, New Haven: Yale University Press, pp 133–55.

Sogge, D. (2002) *Give and take: what's the matter with foreign aid?*, New York: Palgrave.

South, A. (2003) *Mon nationalism and civil war in Burma: the golden sheldrake*, London/New York: Routledge.

South, A. (2004) 'Political transition in Myanmar: a new model for democratization', *Contemporary Southeast Asia*, 26(2): 233–55.

South, A. (2008a) 'Civil society in Burma: the development of democracy amidst conflict', Washington, DC: East–West Center.

South, A. (2008b) *Ethnic politics in Burma: states of conflict*, Oxon/New York: Routledge.

Spires, A.J. (2011) 'Contingent symbiosis and civil society in an authoritarian state: understanding the survival of China's grassroots NGOs', *American Journal of Sociology*, 117(1): 1–45.

Spires, A.J. and Ogawa, A. (2022) 'Introduction: civil society in Asia; challenging and navigating the boundaries of authoritarianism', in A.J. Spires and A. Ogawa (eds) *Authoritarianism and civil society in Asia*, Oxon/New York: Routledge, pp 1–15.

Stammers, N. (1999) 'Social movements and the social construction of human rights', *Human Rights Quarterly*, 21(4): 980–1008.

Stecklow, S. (2018) 'Hatebook: inside Facebook's Myanmar operation; a Reuters special report', Available from: https://www.reuters.com/investigates/special-report/myanmar-facebook-hate/ [Accessed 18 May 2023].

Steinberg, D.I. (1999) 'A void in Myanmar: civil society in Burma', in Burma Center Netherlands and Transnational Institute (eds) *Strengthening civil society in Burma: possibilities and dilemmas for international NGOs*, Chiang Mai: Silkworm Books, pp 1–14.

Steinberg, D.I. (2001) *Burma: the state of Myanmar*, Washington, DC: Georgetown University Press.

Steinberg, D.I. (2010) *Burma/Myanmar: what everyone needs to know*, Oxford: Oxford University Press.

Stokke, K., Klo Kwe Moo Kham, Nang K.L. Nge and Kvanvik, S.H. (2022) 'Illiberal peacebuilding in a hybrid regime: authoritarian strategies for conflict containment in Myanmar', *Political Geography*, 93: 1–14.

Su Mon Thant (2021) 'In the wake of the coup: how Myanmar youth arose to fight for the nation', Brussels: Heinrich Böll Stiftung European Union.

Su Mon Thazin Aung (2016) 'The politics of policymaking in transitional government', in N. Cheesman and N. Farrelly (eds) *Conflict in Myanmar: war, politics, religion*, Singapore: ISEAS, pp 25–46.

Taylor, R.H. (2009) *The state in Myanmar*, Singapore: NUS Press.

Teets, J.C. (2009) 'Post-earthquake relief and reconstruction efforts: the emergence of civil society in China?', *The China Quarterly*, 198: 330–47.

Thawnghmung, A.M. (2004) *Behind the teak curtain: authoritarianism, agricultural policies and political legitimacy in rural Burma/Myanmar*, London: Kegan Paul.

Thawnghmung, A.M. (2008) *The Karen revolution in Burma: diverse voices, uncertain ends*, Washington: East–West Center.

Thawnghmung, A.M. (2018) 'Rural', in A. Simpson, N. Farrelly and I. Holliday (eds) *Routledge handbook of contemporary Myanmar*, Abingdon/New York: Routledge, pp 72–82.

Thawnghmung, A.M. and Htoo, Saw Eh (2022) 'The fractured centre: "two-headed government" and threats to the peace process in Myanmar', *Modern Asian Studies*, 56(2): 504–32.

Thawnghmung, A.M. and Noah, Khun (2021) 'Myanmar's military coup and the elevation of the minority agenda?', *Critical Asian Studies*, 53(2): 297–309.

Thawnghmung, A.M. and Robinson, G. (2017) 'Myanmar's new era: a break from the past, or too much of the same?', *Southeast Asian Affairs*: 237–58.

Thiha, A. (2023) 'It's time to rethink Myanmar's Ethnic Armed Organizations', The Diplomat [online] 24 March, Available from: https://thediplomat.com/2023/03/its-time-to-rethink-myanmars-ethnic-armed-organizations/ [Accessed 18 May 2023].

Thiha, A. and Nilsen, M. (2023) 'Monks and militias in Myanmar', East Asia Forum [online] 10 March, Available from: https://www.eastasiaforum.org/2023/03/10/monks-and-militias-in-myanmar/ [Accessed 18 May 2023].

Thin Lei Win (2019) 'Cracking the glass ceiling in Myanmar media', in L. Brooten, J. McElhone and G. Venkiteswaren (eds) *Myanmar media in transition: legacies, challenges and change*, Singapore: ISEAS, pp 243–50.

Thu Thu Aung and McPherson, P. (2022) 'Monk militia: the Buddhist clergy backing Myanmar's junta', Reuters, 8 December, Available from: https://www.reuters.com/world/asia-pacific/monk-militia-buddhist-clergy-backing-myanmars-junta-2022-12-08/ [Accessed 18 May 2023].

Tin Maung Maung Than (2016) 'Myanmar's General Election 2015: change was the name of the game', *Southeast Asian Affairs*: 241–64.

TNI (2010) 'A changing ethnic landscape: analysis of Burma's 2010 polls', Burma Policy Briefing 4, December, Amsterdam: Transnational Institute.

TNI (2013) 'The Kachin crisis: peace must prevail', Burma Policy Briefing 10, March, Amsterdam: Transnational Institute.

TNI (2014) 'Ethnicity without meaning, data without context: the 2014 census; identity and citizenship in Burma/Myanmar', Amsterdam: Transnational Institute.

TNI (2015) 'Ethnic politics and the 2015 elections in Myanmar', Amsterdam: Transnational Institute.

TNI (2017) 'Beyond Panglong: Myanmar's national peace and reform dilemma', Amsterdam: Transnational Institute.

Tonkin, D. (2007) 'The 1990 elections in Myanmar: broken promises or a failure of communication?', *Contemporary Southeast Asia: A Journal of International and Strategic Affairs*, 29(1): 33–54.

Tsing, A.L. (2004) *Friction: an ethnography of global connections*, Princeton: Princeton University Press.

Turner, A. (2014) *Saving Buddhism: the impermanence of religion in colonial Burma*, Honolulu: University of Hawai'i Press.

UN Human Rights Council (2022) 'Progress made and remaining challenges with regard to the recommendations of the independent international fact-finding mission on Myanmar. Report of the Office of the United Nations High Commissioner for Human Rights.' [online] 21 September, Available from: https://digitallibrary.un.org/record/4008446 [Accessed 18 May 2023].

UNFPA (2017) 'Nationwide youth information corners situation analysis report', United Nations Population Fund/Ministry of Health and Sports, Available from: https://myanmar.unfpa.org/sites/default/files/pub-pdf/YIC_preview.pdf [Accessed 18 May 2023].

Van Tuijl, P. (1999) 'NGOs and human rights: sources of justice and democracy', *Journal of International Affairs*, 52(2): 493–512.

Vigh, H. (2009) 'Motion squared: a second look at the concept of social navigation', *Anthropological Theory*, 9(4): 419–38.

Vrieze, P. (2023) 'Joining the Spring Revolution or charting their own path? Ethnic minority strategies following the 2021 Myanmar coup', *Asian Survey*, 63(1): 90–120.

Wade, F. (2017) *Myanmar's enemy within*, London: Zed Books.

Wai Moe (2010a) 'Students arrested for urging election boycott', Irrawaddy, 29 September, Available from: https://www2.irrawaddy.com/article.php?art_id=19581 [Accessed 2023].

Wai Moe (2010b) 'Pro-election think tank feels the pressure', Irrawaddy, 21 July, Available from: https://election.irrawaddy.com/news/384-pro-election-think-tank-feels-the-pressure.html [Accessed 18 May 2023].

Waibel, G. (2014) 'Grasping discourses, researching practices: investigating civil society in Vietnam and Cambodia', in G. Waibel, J. Ehlert and H.N. Feuer (eds) *Southeast Asia and the civil society gaze: scoping a contested concept in Cambodia and Vietnam*, Oxon/New York: Routledge, pp 1–17.

Walder, A.G. (2009) 'Political sociology and social movements', *Annual Review of Sociology*, 35: 393–412.

Walker, T. (2021) 'Doctor-activist defiant against Myanmar military', VOA News, 15 June, Available from: https://www.voanews.com/a/east-asia-pacific_doctor-activist-defiant-against-myanmar-military/6207031.html [Accessed 18 May 2023].

Walton, M.J. (2008) 'Ethnicity, conflict and history in Burma: the myths of Panglong', *Asian Survey*, 48(6): 889–910.

Walton, M.J. (2012a) 'Politics in the moral universe: Burmese Buddhist political thought', PhD thesis, University of Washington, Available from: https://digital.lib.washington.edu/researchworks/bitstream/handle/1773/21768/Walton_washington_0250E_10956.pdf [Accessed 18 May 2023].

Walton, M.J. (2012b) 'The "wages of Burman-ness": ethnicity and Burman privilege in contemporary Myanmar', *Journal of Contemporary Asia*, iFirst article, 43: 1–27.

Walton, M.J. (2015a) 'The disciplining discourse of unity in Burmese politics', *Journal of Burma Studies*, 19(1): 1–26.

Walton, M.J. (2015b) 'Monks in politics, monks in the world: Buddhist activism in contemporary Myanmar', *Social Research*, 82(2): 507–30.

Walton, M. J. (2016) *Buddhism, politics and political thought in Myanmar*. Cambridge: Cambridge University Press.

Walton, M.J. (2018) 'Reflections on Myanmar under the NLD so far', in J. Chambers, G. McCarthy, N. Farrelly and Chit Win (eds) *Myanmar transformed? People, places and politics*, Singapore: ISEAS, pp 311–18.

Walton, M.J. and Hayward, S. (2014) 'Contesting Buddhist narratives: democratization, nationalism, and communal violence in Myanmar,' Honolulu: East–West Center.

Walton, M.J., McKay, M. and Daw Khin Mar Mar Kyi (2015) 'Women and Myanmar's "Religious Protection Laws"', *The Review of Faith & International Affairs*, 13(4): 36–49.

Ware, A. (2012) *Context-sensitive development: how international NGOs operate in Myanmar*, Sterling, VA: Kumarian Press.

Warr, P. (2020) 'Poverty and inequality in Myanmar: 2005–2017', in J. Chambers, C. Galloway and J. Liljeblad (eds) *Living with Myanmar*, Singapore: ISEAS, pp 125–56.

Watanabe, C. (2014) 'Muddy labor: a Japanese aid ethic of collective intimacy in Myanmar', *Cultural Anthropology*, 29(4): 649–71.

Weiss, M.L. and Hansson, E. (2023) 'Civil society in politics and Southeast Asia in civil society: conceptual foundations', in E. Hansson and M. L. Weiss (eds) *Routledge handbook of civil and uncivil society*, Oxon/New York: Routledge, pp 1–22.

Wells, T. (2020) 'Narratives of donor accountability in support to peace processes: the case of the Joint Peace Fund in Myanmar', *Journal of Peacebuilding & Development*, 15(1): 18–30.

Wells, T. (2021) *Narrating democracy in Myanmar: the struggle between activists, democratic leaders and aid workers*, Amsterdam: Amsterdam University Press.

Wells-Dang, A. (2012) *Civil society networks in China and Vietnam: informal pathbreakers in health and the environment*, Basingstoke/New York: Palgrave Macmillan.

Whaites, A. (1996) 'Let's get civil society straight: NGOs and political theory', *Development in Practice*, 6(3): 240–9.

Williams, D.C. (2012) 'Changing Burma from without: political activism among the Burmese diaspora', *Indiana Journal of Global Legal Studies*, 19(1): 121–42.

Win Tin (2010) 'An election not worthy of support', The New York Times, 30 September, Available from: http://www.nytimes.com/2010/10/01/opinion/01iht-eduwintin.html?_r=0 [Accessed 18 May 2023].

Women's League of Burma (2021) 'Solidarity Message to our Rohingya Sisters and Brothers', [online] 25 August 2021, Available from: https://www.womenofburma.org/statements/solidarity-message-our-rohingya-sisters-and-brothers [Accessed 18 May 2023].

Woods, K. (2011) 'Ceasefire capitalism: military–private partnerships, resource concessions and military–state building in the Burma–China borderlands', *The Journal of Peasant Studies*, 38(4): 747–70.

Woods, K. (2017) 'The war to rule: ceasefire capitalism and state-making in Burma's borderlands', Unpublished PhD thesis, University of California, Berkeley, Available from: https://escholarship.org/content/qt32b98 4t4/qt32b984t4_noSplash_1467b3b0eba33f6aef2bd8d69c39386f.pdf?t= q6z2lq [Accessed 18 May 2023].

Ye Myo Hein (2022) 'One year on: the momentum of Myanmar's armed rebellion', Washington, DC: The Wilson Center/Tagaung Institute of Political Studies.

Ye Myo Hein and Myers, L. (2022) 'Action on Ukraine, quiescence on Myanmar: the limitations of a "democracy versus authoritarianism" framing', Washington, DC: The Wilson Center/Tagaung Institute of Political Studies.

Zarni, M. (2006) 'Thinking politics sociologically: engaging with the state and society in Vietnam and Myanmar/Burma', in Heinrich Boell Foundation (ed) *Active citizens under political wraps: experiences from Myanmar/Burma and Vietnam*, Chiang Mai: Heinrich Boell Foundation, pp 189–200.

Zarni, M. (2012) 'Orientalisation and manufacturing of "civil society" in contemporary Burma', in Z. Ibrahim (ed) *Social science and knowledge in a globalising world*, Kajang: Malaysian Social Science Association, pp 287–310.

Zaw Oo (2006) 'Exit, choice and loyalty in Burma: the role of overseas Burmese in democratising their homeland', in T. Wilson (ed) *Myanmar's long road to national reconciliation*, Singapore/Canberra: Institute of Southeast Asian Studies/Asia Pacific Press, 231–59.

# Index

References to endnotes show both the page number and the note number (172n13).

88 Generation Students 24–25, 38, 56
969 movement 42, 168n11
1988 uprising 21–22

**A**

adversarial framing 93, 110–111
Advisory Commission on Rakhine
   State 46–47
aid
   (de)politicization 123–130, 150
   donor dependency 117–118, 132–135
   expansion 121, 127–128, 163–164
   foreign assistance to civil society 122,
      126–127, 153–154
   restrictions 119–120, 122, 153
All Burma Federation of Student Unions
   (ABFSU) 38, 56, 106
All Burma Monks' Alliance (ABMA) 25, 50
All Burma Students' Democratic Front
   (ABSDF) 39, 40, 59, 168n23
Alternative ASEAN Network on Burma
   (ALTSEAN-Burma) 63, 97,
   124–125
American Center 67, 77, 126, 127
amnesties (prison) 27, 140, 173n3
Amnesty International 63, 131, 151
anti-colonial resistance 17–19, 35, 104,
   168n2, 170n25
Anti-Fascist People's Freedom League
   (AFPFL) 19, 36
Anti-Junta Mass Movement Committee 137
Arakan Rohingya Salvation Army
   (ARSA) 47
Asian Development Bank 127–128, 141
Assistance Association for Political Prisoners
   (Burma; AAPP) 40, 56, 88, 173n2
Association of Southeast Asian Nations
   (ASEAN) 28, 57, 120, 152–153
Aung Kyaw Moe 147
Aung Myo Min 145, 150
Aung San, General 18–19, 36

Aung San Suu Kyi
   house arrest 2, 23, 24
   imprisonment (post-2021 coup) 136, 145
   NLD rule *see* National League for Democracy
   Nobel Peace Prize 24, 131
   political career 22, 45, 158
   Rohingya 44, 47, 131, 147
Australia 120, 124, 126
   donor aid to Myanmar 126
   human rights training 120

**B**

Ban Ki-Moon 57, 150
Bangladesh
   civil society 33
   Rohingya refugees 43, 47, 131, 147,
      152, 172n13
Best Friend, the 50–51, 87, 171n17
Blood Money campaign 154
British
   aid to Myanmar 119, 127
   colonialism 14, 17–19
   *see also* anti-colonial resistance
British Council 67, 127
Buddha Dhamma Parahita Foundation 47
   *see also* MaBaTha
Buddhist
   civil society 34, 35, 37, 38, 49–52, 58, 118, 138
   nationalism 17–18, 32, 35, 42–44, 46, 131, 159
   sangha (monks, nuns) 35, 50–51
   *see also* MaBaTha
Burma Campaign UK 63, 97
Burma Center Netherlands 5, 8, 13, 96, 169n14
Burma Fund 70, 122
Burma Independence Army (BIA) 18
Burma/Myanmar name change 14–15
Burma Partnership 64–65, 88, 91, 104–105, 113
Burma Socialist Programme Party
   (BSPP) 20–21, 36–37, 119
Burman dominance 17, 19, 29, 53, 55, 98,
   110, 155

Burmese Rohingya Organisation UK 131
Burmese Women's Union (BWU) 40, 59
Byamaso Organization 61

**C**

capacity building 70, 118, 119, 121, 164
Capacity Building Initiative 70, 170n22
'ceasefire capitalism' 28, 149
ceasefires 28–29, 52
  civil society development 38, 52–53,
    121, 169n4
  see also peace process, Nationwide
    Ceasefire Agreement
census 43, 54, 128, 166Intro–n1, 173n14
Centre for Peace and Conflict Studies
    (Cambodia) 101, 102, 107, 114–115
Chin
  discrimination 29
  ethnic sub-groups 54
  post-coup military attacks 142
  post-coup resistance 148
China
  aid to Myanmar 120
  arms trade with Myanmar 146
  civil society 75–76, 79–80, 163, 169n9
  UN position on Myanmar 113, 152
Christian civil society see religious organizations
Citizenship Act 20–21, 29, 44, 54
civic space see room to manoeuvre
Civil Disobedience Movement (CDM) 4,
    137, 141, 145, 173n7
civil society
  authoritarian rule 60, 72–76, 79, 85–86,
    161–163
  definitions 7–8, 31–32, 60, 68, 73–74,
    84–86, 161
  diversity and fault lines 49–71
  ethnic organizations 34–36, 39–40, 52–53,
    97, 121, 122, 148
  generations 55–58
  government consultation of 27, 41, 88
  professionalization 32, 67, 68–70, 88,
    132, 160
  relations to the state 79–81, 85–86, 162
  religious organizations 35, 36, 49–52,
    118–119
  representation 33, 55, 62, 68–69, 94, 105,
    156, 158, 165
  respondents 9–12, 67
  role of women 58–60, 68–69, 129, 149
  in (Southeast) Asia 7, 163
  see also CBOs, democracy movement,
    GONGOs, NGOs, 'Third Force',
    welfare organizations
class 7, 29, 66–67, 149, 163
Cold War 19, 119
collective action frames 92–93
Commission of Inquiry campaign
    113–115, 172n18

Committee Representing Pyidaungsu
    Hluttaw (CRPH) 144, 145, 147
Communist Party of Burma
    (CPB) 19, 167n6
community-based organizations (CBOs) 33,
    34, 41, 132
'competitive victimhood' 54, 130
constitution
  1947 19, 20
  1974 20, 23, 75
  2008 25–26, 81, 82, 104, 113, 136, 144,
    155, 168n22
'contingent symbiosis' 79, 162
coup
  1962 17, 20
  2021 2, 83, 136, 137–138, 140
COVID-19 140
Cyclone Nargis 25–26, 57–58, 94, 99–102,
    125–126

**D**

defections see 'watermelons'
democracy movement 39–40, 70, 83, 171n15
  donor aid 122
  position of ethnic nationalities 54–55, 94, 149
  position of women 59
  transnational aspects 63–65, 90–91, 93,
    97–98, 99–102, 159
  see also student activists, exile organizations
democracy promotion 7, 32, 118,
    126–127, 158
Depayin incident 24, 105, 120
diaspora see exile organizations
Dobama Asiayone 18
donor recommendations 163–165
  see also aid

**E**

Ei Thinzar Maung 138, 145, 147
election boycott 81, 91, 103–107, 108–109,
    110–112, 154
elections
  1960 20
  1990 23, 167n12
  2010 26, 72, 81–83, 90, 96–97, 103–114,
    168n13
  2015 44–46, 57
  2020 136
elitism in civil society 67, 69, 70–71, 84
  see also professionalization
Equality Myanmar see Human Rights
    Education Institute of Burma (HREIB)
Esther Ze Naw 138
ethnic armed organizations (EAOs) 20,
    28–29, 141, 147, 166ch2n2
  see also ceasefires, peace process
ethnic nationalities 1, 15–16, 17–19, 46, 143,
    148, 166Intro–n1, 166Intro–n7, 166ch1n3
  federalism 19, 46, 53–55, 144, 148, 169n5

minorities within minority states 54, 169n4, 169n5
political parties 23, 45, 83, 106–108, 110–111, 167n18
victimization 28, 53–54, 82, 114, 130
Euro-Burma Office (EBO) 87, 96–97
European Parliament 150
European Union (EU) 119, 128, 129, 131, 152
exile organizations 39–41, 62–65, 87–88, 95–99, 119, 122
*see also* inside/outside division

**F**

Facebook (Meta) 43–44
farmers *see* rural
federalism *see* ethnic nationalities
Federal Democracy Charter 144
framing 92–94, 110, 154, 160
*see also* collective action frames
Free Burma Coalition (FBC) 63, 96, 119
Free Funeral Service Society 61, 83

**G**

Gambia 47, 131, 155
gender 58–60, 142, 173n5
General Council of Burmese Associations (GCBA) 35, 104
General Strike Committee 138
Generation Wave 56–57, 87, 91, 105
Generation Z 137, 142, 147
genocide 47, 168n14
government-organized non-governmental organizations (GONGOs) 60–62, 122–124
grassroots 66, 68, 134

**H**

hate speech (against Muslims) 4, 42–44
Hsaya San Rebellion 18, 35, 166ch1n2
Htin Kyaw 45
human rights
advocacy 90, 93–94, 101
conceptualizations 13–14, 51, 78–79, 92, 159
international movement 13, 59, 65, 95
norms 13
organizations 40, 53, 63–64, 114, 148
training 64–65, 120
Human Rights Education Institute of Burma (HREIB) 41, 64, 87, 145
Human Rights Watch 101

**I**

ICT for Development Organization 44
independence movement 18, 35
Independent International Fact-Finding Mission on Myanmar (IIFFMM) 47, 131

Independent Investigative Mechanism for Myanmar (IIMM) 131
India
arms trade with Myanmar 146
policy on Myanmar 120
informers *see* surveillance
inside/outside division 31, 62–65, 87–89, 95–102, 122–127, 129
inter-ethnic solidarity 42, 142–143
International Committee of the Red Cross (ICRC) 121–123
International Council of Voluntary Agencies 123
International Court of Justice (ICJ) 47, 131, 150–151, 168n14
International Criminal Court (ICC) 131, 150
International Crisis Group (ICG) 114, 123, 125, 128
international justice 113–114, 130–131
International Labour Organization (ILO) 121, 125
international Non-Governmental Organizations (INGOs) 99–100, 121–122, 123–125, 133–134, 164
intersectional lens 49, 59–60
intra-ethnic diversity 53–54, 129, 149
Islamic civil society *see* religious organizations

**J**

Japan
donor aid to Myanmar 119, 120, 172n4
occupation of Burma 18, 119
Joint Peace Fund 129, 172n12

**K**

Kachin
civil war 42, 46, 82, 108
ethnic sub-groups 54
post-coup military attacks 142
Kachin Baptist Convention (KBC) 36, 52–53
Kachin Independence Army (KIA) 20, 29, 142
Kachin Independence Organization (KIO) 52, 142
Karen
ethnic sub-groups 54
post-coup resistance 148
Karen Human Rights Group (KHRG) 53, 148
Karen National Union (KNU) 19, 36, 52, 141, 148
Kayah State, attack on aid workers 142, 153
Khin Nyunt 24, 28, 77, 121–122, 172n8
Ko Jimmy 139, 169n8
Ko Ni 46–47
Kyaw Moe Tun 149

**L**

labour unions  37, 38, 68, 138
Lanzin Youth Organization  37
LGBTIQ+  60, 142
Letpadan demonstration  46, 129
Letpadaung copper mine  45
Local Defence Forces (LDFs)  145–146
Local Resource Centre  41, 70, 170n23

**M**

MaBaTha  32, 43, 47, 51, 146, 159
  see also Pyu Saw Htee
'marketing of rebellion'  92
Maung Zarni  63–64, 96
  see also Free Burma Coalition
Médecins Sans Frontières (MSF)  123–124, 130
media organizations  39, 40, 91, 99, 122,
  127, 168n8
Metta Development Foundation  52, 62,
  126, 133
military see tatmadaw
Military Intelligence (Service)  20, 77, 87
  see also surveillance
Milk Tea Alliance  143
Min Aung Hlaing  44, 47, 131–132, 136
Min Ko Naing  38, 42, 56, 168n4
Mon
  Literature and Culture Committee  36, 52
  political party positions  107, 148
Myanmar Baptist Convention  51
Myanmar Egress  58, 70–71, 83–84, 91,
  110–111, 170n27
  see also 'Third Force'
Myanmar Maternal and Child Welfare
  Association (MMCWA)  61
Myanmar Peace Center  29, 128
Myanmar Peace Support Initiative  29,
  128, 172n5
Myanmar Police Force  78, 129
Myitsone Dam  41, 42, 143

**N**

National Coalition Government of the Union
  of Burma (NCGUB)  6, 24, 27, 97, 119,
  123, 168n4
National Convention  24
National Democratic Force
  (NDF)  107, 167n18
National Endowment for Democracy  122
National Human Rights Commission  27
National League for Democracy (NLD)
  election boycott  26, 81, 104
  electoral victory  23–24, 27, 44–46, 136,
  167n12, 173n1
  leadership  13
  treatment of civil society  45
  treatment of Muslims  46–47, 131
National Unity Consultative Council
  (NUCC)  144, 155

National Unity Government (NUG)  4, 87,
  144, 156, 173n6
National Unity Party (NUP)  23,
  26, 167n19
Nationwide Ceasefire Agreement
  (NCA)  29, 53, 148, 169n5
natural resources  23, 28, 42, 53
Naypyidaw  24, 120, 138
Ne Win  20, 21, 167n8
Network for Human Rights Documentation
  – Burma  40, 64
non-governmental organizations (NGOs)  8,
  41, 51–52, 68, 76, 132–134
NGO Registration Law  87, 139, 153
'norm entrepreneurs'  108
Norway  29, 128, 172n11

**O**

Official Development Assistance (ODA)  119,
  120, 125, 127, 172n7
Official Secrets Act  47, 75, 139
Organisation of Islamic Cooperation
  (OIC)  130
Organization for the Protection of Race and
  Religion see MaBaTha

**P**

Pandita Development Institute  164, 174n13
Panglong Agreement  19
parahita see welfare organizations
Paung Ku  70, 134, 170n24, 173n20
peace process  46, 53, 128, 129, 169n6
  see also ceasefires, Nationwide
  Ceasefire Agreement
Peaceful Assembly and Peaceful Procession
  Law  27, 45
People's Defence Forces (PDFs)  4, 141–142,
  145–146, 150, 154–155
Phyo Zayar Thaw  45, 57, 139, 169n8
political prisoners  25, 27, 56, 75, 138, 154,
  167n16, 167n17
'popular intellectuals'  67
positionality  5–6
pots and pans protests  137, 143
Progressive Voice see Burma Partnership
Pyoe Pin  70, 127, 170n25
Pyu Saw Htee  146

**R**

Race and Religion Laws  43, 159
Rakhine State
  Advisory Commission  46–47
  Buddhist-Muslim violence  42–44, 130
  Shwe Gas pipeline  40
refugees  28, 47, 129, 172–173n13
Responsibility to protect (R2P)  151
'Roadmap to Democracy'  24–26
Rohingya
  aid delivery  130

citizenship 29, 43, 128, 130–131, 147, 166Intro–n1
    see also citizenship act
  hate speech 44, 143
    see also Facebook
  violence 42, 43, 46–48, 158
    see also genocide, international justice
room to manoeuvre 60, 72–76, 81, 117, 162, 163
rural 35, 45, 58, 65, 66, 69, 74, 85, 169n16
Russia
  arms trade with Myanmar 146
  invasion of Ukraine 150, 152
  UN position on Myanmar 113, 152

S

'Saffron Revolution' 14, 24–25, 167n15
sanctions 13, 64, 95–97, 119–120, 128, 152, 154, 160
Sangha see Buddhist
Shalom (Nyein) Foundation 52, 62
Shan
  ethnic sub-groups 54
  Literature and Culture Committee 52
Shan Women's Action Network 40, 59–60
sit-tat see tatmadaw
social media see Facebook
social welfare see welfare organizations
space discourse (on civil society) see room
  to manoeuvre
'Spring Revolution' 137
State Administration Council (SAC) 2, 136, 141, 149, 150, 152, 156
Special Advisory Council on
  Myanmar 151, 173n11
State Law and Order Restoration
  Council (SLORC) 22–23, 60, 75–77, 121, 167n11
State Peace and Development Council
  (SPDC) 26, 41, 72, 75–77, 104, 167n11
student activists 18, 21, 37–39, 55–57, 106, 168n2
  see also 88 Generation students, All Burma
  Federation of Student Unions, All Burma
  Students' Democratic Front
surveillance 25, 38, 77–78, 83, 88, 122, 157
Susanna Hla Hla Soe 45, 143, 145, 147
Swan Arr Shin 61

T

tatmadaw 154, 167n7
Tay Zar San 137
Thailand
  refugees 28, 39–40, 152, 172n13
  see also democracy movement,
  exile organizations

Telecommunications Law 139, 168n12
Than Shwe 22, 57
Thein Sein
  International Crisis Group award 128
  liberalisation measures 26–27, 41
  peace process 29, 128, 169n5
  State of the Union speech 2012 41, 88
  treatment of Rohingya 42
  see also Union Development and Solidarity
  Party (USDP)
'Third Force' 70–71, 83–84, 87, 90, 106, 110, 128
Thway Thout Ah-Pwe 146
tourism boycott 95, 96
transnational advocacy 90–94, 154, 165
Transnational Institute 8, 169n14

U

U Nu 19–20, 36
U Thant 37–38, 167n9
Ukraine war 150–151, 152, 155
'uncivil society' 8–9, 32
United Kingdom (UK) see British
United Nations Children's Fund
  (UNICEF) 134, 135, 150
UN Credentials Committee 149
UN Human Rights Council 44, 64, 114, 130–131, 152
UN Office for the Coordination of
  Humanitarian Affairs 131, 150
UN Population Fund 128
UN Special Rapporteurs on Human Rights
  in Myanmar
  Paulo Sérgio Pinheiro 113, 124
  Tom Andrews 151
  Tomás Ojea Quintana 113
  Yanghee Lee 130, 151
Union Election Commission (UEC) 136
Union Solidarity and Development
  Association (USDA) 60–61, 101, 122
Union Solidarity and Development Party
  (USDP) 26, 39, 41, 69, 78, 82, 104–107, 136, 173n1
United States (US)
  ambassador to Myanmar 28
  donor aid to Myanmar 123, 126, 127, 135
  see also American Center, democracy
  movement, exile organizations,
  sanctions
Unlawful Associations Act 75, 139, 145, 171ch5n6
urban-rural division 66, 68, 69, 169n16
USAID 128, 135
US Campaign for Burma 64, 96, 113

V

Vahu Development Institute 70, 87
  see also 'Third Force'

Vietnam civil society  60, 75, 79–80, 86, 132, 163
voter education  45, 103, 106, 109

**W**

'watermelons'  144
Welfare organizations (*parahita*)  33, 34, 38, 51, 61–62, 85, 157, 161
Win Myint  45, 136, 145
Win Tin  113
Wirathu  43, 44, 47, 130, 146
Women's League of Burma (WLB)  59, 64, 143
World Bank  128, 141, 172n10
World Health Organization  135
World War II  18, 36

**Y**

Young Men's Buddhist Association (YMBA)  35, 37
Young Men's Christian Association (YMCA)  37, 51
Young Women's Buddhist Association (YWBA)  35
Young Women's Christian Association (YWCA)  37, 51
youth  37, 55–58, 105, 147–148, 169n11

**Z**

Zarganar  57, 83

www.ingramcontent.com/pod-product-compliance
Lightning Source LLC
Chambersburg PA
CBHW070622030426
42337CB00020B/3880